VON STERNBERG

Screen Classics

Screen Classics is a series of critical biographies, film histories, and analytical studies focusing on neglected filmmakers and important screen artists and subjects, from the era of silent cinema to the golden age of Hollywood to the international generation of today. Books in the Screen Classics series are intended for scholars and general readers alike. The contributing authors are established figures in their respective fields. This series also serves the purpose of advancing scholarship on film personalities and themes with ties to Kentucky.

Series Editor

Patrick McGilligan

Books in the Series

Hedy Lamarr: The Most Beautiful Woman in Film
Ruth Barton

The Marxist and the Movies: A Biography of Paul Jarrico
Larry Ceplair

Warren Oates: A Wild Life
Susan Compo

Being Hal Ashby: Life of a Hollywood Rebel
Nick Dawson

Some Like It Wilder: The Life and Controversial Films of Billy Wilder
Gene D. Phillips

Claude Rains: An Actor's Voice
David J. Skal with Jessica Rains

Buzz: The Life and Art of Busby Berkeley
Jeffrey Spivak

VON STERNBERG

John Baxter

THE UNIVERSITY PRESS OF KENTUCKY

Scholarly publisher for the Commonwealth, serving Bellarmine University, Berea College, Centre College of Kentucky, Eastern Kentucky University, The Filson Historical Society, Georgetown College, Kentucky Historical Society, Kentucky State University, Morehead State University, Murray State University, Northern Kentucky University, Transylvania University, University of Kentucky, University of Louisville, and Western Kentucky University.

Editorial and Sales Offices: The University Press of Kentucky
663 South Limestone Street, Lexington, Kentucky 40508-4008
www.kentuckypress.com

14 13 12 11 10   5 4 3 2 1

Photographs from *The Last Command, The Drag Net, Shanghai Express* (Dietrich close-up), *Der Blaue Engel* (production shot), *The Scarlet Empress* (Dietrich–von Sternberg), *The Devil Is a Woman, The King Steps Out, The Shanghai Gesture* (Munson-Tierney and set design), *Jet Pilot,* and *The Saga of Anatahan* are courtesy of the Joel Finler Collection. Portraits of David Stratton and Josef von Sternberg are courtesy of Robert McFarlane. All other photographs are from the author's collection.

Library of Congress Cataloging-in-Publication Data

Baxter, John, 1939–
  Von Sternberg / John Baxter.
    p.   cm. — (Screen classics)
  Includes bibliographical references and index.
  Includes filmography.
  ISBN 978-0-8131-2601-2 (hardcover : alk. paper)
  1. Von Sternberg, Josef, 1894–1969. 2. Motion picture producers and directors—United States—Biography. I. Title.
  PN1998.3.V66.B39 2010
  791.4302'33092—dc22
  [B]
                              2010023313

This book is printed on acid-free recycled paper meeting
the requirements of the American National Standard
for Permanence in Paper for Printed Library Materials.

Manufactured in the United States of America.

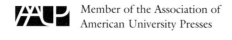   Member of the Association of
American University Presses

For Curtis Harrington, true believer

Those who dream by night in the dusty recesses of their minds wake in the day to find that all was vanity; but the dreamers of the day are dangerous men, for they may act their dream with open eyes, and make it possible.

—T. E. Lawrence (Lawrence of Arabia), *The Seven Pillars of Wisdom*

Contents

Contents

Illustrations follow page 152

The Man Who Asked for Onions

> "Do you have a hobby?"
>
> "Yes. Chinese philately."
>
> "Why that?"
>
> "I wanted a subject I could not exhaust."
>
> —Conversation between Josef von Sternberg and the author

"ONIONS?"

The waiter stared at the man who'd made this request.

We were in the Emerald Room of the Australia Hotel, the most prestigious hotel in Sydney, if not the most modern. Six meters above our heads dangled a huge Italian chandelier. In every direction, tables covered in linen, ironed glossy with starch, extended to infinity. Out of sight a fountain played, while marble nymphs observed us covertly from a jungle of potted ferns.

The table settings, like the décor, belonged to the age of Queen Victoria. Each plate, bowl, dish, cup, and saucer bore the hotel's emblem. The flatware, scratched to dullness by generations of use, had the heaviness of tools—soup spoons like shovels, knives as hefty as trowels. We might be dining in 1967, but we were eating in the style of 1889, when French tragedienne Sarah Bernhardt officially opened the hotel. The register with her signature was displayed in the lobby.

"Yes. Onions," repeated the short man with the gray beard. He didn't raise his head, so he didn't see what we saw: a portly, middle-aged waiter of European origin, judging from his voice, in confusion.

"You mean . . . an onion salad?" the man suggested hopefully.

I suppressed a wince. Even in my brief acquaintance with Josef von Sternberg, I'd learned not to question his orders, nor try to anticipate or interpret them.

The third person at our table was David Stratton, director of the Sydney Film Festival; he was responsible for inviting von Sternberg to Sydney and knew him better.

"Mr. von Sternberg would like some onions," he explained. "Just onions. That's all."

As the waiter retreated, I mentally wound back our conversation to the moment, minutes before, when von Sternberg had cleared his throat and remarked, "You must excuse me. I have a slight cold. Back home in California, I would eat onions and garlic, which cure such things." (He didn't add "it's believed" or "in my opinion." Von Sternberg presented all statements as incontrovertible fact.)

His right hand—the one usually clenched around the handle of his cane—worried at the remains of a bread roll, which he'd reduced to crumbs without eating any of it. Like his low, uninflected voice and the avoidance of eye contact, the fidgeting was another symptom of a nervous temperament rigidly controlled by an effort of will.

"Jules Furthman," I said, guiding the conversation back to films. "You worked with him more than any other person."

This was an understatement. From *The Drag Net* in 1928 to *Jet Pilot* in 1957, his name appeared on almost every von Sternberg film, though in so many forms—credited with writing the screenplay, adaptation, or original story, or even as producer—that their relationship eluded definition.

"I wondered," I went on, "what was your working method?"

"We had no *method*," von Sternberg said. "I simply told him what I wanted done, and he did it."

The waiter materialized at his elbow.

"Your onions, sir."

He deposited two large brown onions by von Sternberg's twitching right hand. The slightest of nods indicated his acceptance.

"Um . . . well," I continued, "when you say you 'told Furthman what to do.' . . ."

But it was no use. For the rest of the meal, von Sternberg responded to my tentative inquiries with an evasion or a lie. If he could be obdurate about onions, he was, on the subject of his work, adamantine. But at least he was responding. Even as noted a critic as Peter Bogdanovich was fobbed off with a succession of "I don't remember"s and "I don't know"s. Some journalists got not even that much—just a silent stare and a snapped, "Next."

The waiter cracked before I did. Standing by the wall, he watched for a few minutes and, when it became obvious von Sternberg had no immediate plans for the onions, returned to wrap them in a napkin. It was bad enough to know they were there, let alone to have to look at them.

Lunch over, von Sternberg rose, took his cane in one hand and the bundled onions in the other, and then, unexpectedly, said to me, "I have some papers in my room that might interest you."

I exchanged a glance with David. What was the etiquette here?

"Er . . . well, thanks," I began.

"If you come with me now," he said firmly, "I can give them to you."

David lifted his hands and bowed his head in acceptance—about all he could do in the circumstances.

An ancient elevator, its linen-fold paneling varnished brown as gravy, took us to the top floor. Leading me along meandering corridors, he unlocked the door of his suite—and we stepped into jungle madness. Skulls as yellow as old ivory grinned from the corners of the room; idols yawned, their torsos gashed with marks of the stone axes that had shaped them. Leaning against overstuffed armchairs were clubs embedded with sharks' teeth. A throne of black wood, topped with more skulls, sat empty, its seat hollowed and polished by generations of chiefs' backsides. It was impossible not to be reminded of "Hot Voodoo," the dance sequence of *Blonde Venus,* made thirty-five years earlier: A gorilla lumbers onto a nightclub stage, to be unmasked as Marlene Dietrich in disguise. As she emerges from the ape suit, dreamily swaying—a nymph shrugging off its chrysalis—a chorus line of beautiful black women circle her, each carrying a *fausse*-African shield decorated with a gaping, fanged mouth that evokes the most extreme of male terrors, the *vagina dentata*—a "vagina that bites."

More artifacts jammed the bedroom. Additional skulls stared through the door. Each idol, mask, and club had, I realized, a twin.

"Duplicates?"

"Of course." Was there the ghost of a smile? "One for my collection, and one to sell."

He handed me a sheaf of papers—the text of an article in some obscure magazine. As we shook hands at the door I saw, over his shoulder on the coffee table, the bundle containing his onions.

Did he spend the next half hour taking his ease on that throne, munching an onion like an apple as he surveyed his hoard? Or did he, the moment the door closed, toss the onions in the wastepaper basket, no longer useful as props in the prank he had played on us? Either way, the mythology of Josef von Sternberg was richer by another anecdote, and the obscurity with which he surrounded himself was one level more profound.

Vienna

> I never knew the old Vienna before the war with its Strauss
> music, its glamour and easy charm.
>
> —Graham Greene, screenplay for *The Third Man*

EVEN IF WE KNEW nothing about Josef von Sternberg, an unhappy
childhood could be inferred from his films. Fathers, if they appear at
all, are tyrants. Mothers sacrifice everything for their children, who
repay them with petulance or indifference. His men both fear and welcome the lash of contempt that their women wield, and women alone
retain their individuality. Summarizing his life, von Sternberg wrote,
"Fear always was first, to be dispelled by aggression, always followed
by guilt."[1] His contemporary, Soviet director Sergei Eisenstein, agreed
about his psychological burdens. "He had a most pronounced inferiority complex. . . . Snobbery could not hide von Sternberg's trauma about
his own inadequacy."[2] In middle age he would write a screenplay called
The Seven Bad Years, about "the adult insistence to follow the pattern
inflicted on a child in its first seven helpless years, from which a man
could extricate himself were he to recognize that an irresponsible child
was leading him into trouble."

He was born Jonas Sternberg on May 29, 1894, in Vienna, then the
capital of the Austro-Hungarian empire. His father, Moses Sternberg,
came from a family of woodworkers but had been inducted into the Austrian army. His mother, Serafin Singer, was the daughter of an instructor

who gave classes in German, the "official" language, to recruits; coming from all corners of the imperial domain, these new soldiers might speak any one of a dozen tongues or dialects. Jonas's parents were unmarried when he was conceived, which scandalized both families. According to his memoirs, Moses and Serafin were "disinherited" when they ignored parental objections to their relationship. Whether there was much to inherit, in fortune or in pedigree, isn't clear, although even a remote aristocratic connection would account for the readiness with which he later permitted the honorific "von" to be inserted into his name.

No photographs of Moses survive, so we know only what von Sternberg tells us: that he was "handsome and intelligent, . . . a marvel at anything mechanical, never idle [and] made friends easily." Moses had apparently written a book on mathematics as a young man, but he was also physically powerful and often beat both his wife and his children. With grudging pride, von Sternberg cites less damning proof of his father's strength, such as the ability to lift a man by his heels and hold him out at arm's length. After being pelted with snowballs by other recruits, Moses, according to his son, "demolished" them. As an Orthodox Jew, Moses could have anticipated their hostility. Discrimination riddled the Austrian army, as it did the French, which was even then railroading Alfred Dreyfus to Devil's Island on a false charge of espionage. The Austro-Hungarian officer class consisted almost entirely of *Judenfressers*—"Jew-eaters," as anti-Semites were called. When Jewish officers showed an embarrassing superiority in the saber duels that provided those dashing facial scars, their gentile comrades promulgated the 1894 Waidhofen Manifesto, which proclaimed that Jews, being ethnically subhuman, were born without honor. Accordingly, they could not be insulted and thus were barred from demanding satisfaction in a duel.

Following his marriage, Moses left the army and rented an apartment at Blumauergasse 25 in Wien II, a district consisting of nineteenth-century tenements. The building still stands, a bleak corner block in a lower-class district (with four floors rather than five, as von Sternberg recalled). Jonas grew up by the light of kerosene lamps, with no piped gas or electricity, and never had enough to eat. Relatives of his mother supported them—a pattern that continued through his adolescence, instilling a lifelong frugality.

Sanitation was primitive. Not surprisingly, vermin proliferated. Hunting fleas and other bugs was the usual preliminary to sleep, and von Sternberg took an intense interest when the maids in nearby apartments (who didn't bother to draw the curtains or lower the blinds) stripped at night to shake their underclothes over dishes of water, drowning the fleas that tumbled out.

Historian Sidney Bolkosky describes fin de siècle Vienna as a battleground of warring extremes: "home to the highest rates of suicide, prostitution, unwed mothers, intrigue, diplomacy of all sorts. Its values included liberal humanism and arch conservatism, patriarchal primacy and, perhaps more significant, misogyny. It was home, too, to Theodore Herzl, the founder of Zionism, and to Adolf Hitler; home, in short to emancipated Jews and to Anti-Semitism."[3] Despite this, von Sternberg retained a romantic affection for the city. "I was born with the fragrance of chestnut blossoms in my nostrils," he wrote, "the perfume of the old trees that stretched in stately procession to the Danube, not far distant. And the first sounds I heard were mingled with the melodies that floated into my crib from the hurdy-gurdies, calliopes and wondrously decorated mechanical music boxes that serenaded the gallantly uniformed soldiers strolling in the Prater and their servant-girl companions."

In November 1897 Moses, who had struggled to find work, joined the flood of Europeans seeking a better life in the United States. Three-year-old Jonas, his younger brother Siegfried, and Serafin, pregnant with daughter Hermine, known as Minna, remained behind. For the next four years he lived in a world colored by the gentler values of his mother—a period he celebrates in *The Case of Lena Smith* and *Blonde Venus*. Her presence also encouraged his precocious sexual instincts. After spying on the maids as they undressed, he watched with interest as the same girls, now wearing their Sunday best, strolled on the arms of their soldier lovers. He also noted how prostitutes congregated wherever there were crowds. As characters in his films, virtuous women held little interest. Almost invariably, his heroines are unfaithful, duplicitous, and promiscuous, if not unrepentant courtesans.

Young Jonas shared the streets with geniuses as well as whores. In painting, music, and literature, Vienna represented the cutting edge of artistic experimentation. The group calling itself the Secession had broken with the swirling curlicues of the Franco-Belgian art nouveau and, via artists such as Gustav Klimt and Egon Schiele, entered the territory of sexual imagery and the unconscious pioneered by another Austrian, Sigmund Freud. In their music, Gustav Mahler and Richard Strauss evoked similar states of mind, while writers such as Arthur Schnitzler wove cynical stories around the soldiers and maids von Sternberg saw "stepping out" on Sundays.

These streams of sensation flowed together in the Prater. An imperial hunting preserve until the emperor presented it to the people of Vienna in 1766, this park became the preferred place for Sunday outings. Food stalls and sideshows appeared, and in 1895, the year after von Sternberg's birth, a major reconstruction transformed it into a permanent amusement area. Two years later the *Riesenrad*—literally "big wheel"—was erected, destined to become as much a symbol of Vienna as the Eiffel Tower was of Paris, and familiar to film audiences from Carol Reed's *The Third Man*.

Serafin told stories of how, as a girl, she had played Snow White in a circus, but it was the Prater that ignited Jonas's taste for spectacle. He evokes it directly only in *The Case of Lena Smith*, but a nostalgia for carnivals is evident from their appearance in *Underworld, The Drag Net, Dishonored, The Devil Is a Woman,* and *The King Steps Out,* as well as the cabarets of *Morocco* and *Blonde Venus*. In his memoirs, von Sternberg rhapsodizes about the Prater: "[its] pirouetting fleas, sword swallowers, tumbling midgets and men on stilts, contortionists, jugglers and acrobats, wild swings with skirts flaring from them . . . a forest of balloons, tattooed athletes, muscle-bulging weight lifters, women who were sawed in half . . . trained dogs and elephants, tightropes that provided footing for a gourmet who feasted on a basketful of local sausages with horseradish that made my mouth water."

In 1889 British author George du Maurier published *Trilby: A Novel.* Set in nineteenth-century Paris, it describes how a tone-deaf Irish street waif, Trilby O'Ferrall, becomes a great singer under the influence of a hypnotist. Although the name *trilby* survives mostly as the term for the soft hat with a creased crown worn by the character in the book, the public imagination was caught by the figure of her malevolent impresario, whom du Maurier invests with all of European society's xenophobia and anti-Semitism.

> [He was] a tall bony individual of any age between thirty and forty-five, of Jewish aspect, well-featured but sinister. He was very shabby and dirty, and wore a red beret and a large velveteen cloak, with a big metal clasp at the collar. His thick, heavy, languid, lustreless black hair fell down behind his ears on to his shoulders, in that musician-like way that is so offensive to the normal Englishman. He had bold, brilliant black eyes, with long heavy lids, a thin, sallow face, and a beard of burnt-up black, which grew almost from his under eyelids; and over it his moustache, a shade lighter, fell in two long spiral twists. He went by the name of Svengali.[4]

Svengali became a synonym for any menacing individual who, acting behind the scenes, directs and manipulates the career of a talented innocent. Once John Barrymore played him in Archie Mayo's eponymous 1931 film, the name became part of the language. Von Sternberg often attracted the label "Dietrich's Svengali." Despite rejecting the comparison in interviews, he encouraged it in his actions, courting dislike and dressing to emphasize his strangeness. At times, the resonance between his behavior and that of the fictional Svengali was eerily exact. "[He] would either fawn or bully," wrote du Maurier, "and could be grossly impertinent. He had a kind of cynical humor, which was more offensive than amusing, and always laughed at the wrong thing, at the wrong time, in the wrong place. And his laughter was always derisive and full of malice."[5]

Love and Other Distractions

Allah be praised for always providing new women.
—Dr. Omar (Victor Mature), in *The Shanghai Gesture*

YOUNG JONAS LOOKED FORWARD to weekends at the Prater all the more because of the ordeal of his weekdays. He hated the yeshiva, which, beginning at age six, he was forced to attend after regular classes to learn Hebrew. He particularly resented the teacher, a "bearded monster" named Antcherl, on whom he partly modeled Professor Rath in *The Blue Angel*.

Fortunately, this misery lasted only a year. Though not exactly prospering in the United States, Moses found enough work to send for his family, but not enough to pay their fares, which Serafin borrowed from relatives. In December 1901, with seven-year-old Jonas, little Siegfried, and baby Hermine, she embarked for New York. Because the Austro-Hungarian empire had only one outlet to the sea, the Adriatic port of Trieste, the family had to travel by train to Hamburg, Germany. Until the ship sailed, they took a room in a boardinghouse, the walls of which crawled with red-brown bugs. By comparison, the fourteen-day transatlantic voyage was uneventful, and after screening at Ellis Island, they joined Moses in the Yorkville district of the Upper East Side of Manhattan. Although, as in Vienna, they had to climb many flights of stairs to reach their new apartment, it offered the relative luxury of hot water, a bathtub, and a dumbwaiter to bring goods from the ground floor.

Moses took menial jobs, including working at the Coney Island amusement park, where he controlled the flow of water that carried boats through the Tunnel of Love. Meanwhile, in 1904, sister Mole (pronounced "Molly," but listed in the 1910 census as "Amelia") was added to the family. Education being free, Jonas enrolled in the local grade school and struggled with English. He soon forgot his German and rarely spoke it for the rest of his life; in fact, when he went to Berlin in 1929 to make *The Blue Angel,* negotiations were conducted in English. According to Carl Zuckmayer, the film's principal screenwriter, multilingual playwright Karl Vollmoeller sat in on discussions with von Sternberg, Emil Jannings, Erich Pommer, and himself "as a kind of interpreter, since none of us spoke correct English at the time and von Sternberg did not like to remember his German descent."[1] Von Sternberg's rejection of his German connections became more pronounced with age. He lied to *Cahiers du Cinema* in 1963, claiming, "I had never been in Germany before [I made *Der Blaue Engel*]. I knew nothing about Germany. I was an American director who had come from Hollywood to make the film."[2]

Migrants pouring into New York made it the world's second-largest city after London. But few of today's residents would recognize it. The Bronx, recently annexed by overflowing Manhattan, remained mostly farmland. Coney Island was still an island, separated from Brooklyn by Coney Island Creek. Oystermen harvested in Jamaica Bay, and fishermen's shanties lined the shores of Manhattan. With the subway not yet completed, horse-drawn streetcars provided public transport, augmented by elevated railroads such as the one that ran down Sixth Avenue. Horses were so common that doomsayers foresaw their accumulated manure blocking entire streets. (Instead, it dried and blew about, spreading intestinal and respiratory diseases.) Pennsylvania Station and Grand Central had yet to be built. Once they were, pedestrians on Park Avenue choked on coal smoke and cinders until the New York Central was electrified in 1912.

Von Sternberg detested this thrusting, greedy metropolis. He would set his first film as a director, *The Salvation Hunters,* in a dockland polluted by industry, where a dredge monotonously claws up mud and deposits it on a scow. As a boy he saw many such dredges at work as Manhattan created new land by dumping garbage and deepened the Hudson and East rivers to accommodate larger ships carrying yet more immigrants. Father and son agreed on the deficiencies of New York, and in 1904, Moses sent the family back to Vienna while he remained in the United States.

Serafin was pregnant, and a third son, Heinrich, was born the following year. Their new home in Vienna, the middle story of a freestanding house, was an improvement over the Blumauergasse tenement. A carpenter's workshop occupied the street level, while in the loft above them, housemaids aired and dried washing. The family scratched along on odd jobs and charity from Serafin's family. Young Jonas found an after-school job grazing circus horses in the Prater, but it lasted only for the summer. During the winter of 1905 he was forced to endure the humiliation of lining up with other poor children for a free overcoat from the city—on which, to make everyone aware of its largesse, the council had embroidered its coat of arms. He unpicked this badge of poverty. In 1960, when the mayor of Vienna proposed to present von Sternberg with a medal, he "described the decoration that had honored me when I was cold." The mayor promised to end the practice immediately.

At eleven, Jonas enrolled in a local *gymnasium,* a form of high school inferior to the more demanding *lyceum.* One of his teachers was Karl Adolph, a former housepainter who later earned a modest reputation as a writer, publishing collections of stories about working-class life in the Austrian capital. Adolph's stories concentrated on the peasant girls, drawn to the city from all over the empire by employment as maids or laundresses, who offered rich pickings to the city's bachelors.

Between eleven and fourteen, von Sternberg's adolescent preoccupation with sex developed into a lifelong interest. Obscene graffiti gave him a knowledge of anatomy, which improved when he gathered in a cellar with some other boys to watch a girl on a swing show herself naked under her skirt. He had a few brushes with homosexuality. A teacher invited him to his apartment, ostensibly to help with his studies but actually to make advances, and an older boy pursued him with poems and even flowers. Jonas claimed to be indifferent, as he was to the men who pressed themselves against him on crowded streetcars.

Because his work deals so frequently but often obliquely with sex, this has invited speculation about von Sternberg's sexuality. Superficially, he was almost obsessively heterosexual. Maria Riva, Marlene Dietrich's daughter, overheard her mother saying, "Of course, Jo, being a Jew, never stops—they always want to do it, all the time! Especially if they are small and have a thing for tall, blue-eyed Christians!"[3] Dissenting opinions come mostly from those who disliked him. Sergei Eisenstein, initially an admirer and then a jealous rival, suggested that von Sternberg was, like himself, homosexual, with a taste for well-built young men, but this sounds more like bile than a serious claim.[4] Screenwriter Frederica Sagor Maas, a friend of von Sternberg's first wife, Riza Royce (and thus no champion of Josef's), commented tartly that the marriage may not have been consummated because, "according to Riza, Josef von Sternberg's equipment was faulty."[5] Obviously it functioned well enough, since he married three times and fathered a son. Less easy to ignore are the indications of masochism, particularly in relation to Marlene Dietrich, his star and lover for almost a decade. If not for reasons of sexual gratification, why would he have stood by, stoically, as a succession of men and women occupied her bed and claimed her affections? To clarify their relationship, in almost every film he made after she entered his life, he included the character of a frustrated, impotent, or abandoned lover, costumed and made up to resemble himself. Only one scene in his work is directly traceable to a childhood sexual experience. While swimming in the Alte Donau, a dammed-off branch of the Danube, he blundered into a group of nude women, who warned him off in the impolite local German. He replicated that moment in one of his most sensual sequences, the opening of *Blonde Venus*, where Herbert Marshall and hiking friends encounter Dietrich and her companions naked in a forest pool.

At thirteen, Jonas did fall in love with a girl. He praised her "graceful posture [and] proud stride," her "lithe and alluring" body and "long swinging braids," and wrote of "trembling for hours on a street waiting to catch a distant glimpse." He was desolate when he saw her kissing a more forward friend. It is inviting to compare her with Dietrich's character in *Dishonored*, who fools rival spy Victor McLaglen with an imitation of a country maiden—dirndl, braids, and all. Despite describing his early sexual stirrings as a "song of the flesh [in the midst of which] we were as innocent as are newly born kittens" and claiming, "I sought only companionship and affection," he had already cast himself as the passive partner, squirming while more confident rivals swept away the object of his desire. Revealingly, he said of this first love, "she permitted me to worship her, and in turn she worshipped herself"—a capsule description of his male protagonists' relationship with women. "There was no guilt in me, no stealth and no fear," he wrote—adding, ominously, "though these chimeras developed with time."

An Artist's Life

Von Sternberg is a painter in the narrowest and broadest
senses of the word.
—Max Reinhardt[1]

VON STERNBERG'S LIFE IN Vienna ended in 1908 when Moses,
who became a U.S. citizen in 1906, decided that the family should
rejoin him in the United States. He'd found steady work in the clothing
business. His naturalization application lists his profession as "furrier,"
and the 1910 census as "lace worker." To signify his commitment to his
adoptive home, Moses changed his name to Morris. On their arrival
in the United States, Serafin became Serafina, Heinrich was renamed
Henry, Hermine became Minna, and Siegfried was known as Fred.
Jonas assumed the more common Josef but never liked the diminutive
Joe. He always signed himself "Jo," a reminder of the original. Since
Moses was naturalized, the entire family automatically acquired U.S.
citizenship.

A million immigrants passed through Ellis Island in 1908, many
squeezing into the tenements of New York's five boroughs. The Sternbergs lived at various addresses around Brooklyn before settling in Nas-
sau County at 57 Lloyd Avenue, Lynbrook, where Morris remained for
the rest of his life. Josef enrolled in Jamaica High School in Queens. He
lasted there only a year before an aunt found him a $4 a week job sweep-
ing up in a millinery shop—one source of the later rumor that he began

working life as "a pants-presser from Brooklyn."[2] From there, he moved to a lace warehouse on Fifth Avenue, probably the one where Morris worked. The 1910 census lists him as "errand boy." His work gave him an intimacy with fabric and lace, but also a contempt for working-class Americans. His colleagues spent their time boasting of whores they had visited, commiserating about their doses of the clap, and indulging in pranks, such as waylaying Josef after work, getting him drunk—for the first and last time in his life, he claims—and pulling down his pants to decorate his behind with the company's date stamp.

Morris's bad temper didn't mellow with age, and he frequently took it out on his family. "He and my father didn't get along," confirms von Sternberg's son Nicholas, "due to my grandfather's rough handling of my father when he was young."[3] It was particularly galling that, after each beating, he required the children to kiss his hand. Eventually Josef stood up to his father when he tried to beat young Fred, a courageous gesture for someone who had stopped growing at five feet five inches tall. Morris never struck his sons again but continued to inflict his ill temper on Serafina, who left him to live with relatives in the Bronx. The 1910 census shows Morris Sternberg as a single parent living in Brooklyn with his five children. The three youngest later moved in with their mother. Seventeen-year-old Josef preferred independence and left home. For the next year he shoveled snow, drove a team of horses to deliver rolls of paper, and sold costume jewelry door to door for a man named Kamanetzky, whom he disliked sufficiently to parody in *The Shanghai Gesture* as the glowering casino appraiser, peering suspiciously through a loupe at items offered in trade. Rather than returning to live with Morris when he was out of work, Josef slept in parks or Bowery flophouses and, he claimed, carried a bone in his pocket to gnaw on, like a dog.

Once the New York Public Library opened in 1911, he spent most of his spare time there. A classic autodidact, he read almost entirely to inform himself. Fiction didn't figure in his curriculum, which favored philosophy, history, and particularly art. On February 17, 1913, an International Exhibition of Modern Art opened in the Sixty-ninth Regiment Armory on New York's Lexington Avenue. Mounted by the Association of American Painters and Sculptors, it aimed to demonstrate that local artists deserved comparison with the best in Europe. Many of the 300 artists who contributed 1,250 paintings and sculptures to the Armory Show, as it became known, were U.S.-based, including George Bellows, Mary Cassatt, Childe Hassam, Edward Hopper, and James McNeill Whistler. Others were Europeans exhibiting in the United States for the first time. They included Wassily Kandinsky, Pablo Picasso, Paul Cezanne, and Marcel Duchamp, whose *Nude Descending a Staircase* fascinated artists but aroused derision in the papers.

Four thousand people attended on the first day, and von Sternberg was among them. "That was an enormous influence on him," said Meri von Sternberg, his third wife, "and [he] often talked about what he saw there."[4] He returned frequently, indifferent to the furor. He was already developing a taste that would lead him to sketch and paint—not very successfully—and experiment with still photographs. Later, he amassed one of Hollywood's finest collections of modern art and commissioned new works, including portraits of himself by David Alfaro Siqueiros, Rudolf Belling, and Boris Deutsch. Jesse Lasky Jr. wrote that "he was always saving himself from oblivion with the immortalising attentions of sculptors and painters. One could frequently find him posing in his office while developing one of his scripts."[5] This is an exaggeration, although he did allow Siqueiros to observe him at work to create some preliminary sketches for his portrait.

Von Sternberg's first discovery about the cinema was also his most important: there was little new in the movies. Painters had long since solved any visual problems. This insight shaped his attitude about motion pictures. Aeneas Mackenzie wrote in a 1936 essay, "Leonardo of the Lenses," that "the screen is his medium—not the cinema."[6] "His purpose is to reveal the emotional significance of a subject by a series of magnificent canvases."[7] Von Sternberg agreed. "I don't make movies. I make motion pictures." He regarded the cinematic image as a painter sees a canvas. "A frame is made to contain the performer," he wrote of his technique; "a background is evoked, every ray of light aids or detracts; foreground is interposed; the very air becomes part of the effect." He defined art as "the compression of infinite spiritual power into a confined space," and his particular skill as bringing his subjects into "a dramatic encounter with light."

He scorned narrative. The need for screenwriters always irked him, and he clashed with them repeatedly. Asked what importance he attached to scripts, he snapped, "None." Where other filmmakers emphasized a point with dialogue or a close-up, von Sternberg moved the character from darkness into light. One can imagine him formulating this technique while walking the city streets, watching how light from a street lamp fell on people moving toward and then away from it, or how shadows textured the face of a person who stepped close to a curtain.

He communicated in images, not words, and his medium was light. He moved characters and objects in and out of it, dipping them in silver, dissolving them into a flow of smoke, veils, nets, feathers, fog. "Shadow is mystery and light is clarity," he said. "Shadow conceals—light reveals. To know what to reveal and what to conceal, and in what degrees to do this, is all there is to art." Documentary filmmaker John Grierson dismissed von Sternberg's work with the glib accusation that "when a director dies, he becomes a photographer,"[8] but the gibe backfired, since von Sternberg agreed with him: virtuosity with the camera was indeed a "prime requisite" of a director.

The World, the Flesh, and William A. Brady

Motion pictures are just a fad.

—William A. Brady to Adolph Zukor

UNTIL THE MID-1920S, the East Coast film industry, particularly the studios in Astoria, Queens, and Fort Lee, New Jersey, rivaled that of the West. Most cinemas were in the large eastern cities, and in addition to providing a pool of actors, artists, and technicians, New York housed the banks that funded production.

Jules Brulatour dominated Fort Lee. He wasn't French but had been born in New Orleans. As well as monopolizing the supply of Eastman raw film stock, Brulatour processed it and warehoused the completed motion pictures. The studios he built at Fort Lee attracted both American producers and French film companies such as Éclair and Pathé, which made films for both markets. With the outbreak of war in 1914, the French halted U.S. production. Local companies faltered as well, no longer able to rely on European sales. Fort Lee was rescued by Lewis J. Selznick. Raising money on Wall Street and enlisting Brulatour as an ally, he formed the World Film Company by combining a number of independents, including Brulatour's Peerless, William A. Brady's Paragon, and Arthur Spiegel's Equitable. He also recruited the unemployed French filmmakers.

William Aloysius Brady emerged as the driving force of World, his importance signaled by the company's slogan, "World Pictures—

Brady-made." Beginning as a street newsboy, he had been an actor, playwright, producer, theater builder, and fight promoter. With his brusque manner and clothes dusted with cigar ash, Brady brought a sense of the barroom and the boxing ring to the movies he financed and circulated, which numbered about twenty a year between 1914 and 1917. To service his prints, he acquired a small company whose owner had developed a system for cleaning and repair. Among its employees was Josef von Sternberg.

Von Sternberg dated his own discovery of the cinema to around 1910 and his days of "sleeping rough," when a nickel or dime would buy a few hours off the streets in a warm if smelly and noisy nickelodeon. But the film *Fun in a Chinese Laundry,* whose title he borrowed for his autobiography (it was two films, in fact, since both Lubin and Edison used the name), was made in 1901, suggesting an earlier acquaintance.

In the summer of 1911, in Prospect Park, Brooklyn, he took shelter under a footbridge during an electrical storm. Two girls joined him, one of whom fainted when lightning struck a nearby tree. After the storm the girls took him to meet a friend, who showed off the machine his father had constructed in his basement for repairing films. By the time Josef left, he had a job cleaning and patching films and mending torn sprocket holes. He also ferried prints by motorcycle between the city's cinemas—the most important part of his work, since his employer appears to have indulged in the lucrative practice of "bicycling." After cleaning a print, he would rent it illegally for a day or two before returning it to the film exchange that collected fees on behalf of producers.

World's purchase of the film repair company transformed von Sternberg's life. For a while he continued to service prints, but Fort Lee offered many opportunities. "Shortly after graduation from the bench where sprocket holes were mended," he wrote,

> I was made head of the shipping department centered in a film laboratory, and entrusted with the task of seeing to it that the theatres promptly received their copies. As films are usually completed barely in time to reach a theatre, this meant that not only had I to watch the films being hauled out of the developing tanks

to be dried on giant drums but I also had to mount them swiftly on metal reels, pile them into an old battered Ford, and then drive them through a storm-lashed New Jersey coast road to a Hoboken express office to make certain that the films would reach their destination in time.

From shipping he graduated to editing. Von Sternberg told his son that he won a promotion when his boss was fired for graft—perhaps a consequence of the earlier "bicycling" scam—but his memoirs contain a more glamorous version. He was viewing a film to check the print quality when its director, Harley Knoles, asked his opinion. Von Sternberg questioned the use of "Adirondacks" in an intertitle. "Why not just say 'mountains'? Nobody knows where the Adirondacks are anyway." A few days later, Brady arrived unannounced in the office, planted his backside on von Sternberg's desk, and offered him "all the money in the world" to take over cutting, editing, and writing intertitles. The promised fortune was only a $5 raise to $35 a week, but he was glad to get it. Over the next two years he cut, he estimated, a hundred productions. He also "doctored" failures, reediting them and inventing intertitles to cover lapses in continuity. Although he later described himself as Brady's "assistant," his 1917 draft card gives his profession as "lab expert," a much lowlier role. However, his speedy rise in the company is unquestioned.

Not that it was a difficult industry in which to flourish. Most films of the time were either knockabout comedies or stagy melodramas created by people who treated these "galloping tintypes" as a source of quick cash. The French filmmakers absorbed by World took a different view, and it was they who most influenced the young von Sternberg. Directors Maurice Tourneur, George Archainbaud, Émile Chautard, and Albert Capellani; cameramen René Guissart, Lucien Andriot, and Jacques Bizeul; and designer Ben Carré operated as a separate unit, even speaking French on the set. In von Sternberg's three years at World, they taught him the elements of lighting and the camera. He worked with Tourneur, Carre, and Chautard on Tourneur's 1917 *A Girl's Folly*, a behind-the-scenes comedy about two actors who fall in love while making a western, but didn't, as it was rumored, appear in the film.

His first teacher was Tourneur, whose technique favored small, precisely directed lights rather than the system of wall-to-wall illumination preferred by directors trained in the theater. The dapper Chautard, an ex-actor, was the most approachable of the group, but as he spoke little English and von Sternberg no French, the bilingual Bizeul translated. Von Sternberg became Chautard's protégé, a favor he returned by giving Chautard small acting jobs in *Morocco, Shanghai Express,* and *Blonde Venus.*

Chautard demonstrated the unwritten rules by which text becomes a motion picture. Many of these involved objects and the way they appear on screen. A prop, once introduced, assumes a significance out of all proportion to its place in the story. If the audience sees a telephone or a door, they expect the first to ring and the second to open—an illustration of the principle laid down by Anton Chekhov and known as "Chekhov's gun": "One must not put a loaded rifle on stage if no one is thinking of firing it." Von Sternberg went further, however, realizing that objects and actions offer richer opportunities for communication than words do. A woman taking a man's cap and placing it on her own head, or sewing up a torn pocket on his shirt, can define their relationship more subtly than dialogue.

Ernst Lubitsch would exploit this insight with the so-called Lubitsch Touch. In *The Love Parade,* Maurice Chevalier confiscates a pistol from the jealous mistress who is about to shoot him and tosses it into a drawer with half a dozen others. The king in *The Merry Widow* emerges from the queen's boudoir buckling on a sword, only to realize that the belt belongs to a much slimmer man—her lover (Chevalier again), who slipped in as he left. Von Sternberg employs this device in *Morocco.* Legionnaire Tom Brown, visiting singer Amy Jolly in her dressing room for the first time, reaches, without looking, for a fan, which he's surprised to find is not in the usual place. But von Sternberg's use of the technique extends well beyond sight gags. Props become elements in a subliminal language. As Siegfried Kracauer says of *The Blue Angel,* "There is a promiscuous mingling of architectural fragments, characters and nondescript objects. Lola-Lola sings her famous song on a miniature stage so overstuffed with props that she herself seems part of the décor. . . . The persistent interference of mute objects reveals the whole milieu as a scene of loosened instincts."[1]

Carnivals, masks, streamers, balloons, hats, puppets, statues, dolls, and toys run through his work, generally with some sexual connotation. His films often contain the phallic image of a pole topped with a bulbous knob, a hat, a skull, or a large shell. But von Sternberg reserved a special affection for feathers and birds. They are so ubiquitous in his films that it's impossible to assign a single "meaning" to their use. The first shot of his first film as director, *The Salvation Hunters,* is of a seagull perched on a piece of flotsam. Birds permeate his subsequent work: Rath's dead canary in *The Blue Angel;* the feathers of Lola-Lola's postcard portrait; the aigrettes of "Feathers" McCoy in *Underworld* and "Ritzy" in *Thunderbolt* and the feathered caps of "The Magpie" in *The Drag Net;* doves cooing to Helen Faraday in *Blonde Venus;* imperial eagles in *The Last Command, Dishonored, The Scarlet Empress,* and *I, Claudius;* birdsong in Concha's house in *The Devil Is a Woman,* plaster storks in her cabaret, and the silly duck she carries when trying to pass for a peasant; and most potent of all, the black plumes of Shanghai Lily's hats in *Shanghai Express.* Even in his last film, *The Saga of Anatahan,* Keiko waves like a trapped bird to the waiting ship, and the castaways carve toy boats that will carry them away, in the words of von Sternberg's commentary, "on the wings of their longing."

When he brought Marlene Dietrich from Berlin in 1930, he gave her daughter a crimson and blue macaw. He also ordered Paramount studio carpenters to build an aviary in her garden and stocked it with exotic species. Even six-year-old daughter Heidede intuited that her mother's newest friend "must have a thing about birds."[2] However, the captives in the aviary, chosen for their looks rather than compatibility, pecked one another to death, suggesting that von Sternberg's interest was not ornithological but extended only to birds' decorative qualities. As Raymond Durgnat wrote of these and other details in von Sternberg's films, "They are not so much symbols (i.e., a code for something else) as carriers of atmosphere."[3] Further obscuring their significance, von Sternberg didn't keep birds as pets, preferring dogs; nor did he write about them with any special enthusiasm.

We can only guess at the connection he intends us to see between the pigeons that flap away from the windowsill when Olga Baclanova shoots her unfaithful husband in *The Docks of New York* and the stone eagle Gustav von Seyffertitz eyes in the courtyard where X-27 has just gone to her death in *Dishonored*. Perhaps some sense of freedom attained or denied, responsibility accepted or flouted, love won or lost—and always the reminder that love, freedom, even life can disappear in a batting of wings, leaving no souvenir more substantial than the scrap of a plume, a hint of infinite possibility, that drifts down to "Rolls Royce" in *Underworld* as "Feathers" descends into his squalid life. In the manipulation of such materials, von Sternberg has no peer. "He can convey sensuality in a manner which baffles the censors," wrote one admiring journalist. "They cannot put their finger on it."[4]

In the emerging industrialized Hollywood, von Sternberg's expertise in cinematography, design, and editing represented both strength and weakness. Sergei Eisenstein believed that having risen through the ranks from editing exacerbated von Sternberg's sense of inferiority. Some colleagues even perceived his skill in lighting as a demeaning inclination to perform tasks not the province of the director, who, it was felt, should concentrate on performances and leave technical matters to cinematographers and set designers. Directors trained in Germany often wore white gloves on the set, signifying a refusal to soil their hands with anything physical, even the moving of a chair. This separation of skills irritated von Sternberg. Long before the ideologues of the *nouvelle vague* asked, "If film is an art, who is the artist?" and decided that the answer was usually "the director," he had reached the same conclusion. "Whereas a painter uses his brushes, canvas and colors, following only the bent of his imagination," he complained, "the film director has to consider other men and human material." He didn't hesitate to step on the toes of technicians. On *Shanghai Express* he climbed on top of a locomotive to paint in shadows that the director of photography had failed to provide, and on *Crime and Punishment* he not only dabbed paint on sets but also physically moved equipment. Nor did his practice of scrawling graffiti across mirrors and walls or plastering sets with posters endear him to art directors. Although the exclusive American Society of Cinematographers honored him with the first membership ever conferred on a director, and many lighting cameramen acknowledged him as an equal, if not their master, just as many resented him. He was to learn that "human material" could harbor a grudge for a dismayingly long time.

In Uniform

The apparel oft proclaims the man.

—William Shakespeare, *Hamlet*

IN APRIL 1917 THE United States entered the European war. As Hollywood whipped up hatred of the Hun in its films, Douglas Fairbanks, Mary Pickford, Charlie Chaplin, and other stars toured the nation, selling bonds. In July Congress ordered the Army Signal Corps to obtain photographs and create a comprehensive pictorial history of the war. With U.S. troops already in France and General John Pershing installed in Paris, the Signal Crops hurriedly formed a Photographic Section. Moviemakers who had been peeling potatoes, drilling, or learning the workings of an Enfield rifle were whisked to Columbia University in uptown Manhattan, where the School of Military Cinematography ran a six-week course for combat cameraman and photographers. Among them was Victor Fleming, former cameraman for Douglas Fairbanks and later director of *Gone with the Wind,* as well as future directors Wesley Ruggles; Ernest B. Schoedsack, creator of *King Kong;* Henry Hathaway, who would work as von Sternberg's assistant and second unit director on *Morocco* and other films; and Lev Milstein, who, as Lewis Milestone, showed war from the German side in *All Quiet on the Western Front.*

Josef Sternberg and his brother Fred enlisted on the same day, June 5, 1917. Jo gave his profession as "lab expert" and his address as the

World studios; Fred was listed as "salesman" with Sternberg Brothers, 902 Broadway. Jo went to the Signal Corps, Fred to the Marine Corps. Their ready acceptance into the armed forces is surprising, given the prevailing anti-Teutonic hostility. Many actors with German names adopted something more Anglo-Saxon for the duration. Gustav von Seyffertitz, who later acted in *The Docks of New York, Shanghai Express,* and *Dishonored,* became "G. Butler Clonebaugh," and von Sternberg's future scriptwriter Jules Furthman used the noms de plume "Stephen Fox" and "Julius Grinnell." But apparently an Austrian-born editor with an unrepentantly German name working at the heart of the U.S. war information effort aroused no suspicion. His posting even made the trade paper *Moving Picture World,* which reported, "Joe Sternberg has been stationed at Columbia University, where he will be engaged in important work connected with the preparation of a film which will be used as an aid to training recruits." It was a milestone of sorts—his first citation in the "trades," where he would appear with some regularity. Von Sternberg probably planted the story himself.

Von Sternberg's training films attracted attention, particularly one on the use of the bayonet. According to a 1931 profile, "officers at the cantonments had been complaining that they could order the dough-boys to attend showings of these educational pictures, but they could not command them to stay awake. Von Sternberg, wholly uninhibited by censorship for once, began a lesson on the bayonet with a few feet showing what knife wounds looked like. Enthusiastic reports reached the War College; the men had stayed awake, not only during the show, but most of the night as well."[1] Fred was less fortunate. Caught in a gas attack at Belleau Wood in June 1918, he was invalided home. Subsequently the French government awarded his unit, the Fourth Brigade of Marines, a collective Croix de Guerre for courage. After the war Fred found work as a film projectionist, but he never fully recovered his health and died in 1936.

In July 1915 von Sternberg was in Chicago when the steamer *Eastland* capsized while ferrying employees of the Western Electric Company back from a picnic, causing 844 people to die. "I wept while the bodies were carried off in truck after truck," he wrote. Such emotion wasn't typical, since he was already formulating a rebarbative personal style. Jesse Lasky Jr., son of the man who cofounded Famous Players–Lasky, remembered "a short, somewhat hunched figure, opinionated, pompous, seemingly unhumorous, introverted and vain, [who] looked like hell."[2] Much calculation went into this image. At a time when fashion favored a clean-shaven face and neatly trimmed hair, gleaming with pomade, von Sternberg wore his hair long, letting it droop over his pale forehead, conferring a poetic melancholy on his deep brown eyes. Describing him in middle age, Sergei Eisenstein wrote, "He was short, greying, with a slightly artistic haircut. He sported a greyish moustache which drooped unevenly on either side."[3] The moustache was a relatively late addition. In 1922, while on location in Wales as assistant director on Alliance's *Love and a Whirlwind,* von Sternberg shared a room with actor Clive Brook, who found him staring into the mirror one morning.

"Which is more horrible?" he asked. "With a moustache or without one?"

When Brook queried the need to look horrible, von Sternberg replied, "The only way to succeed is to make people hate you. That way they remember you."[4]

This remained his doctrine, accentuated by a studied, often exaggerated choice of clothes and accessories. He favored red or black shirts and jackets in fabrics and colors that most people shunned but that caught the eye—acid green or a bilious beige—accentuated by contrasting white or yellow shoes. Eisenstein noted a "passion for jackets and short square-cut coats."[5] Before he could afford tailoring, von Sternberg bought these secondhand. Though well made, such hand-me-downs were seldom the right size. "He buys his suits to fit the man he'd like to be, about three sizes too large," jeered Joseph L. Mankiewicz. "He gets in his pants with a step-ladder, and takes three steps before the suit moves." Allowing for the malice behind it, the comment is apt. Von Sternberg saw himself as physically larger than he was. Once he became wealthy, he continued to wear well-padded suits and heavy coats that sometimes reached his ankles, while the collars rose above his head. He chose the grandest cars, unconcerned that they dwarfed him, and he kept the largest or most aggressive breeds of dog—Great Danes and Dobermans.

More observant people admired the calculation that went into his wardrobe. Like Woody Allen closer to our own time, he expended money and effort on appearing casual. Berlin painter George Grosz remarked, "His outer garments were . . . always, naturally, made to measure by the very best tailors. The lapels . . . were cut like a shawl collar and without buttonholes. Moreover, he favoured waistcoats with long sleeves, as did the equally individualistic Bert Brecht. Von Sternberg also wore soft, broad, comfortably-cut shirt-collars with elongated, slightly protruding points. . . . It all hinted at a 'closet' unconventionality, the kind that did not offend too grossly against the rules of gentlemanly dress."[6] He particularly intrigued visitors from Britain, where clothes signified social class. Two English guests on the set of *The Docks of New York* in 1928 were sufficiently struck to describe a typical von Sternberg costume. "His rough tweed Norfolk jacket was sportive. His fat walking cane betokened a dash of the country squire; his full-bottomed, well-creased flannel trousers, white with a narrow blue line, hinted at the fashionable beach club; while his shoes, white buckskins with black decorations, lent a touch of lawless fantasy."[7]

For a model in both his personal style and his work, von Sternberg looked no further than Erich von Stroheim. Both were physically short and self-educated and had been brought up poor in working-class Vienna. But where von Sternberg was retiring, von Stroheim, a born actor, blustered his way to celebrity. Casually accessing a "von" to suggest aristocracy, the actor shaved his head, screwed a monocle into his eye, and adopted a variety of quasi-military uniforms, accentuated by a riding crop or cane. Humorist and scriptwriter S. J. Perelman wrote admiringly of von Stroheim's screen persona: "his stiff-necked swagger, his cynical contempt for the women he misused, and, above all, his dandyism—the monogrammed cigarettes, the dressing gowns with silk lapels, the musk he sprayed himself with to heighten his allure." A publicist labeled him "The Man You Love To Hate."[8]

Von Stroheim had never been near a film studio before arriving in the United States, but this didn't prevent him from affecting the white gloves of a director. Von Sternberg was among the admirers who adopted the custom, but gloves were only one element of his costume, which changed from film to film. He might arrive for the first day of shooting in a silk dressing gown. On others, he wore a boilersuit, a solar topee with high riding boots and breeches, a velvet coat and beret, or a robe with a scarf wound round his head like a turban—always with his cane and, in time, a huge megaphone or public-address system. With such accessories, his small stature, low voice, timidity, and lack of education evaporated. No actor cast as an artistic genius could have entered more completely into the part.

One element of his wardrobe gave particular offense. "They'll tell you he's arrogant and impudent," wrote a journalist, "a four-flusher and a faker, and they point with telling effect to his cane. Hollywood, you must understand, doesn't go in for canes. Plus-fours, puttees and polo shirts, maybe, but no canes." Von Sternberg responded by sporting even more ostentatious examples. George Grosz was almost alone in realizing that the canes were not just fashion accessories. "In Germany [canes] were still the hallmark of a 'gentleman,'" he wrote, "and, along with gloves and a leather briefcase, identified the former *Corps* [fraternity] student, managing director or social climber. . . . In von Sternberg's hand, moreover, the simple walking stick was also a sort of fetish or magic wand, something that brought good luck to those who carried it and misfortune to those who mislaid or forgot it." Initially, von Sternberg insisted to Grosz that he wasn't superstitious, then conceded that the canes had a ritual significance. "This stick has powers one can't explain," said Grosz, "just like a divining rod."[9] (Nicholas von Sternberg confirms, "My father was very superstitious. He particularly hated a black cat crossing his path."[10] Black cats play an ominous role in some of his films, notably *Underworld, Thunderbolt*—the criminals frequent a bar called The Black Cat—and *Dishonored,* in which secret agent Dietrich takes her pet on every mission, even in the open cockpit of an aircraft, and is eventually betrayed by it.)

As von Sternberg attained more independence, he widened his personal image into an entire lifestyle. For a time, whenever he ate in a restaurant, he demanded that a plate with six black grapes await him at the table. To maintain an impression of creative dominance, he held script conferences or auditions in secret, locking the doors and permitting no one to enter or leave. On the set, nobody was allowed to make the slightest noise. He even banned watches, claiming that their ticking distracted him. Food and drink were forbidden on the set. These rules were quite common among European directors such as Max Reinhardt; if a visitor didn't respectfully remove his hat, Reinhardt would snatch it off his head and throw it into the wings. "Everyone in Hollywood has . . . a 'gag,'" wrote the *New Yorker* in 1931, defining this as "some trait or mannerism [or] role which attracts attention." British actors formed the Hollywood Cricket Club and staged kipper breakfasts or fish-and-chip suppers. Russians gathered at the Russian-American Art Club to hear the songs and dances of czarist days. American actresses married European aristocrats and flaunted them at garden parties. However, as the writer concluded admiringly, "von Sternberg's gag has been von Sternberg."[11]

Over There

How Ya Gonna Keep 'em Down on the Farm (After
They've Seen Paree)?
—Song by Joe Young and Sam M. Lewis, 1918

BY THE TIME THE war ended with the armistice of November 1918,
von Sternberg had left the Army War College and was attached to the
Medical Corps in Washington, D.C. He wasn't demobilized until 1919,
and then only after William Brady intervened. He found the film industry much changed. In 1916 Brady had forced Lewis Selznick out
of World and switched to stage-bound melodramas that exploited his
Broadway connections. These proved so unpopular that he sold his interest back to Selznick in 1918, having lost millions for his backers and
instilled a caution about investing in the cinema that persists on Wall
Street today.

With World nearly defunct, von Sternberg looked for other work in
New York but had little success. Some of the French artists and technicians from Fort Lee were back in Paris, but Émile Chautard remained.
He hired von Sternberg as his assistant on the 1919 adaptation of
Gaston Leroux's detective story *The Mystery of the Yellow Room* and let
him direct a few scenes. In August 1920 he worked for two weeks as
assistant on *Twisted Souls,* a country house murder melodrama directed
by George Kelson, a former World director who frequently worked as
assistant to Harley Knoles. Stage magician Howard Thurston appeared

in the film as an upright Western spiritualist who unmasks the methods of fake mediums from India. Von Sternberg also received credit (as "Jo Sternberg") as assistant to Wallace Worsley (later director of *The Hunchback of Notre Dame*) on *The Highest Bidder*, released in 1921. It marked his first meeting with actor Lionel Atwill, his alter ego in *The Devil Is a Woman*.

With the industry migrating west, von Sternberg turned to Hollywood, which was flourishing as the public developed a taste for spacious action films. Unwilling to pay for a sleeping berth on the train, he sat up for the entire five-day journey, sustained by sandwiches. But Los Angeles proved no paradise. After New York, with its teeming crowds, public transport, and easy access, the emptiness disquieted him. He saw "only a barren village, [and] after a week of walking along empty streets lined with eucalyptus trees, not having seen a single soul connected with films, I made my way back again."

War had shattered the cinemas of Germany and France, allowing the U.S. industry, fat on three years free of competition, to devour most continental theater chains, production facilities, and talent. Any European director or performer of conspicuous ability quickly received an invitation from Hollywood. All the same, von Sternberg felt a greater affinity with European methods than American ones, and he crossed the Atlantic on a cattle boat in 1921. He went straight to Vienna, visiting the city six times that year. On each occasion he lived at Gartnerstrasse 9, listing his profession as "film director." (The apartment apparently belonged to a relative, since he also stayed there in 1925.) He looked up his old teacher Karl Adolph, who had won a late reputation for his writing. No doubt pleased to be described by his ex-pupil as "an old-fashioned man who knows [the Viennese] better than any man alive today,"[1] Adolph authorized him to make an English version of his 1914 *Tochter,* a series of stories about working-class life that reflected his years spent as a housepainter. On May 24 von Sternberg called on Arthur Schnitzler, but overcome with nerves, he couldn't stop talking. Schnitzler had to remind his visitor that he had come to hear the thoughts of the author of *Reigen* and *Traumnovelle,* not vice versa. "But," von Sternberg said, "he told me he had never listened to such a cultured and interesting talk." For the rest of his life, an inscribed photograph of Schnitzler hung in his office. Of his boldly sexual plays and tales, he said, Schnitzler "was the first one to give me artistic courage."

From Austria he went to England, where he bought a Triumph motorcycle and crashed it, breaking a kneecap. Looking for work, he gravitated to the Alliance Film Corporation, formed by advertising entrepreneur Sir David Higham. Its fourth production, an adaptation of the opera *The Bohemian Girl,* was being directed by Harley Knoles, who remembered von Sternberg from World. Knoles hired him as second unit director and sent him to Hungary to shoot background footage. He also worked on 1922's *Love and a Whirlwind,* codirected by D. Duncan MacRae and American Harold Shaw and featuring Clive Brook, who later became a favorite von Sternberg actor. No additional work followed, however, and after a period of "aimlessly flounder[ing]" in England, he rode his bike to Italy, determined "to see every church."

In 1922 a publisher called the International Editor issued von Sternberg's translation of Adolph's *Tochter* as *Daughters of Vienna,* "freely adapted from the Viennese." Von Sternberg had translated Adolph's text literally, changing little except to remove elements that might confuse English readers. In later years he disparaged this attempt at literature. On a copy signed in Carmel, California, in 1930 he wrote, "Curious how a man's sins crop up in unexpected places." Two editions were supposedly issued: a regular printing, probably of 500 copies, and a luxury printing of 250 copies signed by von Sternberg, Adolph, and Karl Borschke, who contributed the postage stamp–sized drawings that headed each chapter. But the history of this little book, von Sternberg's only extended piece of writing before the 1965 publication of *Fun in a Chinese Laundry,* bristles with inconsistencies. The International Editor, despite claims of having offices in London, New York, and Vienna, apparently never published anything else. Nor has any copy of the limited, signed edition ever appeared for sale. The printer, Frisch and Co., published art books and luxury editions of Schnitzler—who, one might speculate, had some part in what appears to have been a "vanity" project.

Out There

> I can't talk about Hollywood. It was a horror to me when I was there and it's a horror to look back on. I can't imagine how I did it. When I got away from it, I couldn't even refer to the place by name. "Out there," I called it.
>
> —Dorothy Parker

FOR MORE THAN FORTY years, French director Robert Florey served as an unofficial consul to Europeans visiting Hollywood. He and von Sternberg became friendly when the latter, close to his thirtieth birthday, made a second stab at California. This time he lodged in a bungalow near the corner of Vine Street and Hollywood Boulevard—only two blocks, he later noted wryly, from where a star sunk in the pavement commemorates his work. His accommodations were spartan—a single room with a Murphy bed that served as a bureau by day and folded down into a bed at night. He ate alone at nearby Musso and Frank's, an old-fashioned restaurant with high-backed wooden booths, where he could linger for hours. He was never without a book, usually pocket editions of works by philosophers and historians. Thin and quiet, he exuded an air of brooding melancholy, emphasized by his black shirts, floppy hairdo, and heavy moustache.

In his ancient car, he made the rounds of the many small studios, soon to be absorbed by evolving "majors" such as Paramount and Metro-Goldwyn-Mayer (MGM). He may have worked for minor director Lawrence Windom, but it's not known on what film. He did encounter Hugo Ballin, a former art director at World. Ballin's wife Mabel had acted there, and in the hopes of reviving her career, Ballin had formed his own company to film Thackeray's Napoleonic novel *Vanity Fair*, with Mabel as its scheming heroine Becky Sharp. Von Sternberg served as his assistant, after which he looked for work at Grand-Asher, the low-budget studio of Harry Asher, where Roy William Neill was about to direct *By Divine Right*. Mildred Harris, ex-wife of Charlie Chaplin, played a stenographer stalked by her lecherous employer. Like most Asher productions, this one hung by a shoestring. Its high point, a train wreck, wasn't even original but was assembled from miniatures and stock footage. At their interview, Neill, reasonably, asked what the newcomer von Sternberg knew of local conditions. Von Sternberg claims that he went to the window and whistled piercingly. By doing so, he told a startled Neill, one could summon a dozen men with intimate local knowledge but none with his filmmaking skill. Either impressed or desperate, Neill hired him as both assistant director and script editor.

Directors such as Ballin and Neill aroused only his scorn—which, in his determination to have everyone hate him, he made no attempt to hide. In 1931 the *New Yorker* remarked, "The accepted thing for the man who has risen is to appreciate the niceties of *noblesse oblige*. One may be haughty to associates of lesser days, but one should be kind. On the contrary, von Sternberg is likely to make cutting remarks. He ferrets out little weaknesses and comments on them. He opens himself to the accusation that he attempts to pay back old scores, and nurses grievances born of early hardships."[1]

His model of what a filmmaker could and should be remained Erich von Stroheim, even though, in 1924, the two men probably hadn't met. When von Stroheim was making *Blind Husbands* and *Foolish Wives*, von Sternberg was in Europe, and by the time he returned, von Stroheim was on location with *Greed*. Nevertheless, he called him "unique and inimitable," an artist who "invested his films . . . with an intensity that bristled and proclaimed him."

During 1924, nobody in the movie business talked about much except *Greed*, which von Stroheim had been shooting for months in the Sierra Nevada and Death Valley. Halfway through, the company sold out to Louis B. Mayer's Metro Pictures, creating the foundations for MGM. The cinema of epic personal vision collided head-on with the studio product, oriented entirely on profit. The result was a foregone conclusion. Thalberg ordered *Greed* reduced to two hours from the original nine. Before the cuts began, von Stroheim screened the full version for critics and friends. Von Sternberg called it "a powerful and singular demonstration of how a director can influence his performers." It inspired him to begin the screenplay that would become his first feature, *The Salvation Hunters.* "We were all influenced by *Greed*," he said.

Also in 1924, von Sternberg met Viennese producer Max Reinhardt, who was visiting German playwright Karl ("Peter") Vollmoeller in Hollywood, where the writer lived for part of the year. Reinhardt trailed glory. He directed theater companies in both Germany and Austria, including the intimate Kammerspiele in Vienna, where new styles of performance and design were being developed. His productions afforded writers such as Vollmoeller and Hugo von Hofmannstahl almost unlimited opportunity for experimentation, and his acting school produced Europe's most gifted performers.

Given models of upward mobility such as von Stroheim and Reinhardt (born Maximilian Goldmann), it isn't surprising that Josef Sternberg emerged from *By Divine Right* with a "von" in his name, signifying a descent from aristocracy. He credited this ennobling to actor Elliott Dexter, who had a hand in the production and supposedly wanted to "even up" the length of the names as they appeared in the credits. Since Sternberg, normally punctilious about the tiniest detail, was uncritical of this addition, it's likely that he connived at it. (Director Neill would not have objected, since his own name was adapted from the cumbersome "Roland William Neill de Gostrie.") European aristocracy contained almost no acknowledged Jews, and none with a genealogy so precisely documented as to rate the honorific "von," but Dexter neither knew nor cared. Those who did recognize the counterfeit—Dietrich among them—laughed it off as "just Hollywood."[2]

By aggrandizing himself, von Sternberg may have hoped to end rumors that he was not named Sternberg at all, nor was he Viennese. "It was generally believed," said Jesse Lasky Jr., "that he was actually Joe Stern from Brooklyn, and the rest arrogant fabrication."[3] Sternberg professed to be stung by this charge. In 1963 he told an interviewer, "I once offered $50,000 to anyone who could produce any proof that my name is Joe Stern; I've never had to pay it." However, speaking of the period around 1926, he acknowledged, "At that time I was known as Joe Stern."[4] This was certainly the name he used in 1929 when he worked briefly at Paramount's British studios, supervising the construction of its sound recording facilities. At various times he was credited as "Joe," "Josef," or, as on *The Highest Bidder* in 1921, "Jo Sternberg." Adopting "von" may have been the conclusion of the process of refining his name as he had his appearance. Once the decision was made, he adhered to it ferociously. Successive secretaries would inform callers that there was no "Mr. Sternberg" and that his family name began not with an "S" but with a "v."

The accusation that he was "a pants presser from Brooklyn" was not so easily corrected. He did begin his working life in the garment trade, though not as a tailor. However, the image of the new California moviemakers as jumped-up graduates of New York's sweatshops (which many were) appealed to the gentile businessmen now looking with interest at the West Coast film industry. Joseph Kennedy, sometime lover of Dietrich and father of future president John Kennedy, jeered, "Look at that bunch of pants-pressers in Hollywood, making themselves millionaires. I could take the whole business away from them."[5] Not one to make idle threats, Kennedy bought control of the Film Booking Office (FBO) studio, which underwrote the next film on which von Sternberg worked. Within a few years Kennedy owned a substantial segment of the U.S. film industry.

FBO subsisted on westerns, animal films, and dramas based on front-page news. One such revelation concerned Paris-based quack surgeon Serge Voronoff, who claimed that he could restore youth and prolong life by transplanting or injecting into his patients tissue from the testicles of monkeys that he raised in a private zoo on the Côte d'Azur. In 1923 Gertrude Atherton's novel *Black Oxen* imagined a socialite rejuvenated by this pseudoscience, and the following year Frank Lloyd filmed it. On its coattails, Paul Bern, future MGM producer and ill-fated husband of Jean Harlow, wrote a similar screenplay called *Vanity's Price*. Anna Q. Nilsson played aging actress Vanna du Maurier, restored to beauty by "Steinach glandular therapy" at the cost of mental instability and outbursts of murderous rage.

Von Sternberg asked Neill for a job as his assistant, suggesting a salary of $150 a week. His credentials were, he pointed out, impeccable. Not only had he been born in the city where some of the story took place; he had also met Serge Voronoff in Paris. Whether or not Neill believed him, von Sternberg was hired at $100 a week. All went well until, three weeks into the thirty-day shoot, studio head Pat Powers invited von Sternberg to take over direction. Neill, he said, was about to be fired for insulting him. When von Sternberg hesitated, Powers suggested that any loyalty to his former director would be misplaced, since Neill had called him "worthless." Loyalty didn't come into it, von Sternberg replied. He simply despised the story.

Neill quit, leaving a love scene and Vanna's surgery still to be shot. Von Sternberg agreed to finish the film in return for a $50 raise and a new set for the hospital sequence constructed to his specifications and inspired, he later claimed, by Rembrandt's painting *The Anatomy Lesson of Dr. Nicolaes Tulp*. Circular, it had steeply raked seats, allowing students to look down on the operation—a design replicated in the terraced cabaret of *Morocco* and the gambling pit of *The Shanghai Gesture*. In this case, von Sternberg "instructed one of his actors to show disgust. Another had been told to lean over toward the man next to him and leer, as though some obscene remark had passed between them. A third looked amused."[6] *New York Times* reviewer Mordaunt Hall, while dismissing *Vanity's Price* as piffle, found this scene memorable. "The operating room in Vienna is shown, with visiting surgeons studying the operation on Vanna through field glasses. One surgeon shakes his head, knowing that the woman's vanity is bound to suffer by the effect the Steinach treatment will have on her mentality."[7] On the strength of reviews like Hall's, FBO elevated *Vanity's Price* to its list of "Gold Medal Specials," released under its Gothic Films banner. Powers offered von Sternberg a contract, but he turned it down. He'd had a better offer from an unexpected source.

Photographing a Thought

Charlotte: Oh, Henrik, stop playing that gloomy music.
Henrik: It isn't gloomy. It's profound.
—Hugh Wheeler, *A Little Night Music*

SO LOW WAS VON STERNBERG'S opinion of the man who helped him make his first feature that he doesn't even mention his name in *Fun in a Chinese Laundry.* Instead, he simply calls the man "Kipps," after his best-known acting role. Five years his junior, Arthur George Brest, a brash Scot who preferred to be billed as "George K. Arthur," was a man on the make. In 1921, while living in London, he had learned that U.S. director Harold Shaw planned to film H. G. Wells's novel *Kipps,* about a maladroit shop assistant who inherits a fortune but stumbles when he tries to enter high society. A number of candidates for the part were sent to meet Wells, one of whom was Arthur. The actor "accidentally" knocked over a valuable vase in the writer's home, in effect turning a get-acquainted visit into an audition. "My bewildered embarrassment and contrite (though mute) apologies worked the miracle," he explained.[1]

After *Kipps,* Arthur snared small parts in two movies with D. W. Griffith star Mae Marsh. He also pursued Charlie Chaplin, Mary Pickford, and Douglas Fairbanks when they visited London. Arthur became so convinced of his own eventual stardom that he abandoned his new wife and sailed for the United States in December 1922. It has been suggested that Arthur and von Sternberg met on that transatlantic crossing, but the latter had actually returned two months earlier. It's possible, however, that they knew each other in London, since *Kipps* director Shaw also directed *Love and a Whirlwind,* on which von Sternberg was an assistant. By the time *Vanity's Price* came out, they were sufficiently friendly for Arthur to show von Sternberg a screenplay he'd written, *Just Plain Bugs,* and ask him to direct it—starring himself, naturally. Arthur even claimed to have raised $6,000—supplied, he whispered, by Chaplin.

At this point, their stories diverge. Von Sternberg says he offered to write a better script as a showcase for their talents, but Arthur says the script already existed. He also denies claiming that Chaplin was involved. According to Arthur:

> We . . . divided up the necessary capital into sixteen shares. I had
> five and a half shares, von Sternberg four and my sister Doris Lloyd
> two. We were short of the rest of the money—about £400—and
> you can guess what luck I had trying to persuade the film people,
> who are used to films costing at least $25,000, to put money into a
> picture which was only going to cost so little. However, we started,
> borrowing a studio and using old scenery, which we "dressed up"
> ourselves. Eventually things got so bad that we were able to make
> only four hundred feet of film at a time as we raised the money.[2]

Von Sternberg calculated that by staging most of the action outdoors, he could shoot for three weeks on Arthur's $6,000. "I had in mind a visual poem," he wrote. "Instead of flat lighting, shadows. In the place of pasty masks, faces in relief, plastic and deep-eyed. Instead of scenery which meant nothing, an emotionalized background that would transfer itself into my foreground. Instead of saccharine characters, sober figures moving in rhythm. . . . And dominating all this was an imposing piece of machinery: the hero of the film was to be a dredge."

As a first step, he rowed out to the dredge perched on a barge in San Pedro harbor and persuaded the operators to let him shoot there. Meanwhile, a cast and crew were rounded up. Cinematographer Eddie Gheller, though moderately experienced, probably acted mainly as the camera operator, given von Sternberg's intimate knowledge of film lighting. The assistant director, credited variously as "Peter" or "George Ruric," was George Carrol Sims; later, as "Paul Cain," he would write for crime pulps such as *Black Mask,* as well as scripting two distinctive thrillers: Edgar Ulmer's *The Black Cat,* with Boris Karloff and Bela Lugosi, and *Grand Central Murder.*

Von Sternberg and Arthur always claimed that they chose their cast from the bit players who hung around the studio gates—the group characterized in *The Last Command* as "the bread line of Hollywood." In contrast to his denial of credit to the more important collaborators, von Sternberg remained loyal to these performers and even inserted a panel into the credits of *The Shanghai Gesture,* praising its "large cast of HOLLYWOOD EXTRAS, who, without expecting credit or mention, stand ready day and night to do their best—and who at their best are more than good enough to deserve mention." Claiming that such people made up the cast of *The Salvation Hunters* was a good story, but untrue. Arthur was thoroughly experienced, and Robert McIntyre, an MGM casting director, helped out by recommending other talented and reliable candidates. Olaf Hytten, a fellow Scot who played a deckhand ("The Brute"), had twenty films to his credit. Otto Matiesen, aka "The Man" (or, more accurately, "The Pimp") who lures "The Girl" into prostitution, played Napoleon in Ballin's *Vanity Fair.* Even six-year-old Bruce Guerin ("The Child") had appeared in a dozen movies. In the least likely piece of casting, "The Woman," drab companion of "The Man" and, by implication, a whore (an intertitle describes her as having "fallen as low as her stockings," signaling a "fallen woman"), was played by Nellie Bly Baker. She was Charlie Chaplin's secretary but took acting roles on the side, notably as a stern-faced masseuse in *A Woman of Paris.* Her involvement with Arthur suggests that she was his mole in the Chaplin organization.

The only true newcomer was his star. Georgia Hale, a nineteen-year-old "dress extra" he'd met on *Vanity's Price.* Impressed by her "sullen charm," he'd lent her *Daughters of Vienna* and promised her a great future. Possibly they became lovers, although Hale's sentimental memoirs, *Charlie Chaplin: Intimate Close-Ups,* insist the relationship was platonic, with Sternberg a solicitous friend, urging her to read more, and fretting about their stuttering careers. When, following the success of *The Salvation Hunters,* he took her to dinner in his new red Packard, offered her a diamond ring in lieu of a salary, and proposed marriage, she turned him down. He'd been supplanted by Chaplin, who was grooming her as his next lover and star.

Von Sternberg's synopsis of *The Salvation Hunters* was curt: "Three derelicts live on a mud scow from which circumstances and environment release them after poetically conceived tribulations." On screen, he amplifies his theme in a wordy foreword. "There are important fragments of life that have been avoided by the motion picture because Thought is concerned and not the Body. A thought can create and destroy nations—and it is all the more powerful because it is born of suffering, lives in silence, and dies when it has done its work. Our aim has been to photograph a thought. A thought that guides humans who crawl close to the earth—whose lives are simple—who begin nowhere and end nowhere." Boiled down, this equates to "the will to achieve an end can triumph over force of circumstances"—a belief that motivated von Sternberg all his life and, one suspects, he first encountered in Ralph Waldo Emerson's essay "Self-Reliance."

The "derelicts" of *The Salvation Hunters* are The Boy, The Girl, and The Child. The Girl and The Child live on the dredge, which, in some manner that is never clarified, is responsible for their orphaned situation. The Boy mopes around the harbor, brooding on the gulls, the rusting scrap iron along the water's edge, and the fishermen mending nets. Meanwhile, the dredge tirelessly drops its claw into the water, drags up mud, dumps it, and returns for more, indifferent to the fact that with each load, an equal quantity of earth crumbles from the bank. Convinced that fate intends something better for them, The Boy suggests that the three move to the city. Von Sternberg wastes no time showing Los Angeles as a palm-shaded paradise; instead, he relocates them in a slum of dirt streets and wooden shacks in what was then Chinatown. Hopeless and hungry, they are approached by The Man, who offers them a room until they get on their feet. His companion, The Woman, is ready to feed them as well, but The Man stops her. "Hunger," he explains in a memorably insidious intertitle, "will whisper things into their ears that I might find it troublesome to say." In case we don't grasp that he's Satan incarnate, von Sternberg poses The Man against a set of goat horns attached to the wall, so that they appear to grow from his head.

Finding no work, The Boy returns with just a stick of gum. The Girl starts to look more favorably on whoring and, reluctantly, drags herself downstairs and into the street. Ignoring "Jesus Saves!" chalked on a boarded-up window, she almost immediately picks up The Gentleman, a dapper individual with a cane. He follows her to the room, where, to his confusion, The Boy and The Child are waiting while The Man lurks outside the door. Understandably spooked, he gives some money to The Child and flees. The Gentleman was played by another veteran of *Vanity's Price.* "Stuart Holmes, the famous 'villain,' had an evening to spare and played a part for us," recalled von Sternberg. "It cost [$100], and he insisted on being paid beforehand, but his name was worth it."

Following this disappointing encounter, The Man offers to take everyone on a drive. Their destination is a tract of the then-deserted San Fernando Valley, where the only mark of settlement is a real estate agent's sign announcing, "Here Your Dreams Come True." When The Man tries to seduce The Girl, there's a fistfight in which The Boy triumphs. After this, the three derelicts march down the road to the optimistic intertitle, "It isn't conditions, nor is it environment—our faith controls our lives!" As a synopsis of the time suggested, "This is where you cheer."

Even though it was shot almost entirely outdoors, *The Salvation Hunters* has the look of a studio film. The dockside exteriors display a back-lot evenness of tone. As a photographer, von Sternberg understood how Alfred Stieglitz and Edward Steichen distilled beauty from urban squalor. According to critic Peter Wollen, all his films occur in "heterocosms"—fantasy cities where the real and imaginary intersect, as in dreams. Though the Atlantic separates the waterfront of *The Docks of New York* and the streets of Lubeck in *The Blue Angel,* von Sternberg's vision integrates them. Decorative elements from *The Salvation Hunters* turn up in all his later films, suggesting that, rather than reflecting actual locations, they make up part of his mental furniture. The "Here Your Dreams Come True" billboard foreshadows similar signs in *Un-*

derworld and *Blonde Venus*. The newspaper pinups and chalked words that decorate walls, as well as a dockside announcement in Chinese, reappear in *Dishonored* and *Shanghai Express*. Stuart Holmes's Gentleman, a reserved figure with a moustache, a three-piece suit and a cane, provides the model for von Sternberg's own appearance and style and represents a recurring character in his films. Equally, Georgia Hale, though lacking the intensity of Marlene Dietrich or Evelyn Brent, is the prototypical von Sternberg heroine—brooding, self-destructive, a focus and motivation for the humiliating actions of the men she fascinates.

In its simplicity and reticence, not to mention its acceptance of poverty and prostitution, *The Salvation Hunters* was ahead of its time. It anticipated the end of stage melodrama as the model for film narrative and acting. But prophets are always without honor, and von Sternberg was no exception. The premiere in a tiny Sunset Boulevard theater ended in chaos. "The members of the cast were in the audience which greeted my work with laughter and jeers," he wrote, "and finally rioted." Not by nature inclined to philosophical resignation, he took the reaction as a personal affront. "[The film] started as a promotion idea for myself, but it became a Cause. I became ill with neuritis. Then, at the preview, the audience laughed for an hour. My neuritis left me."[3] In his eyes, the rejection of *The Salvation Hunters* proved the Nietzschean dictum: "That which does not kill you makes you strong."

In desperation, Arthur, who had already sold his car, took extreme measures to get the film launched.

I tried to get Charlie Chaplin to see it, as I know him pretty well. Some time passed, and one Sunday evening at eleven o'clock Charlie rang me. He seemed frantically excited about our picture, asked me to go to see him at once, and said he thought the whole industry would go mad about it. Charlie telephoned Douglas Fairbanks and asked him to come and see *The Salvation Hunters* but he was out. The next morning Charlie told me he thought we had the greatest picture ever seen. Douglas Fairbanks promised me he would see the picture, but I knew that was a matter of time. Every evening he was seeing films at his house after dinner, and I persuaded his butler, who also projects the films for him, to squeeze

The Salvation Hunters in. [Chaplin] told me afterwards he was "bewildered at the success of this unknown director." Within a quarter of an hour of my going to see him at his request, Douglas Fairbanks had bought a quarter share in the picture for a sum exceeding many times its cost [von Sternberg says $20,000] and had promised to put *The Salvation Hunters* on the market for us.[4]

Since Arthur had sold his car, they hired one so they could arrive at United Artists in style. Confused by the unfamiliar controls, they couldn't find the brakes and came to a stop only by crashing into the gate.

Those who knew Chaplin's sensitivity about his lack of education were unsurprised by his support of *The Salvation Hunters*. To extol such an "arty" production bolstered his intellectual credentials. Was he genuinely impressed? Probably not. He invested no money himself, and after the film went on general release in February 1925, he distanced himself, leaving his partners in United Artists, Mary Pickford and Douglas Fairbanks, holding the bag. In 1929 he would similarly exploit the Dali/Buñuel surrealist short *Un Chien Andalou,* screening it a number of times at his home and declaring it a masterpiece, only to dismiss it in private as "a stupid film." When May Reeves, his girlfriend at the time, asked why, he told her, "Oh, one has to keep people amused, and look up-to-date."[5]

A Genuine Genius

> I don't think Josef von Sternberg is working anywhere. I
> think he's a genuine genius again.
> —Walter Winchell, 1926

WITH UNITED ARTISTS BACKING it, *The Salvation Hunters*
looked like the salvation of everyone involved. Georgia Hale became
Chaplin's mistress, then his leading lady in *The Gold Rush*. George
Arthur won some acting roles, including in a couple of von Sternberg
films, and he later became a successful producer of short features, but
von Sternberg never mentioned him in interviews. As he would do with
increasing frequency, he wrote a collaborator out of his life.

The director himself was feted. The *New Yorker* took pleasure in
writing up his exploits as a case of a smart East Coast Jew putting one
over on dumb West Coast goyim. "Joseph Sternberg drifted from the
East Side, via Broadway, to Hollywood, a well-frayed shoestring pinned
carefully in an inner pocket. He returns Josef von Sternberg, the 'von'
having blossomed under the beneficence of the Californian sun. Out
of experiences with butterfly movie companies, he wrought *The Salvation Hunters,* one of the most discussed of the current reticent dramas.
Forty-seven hundred dollars was Mr. von Sternberg's producing capital,
garnered in reluctant fives, tens and twenties by a native salesmanship
which would see nothing incongruous in attempting to peddle grand
pianos from a pushcart."[1]

Not to be outdone by Chaplin, Pickford signed von Sternberg to a two-film contract. As part of the publicity buildup, he was photographed chatting with baseball star "Babe" Ruth (one struggles to imagine on what topic) and strolling on the lawns of "Pickfair" with Doug and Mary. "I believe him to have those qualities of freshness and originality for which we have long been seeking," trilled Pickford. "He is a master technician and has a sense of drama possessed by few."[2] But her offer was a poisoned chalice. Habitually, she vacillated between aspiring to be considered a serious actress and clinging to her position as "America's Sweetheart." Von Sternberg, after a research visit to Pennsylvania, submitted the outline of another von Stroheim–influenced melodrama called *Backwash,* in which Pickford would play a blind girl living in the squalor of industrial Pittsburgh. Most of the film would be subjective camera, with the action, including a cameo for Chaplin, taking place in her mind. As in *The Salvation Hunters,* he foresaw images of poverty, dirt, and urban ugliness.

After reading it, Pickford hurriedly backpedaled, according to von Sternberg. "My star-to-be," he wrote acidly, "asked me to wait ten weeks, to accustom herself to the idea while she made a 'normal' film with a 'normal' director"—in this case, Marshall Neilan. After that, their contract lapsed by mutual consent. Subsequently, Pickford professed to find him ridiculous. "He proved to be a complete boiled egg," she scoffed. "The business of '*von*' Sternberg, and carrying a cane, and that little moustache! I'm so glad I didn't do the film." Her rejection, however, is suspect. Playing a blind girl would have been nothing new for her. She had already done so in *A Good Little Devil,* one of her earliest stage successes. Von Sternberg also told Sergei Eisenstein that she took *Backwash* sufficiently seriously to prepare for the role by spending time in a home for the blind, studying their behavior. It's more likely she pulled out once *The Salvation Hunters* proved to be a flop. It played for less than a week in New York and only sporadically elsewhere, losing most of the Pickford-Fairbanks investment. She didn't mind displaying her acting skills in an atypical role, but only if it was also a commercial success.

The Salvation Hunters put its director on the map, however, and the big studios made offers, if only to ensure that competitors didn't grab a potential moneymaker. B. P. Schulberg, West Coast production manager of Famous Players–Lasky (soon to be renamed Paramount Publix) was interested, but von Sternberg elected to sign an eight-film contract with MGM. The decision was ill-advised. The richest of the big companies, MGM was also the most rigid, with a factory ethic to which every employee was subordinated. To von Sternberg, however, one fact counted more than any other: Erich von Stroheim was on its payroll, which made the offer irresistible. In only a short time he realized his error. That he had become just another cog in Louis B. Mayer's machine was emphasized when he was ordered to line up with every other director and technician to be photographed for a promotional film celebrating the studio's concentration of talent. He stands glowering at the camera, smoldering cigarette in hand. But predictably, he is at the shoulder of his hero, who, in duster and floppy driving cap, looks like he's on his way to a spin in the country.

While waiting for his first assignment, von Sternberg drove to the studio every day with Robert Florey, who had become his assistant. After telling his secretary not to disturb him, he would drape a red shawl around his shoulders, as men did in the coffee shops of Vienna, and play Florey at chess. Periodically, he completed odd jobs for Mayer. These included directing a screen test for the Moscow-based Jewish Habima Theatre Company, whose forty members arrived in the United States in December 1926. They would tour for two years until the group fragmented, some remaining in the United States, and others moving to Tel Aviv to become the nucleus of the National Theatre of Israel. The test, the producer told von Sternberg, was a courtesy and a gift to the company, which was too distinguished to lower itself to make a film, least of all in Hollywood. No admirer of expressionist acting, in which emotions are externalized, often in exaggerated gestures or shouts, von Sternberg was secretly pleased when the performers, flinging themselves around the soundstage and shouting "Prostitute!" demonstrated that they had no movie potential whatsoever. Knowing nothing of acting technique, he distrusted those who did. In *The Docks of New York*, Olga Baclanova played her role as she had learned to do in Russia. "Just because you were at the Moscow Art Theatre," he told her, "don't think that you understand everything." He bullied her, as he did many performers, to the point of tears, which resulted in the unrehearsed effect he desired. Years later, meeting in Europe, she told him, "I only began to make pictures when you started to yell at me."

Irving Thalberg, head of production at MGM, finally assigned him a British novel by Alden Brooks, published in 1924 as *The Enchanted Land* and in the United States as *Escape*. Brooks, a survivor of the Somme, based it on the war experiences of his friend, painter Matthew Smith, who was hospitalized for a year with shrapnel wounds and shell shock. The book's main character, Dominique Prad, a frustrated artist, almost dies on the battlefield. Convalescing, he swears he will "never do anything else in future but live life, beautiful life, to the full, as it should be led." Back in Paris, he reluctantly takes over the family silk-weaving factory, which supports a gaggle of parasitic relatives and rapacious prospective in-laws. After attempting suicide, he's placed in a rural "rest home," from which he flees, pursued by his fiancée's father and a posse of police. Meeting a gypsy girl, Silda, he joins her band in the woods, where he settles down to a life of art.

Expedience rather than appropriateness dictated the choice of this subject for von Sternberg. King Vidor's *The Big Parade,* a romance between a wounded American soldier and a French peasant, had been the decade's biggest hit for MGM. Thalberg wanted something similar and assigned the same actress, Renée Adorée, to the film. Von Sternberg worked on the scenario with Alice D. G. Miller, daughter of the better-known Alice Duer Miller. The younger Miller began her career with D. W. Griffith, whose sentimental tastes were evident in her writing for films such as *Slave of Desire, So This Is Marriage,* and *Lady of the Night.* We know nothing of how *Escape* was adapted, but much can be inferred from its incongruous new title, *The Exquisite Sinner.* Opposite Adorée, Conrad Nagel, a favorite of Louis B. Mayer, played Dominique. Von Sternberg found a small role for George K. Arthur. A young model from Montana named Myrna Loy, who had posed for photographer Harry Waxman, was lightly draped in netting and plastered with white greasepaint to play a "living statue" in an artist's studio—her Hollywood debut.

With Florey as "technical adviser," von Sternberg tried to instill some French atmosphere into the film. Although they visited Quebec to scout locations, MGM insisted on recycling a chateau set left over from 1923's *In the Palace of the King*. The rest was shot in a village mocked up on the back lot. Von Sternberg did his best to personalize the sets, pasting up posters and daubing walls with graffiti. Determined to show he was his own man, he had a large sign painted with the words "Please BE SILENT Behind Camera." (As a joke, the actors posed for a photograph with von Sternberg and the sign, fingers to lips. He did not appear amused.) On location, he arrived wearing another pawnshop find, a bulky fur-lined overcoat that had belonged to a Shakespearean actor. However, he reserved his special performance for the first day of shooting. Florey was a witness:

> Thirty gendarmes were supposed to march into a Breton village. . . . At 8.45 von Sternberg arrived on the set. All the actors were lined up. He passed before them in review, inspecting them from head to foot, their sergeant-major waiting at a respectful distance. When he arrived at the twenty-first gendarme, von Sternberg stopped, hypnotising the poor man. Then he turned to the technicians and shouted angrily, "What do you take me for? For [Fred] Niblo or [King] Vidor? Who do you think I am?" Enraged, he began rapping on the camera with his cane, to the alarm of Max Fabian, the cameraman. "Get me the head of production. I will not permit you to mock me" etc. [His producers] arrived at the gallop, and von Sternberg exposed the reason for his protest. "A button is missing from the tunic of this gendarme. I will not endure an insult of this sort!"[3]

Having just endured three months of such behavior from von Stroheim on *The Merry Widow*, MGM bridled at getting it from a near unknown. All the same, such antics might have been tolerated if the completed film had been good, but opinions on *The Exquisite Sinner* were divided. Somewhat puzzlingly, given von Sternberg's solemnity, Florey called it "full of interest, and . . . the humour of which von Sternberg was a master."[4] On surer ground, he praised the luminous photography, with its shadows and silhouette scenes. Even John Grierson acknowledged the beauty of the sequence in which Dominique marries Silda in the forest. The *New Yorker* described it as "harsh and beautiful and sincere."[5] But preview audiences found the film obscure. A studio assessor agreed. While conceding that "Mr. von Sternberg has a photographic talent all his own," he complained, "in vain we are looking in the picture for the theme of the story—the longing of a man for freedom." Rewritten intertitles didn't help, so producers Hunt Stromberg and Eddie Mannix were directed to find a solution. Ideas were solicited from staff members. In August the studio accepted a proposal from husband-and-wife team Hope Loring and Louis Lighton, who had fabricated a screenplay from a flimsy short story called "It" by Elinor Glyn. They suggested remaking *The Exquisite Sinner* as a screwball comedy. "Ninety-nine people out of a hundred want MONEY!" they wrote. "And these ninety-nine would feel that any man who runs away from money—just because he wants to PAINT—is crazy! THEREFOR we suggest the following angle—FARCE COMEDY—on the story."

Phil Rosen shot the new version, eliminating most if not all of von Sternberg's footage. Florey remained as assistant director, fuming as Rosen discarded Adorée's authentic costume of head scarf, earrings, and simple dress for a Breton bonnet, laced bodice of the sort worn by Swiss milkmaids, flowered apron, and wooden clogs. Silda became "Marcelle," and Dominique was renamed "Edmond Durand." The studio reader, who rated the new version "pretty good," warned, "we mustn't look . . . for the spiritual significance of the original [story]. The story is told on the screen in a brisk and logical manner which unifies the plot and holds the attention of the audience." But new previews didn't confirm this judgment. Despite more retakes, and retitling as *Heaven on Earth,* the film remained a flop.

While the studio hacked at *The Exquisite Sinner,* von Sternberg was assigned a melodrama of the Parisian underworld, *The Masked Bride.* Gaby, a onetime thief but now a dancer in a Montmartre café, meets Grover, an American millionaire. They fall in love, but before they can be married, Antoine, her former partner in both dancing and burglary, forces her to steal a necklace from Grover, threatening to kill her lover if she doesn't. Both are caught, but Grover, realizing that Gaby did it for love, marries her anyway. The studio assigned two actors from von Stroheim's *The Merry Widow* to the film: Mae Murray as Gaby, and Roy

D'Arcy as the Prefect of Police. In addition, Ben Carré, one of the old French contingent at World, designed the production. But news of the mutilation of *The Exquisite Sinner* stretched von Sternberg's patience too far. After two weeks he ordered cinematographer Oliver Marsh to turn the camera to the ceiling and film the rafters as an expression of contempt, and he left the set. Shortly after, MGM terminated his contract.

On August 12, 1925, von Sternberg went public in the *Los Angeles Times.* "I was given very little choice in the selection of my story, or the cast," he complained, "or opportunity to aid in writing the scenario, titling, editing, or even in methods of direction. . . . I am glad that the break has been made, and think it is a fine thing for me." Christy Cabanne finished *The Masked Bride.* Von Sternberg disowned the film, and he never forgave MGM. Throughout his tenure at Paramount in the 1930s, a board in his outer office listed past projects, with comments on their fate. After "Opus # 1. *The Salvation Hunters*" came "Opus # 2—*The Exquisite Sinner,*" with the note "(Sabotaged by Thalberg)."

With time on his hands, von Sternberg continued writing. His one fiction success was a short story, "The Waxen Galatea." Published in 1925 in the trade magazine *The Director,* it describes a repressed young man whose sexual ideal is represented by a shop-window mannequin made of wax. Finding a woman who resembles the dummy, he falls in love with her, only to despair when she chooses a rival. Embittered, he returns to the abstract love of the inanimate figure, forever perfect, forever faithful. The story has significant resonance with von Sternberg's private life. All three of his wives were younger, unassertive women he could dominate, and in Marlene Dietrich he found a performer willing to let herself be molded to his ideal.

A by-product of Chaplin's patronage was the opportunity to socialize with the star and his cronies, who gathered for breakfast at Henry's, a Hollywood Boulevard café not far from the studio. Another customer was an actress with a formidable profile named Riza Royce. She had arrived in Los Angeles in August on a contract from B. P. Schulberg, having graduated from the *Ziegfeld Follies* to some minor success in Broadway comedies. But Royce was making little headway, despite efforts by her friend, screenwriter Frederica Sagor, who provided room and board until the actress found more work. It's hard to imagine the reticent von Sternberg picking up a girl, but he bought Royce a cup of coffee and a doughnut and invited her to join Chaplin's table. She soon became a fixture there, and in his life.

Three Sheets to the Wind

What decadent rubbish is this?

—Madame Arkadina in Anton Chekhov's *The Sea Gull*

VON STERNBERG'S ACCOUNT OF the next episode in his career was laconic. "During a period when I was confronted with failure," he wrote, "[Charles Chaplin] asked me to direct a film for him. This was quite a distinction, as he had never honoured another director in this fashion, but it only resulted in an unpleasant experience for me."

The film, variously known as *Sea Gulls* (its official title in the Chaplin studio records) or *The Sea Gull,* was retitled by von Sternberg *The Woman Who Loved Once* and then, definitively, *A Woman of the Sea* by Chaplin, to remind people that leading lady Edna Purviance had starred in his own *A Woman of Paris.* Purviance was one of many old girlfriends Chaplin left behind as he strove single-mindedly for success. Evidently feeling guilty about abandoning her, he kept her on salary all her life and tried to restart her career from time to time.

Innocent and winning as she appeared in *The Immigrant* and other Chaplin films, Purviance was not a natural actress. "I suffered untold agonies," she wrote. "Eyes seemed to be everywhere. I was simply frightened to death." Von Sternberg claimed she found relief in alcohol—corroborated by an incident on New Year's Day, 1924. At a party at Purviance's house, attended by her fiancé Courtland Dines and her actress friend Mabel Normand, Dines was shot and wounded

55

by Horace Greer, Normand's chauffeur. Police found quantities of then-illegal liquor in the house, and Greer was charged with attempted murder. His attorney described the party as a "Roman saturnalia" and his client—though admittedly an ex-con—as the "only clean soul in the midst of a bunch of drunks." With *A Woman of Paris* still in the theaters, the case caused comment, and some exhibitors pulled the film. A scandal appeared imminent. However, the April 1924 trial showed every indication of strings being discreetly pulled, probably by Chaplin. Greer declined to testify about the party, supposedly out of respect for Normand, and the jury returned a speedy acquittal.

Following this incident, Purviance's nervousness increased. She didn't work for more than a year and in August 1925 left for a long rest in Europe. She stopped off in New York to see Chaplin, where he was dallying with his latest lover, Louise Brooks. He told her that if any European film project caught her interest, he might be willing to invest in it. That November, Chaplin spent some time 300 miles north of Los Angeles near Monterey, where his friend Harry Crocker owned the stretch of coast near Carmel that is now Seventeen Mile Drive and Pebble Beach golf course. He returned to Los Angeles with the idea of setting a future production there. When Purviance arrived back in December 1925, he offered to star her in such a film and proposed von Sternberg as the director and writer.

To von Sternberg, the promise of Chaplin's near-limitless resources and prestige seemed the answer to every prayer. But people still argue over the part played by Chaplin in the conception and eventual destruction of what became *A Woman of the Sea*. One of the few movie professionals with firsthand knowledge of the project was John Grierson, an aggressive young Scot in California on a three-year Rockefeller research fellowship to study the psychology of propaganda. A few years later, back in Britain, he would put his findings to work by launching what he christened the "Documentary Film movement."

Taken under Chaplin's wing, Grierson saw *The Salvation Hunters* and met von Sternberg, whose character didn't measure up to the Scot's harsh standards. "It struck me that sensibility of his peculiarly intensive and introspective sort was not a very healthy equipment for a hard world," he wrote. "A director of this instinct is bound to have a solitary and (as commerce goes) an unsuccessful life of it. Von Sternberg, I think, was weak."[1] In Grierson's recollection of *The Sea Gull*, "the story was Chaplin's, and humanist to a degree; with fishermen that toiled, and sweated, and lived and loved as proletarians do."[2] Chaplin, he said, admired Charles Dickens and had detected a similar sympathy for ordinary people in *The Salvation Hunters*. A Dickensian spirit was intended to pervade the film—a point that, Grierson insists, was made clear to von Sternberg before work began. If this is correct, von Sternberg either failed to grasp Chaplin's wishes or ignored them—more likely the latter, since it wouldn't be the last time he acted so autocratically.

Harry Crocker showed von Sternberg around Monterey. The net-draped docks, clapboard shacks, and wind-contorted, salt-silvered cypresses of the rocky coastline suggested obvious locations for a drama. Within a few weeks, he had composed a scenario about two sisters from a fishing family. Joan, the Purviance character, is lovable and playful—ideal wife material. In contrast, the glamorous Magdalen, though courted for years by solid but dull fisherman Peter, still hungers for adventure, and she gets it when a novelist visits Monterey. Both sisters are smitten, but it's Magdalen he takes back to the city with him. Joan and Peter marry and remain in Monterey, where, in the words of the closing intertitle, "the sea—made of all the useless tears that have been shed—grows neither less or more."

This was no Dickensian fable of simple fisherfolk, as Chaplin would have known if he had read the scenario. However, he apparently did not. Perhaps he was too busy filming *The Circus*, or von Sternberg may have "forgotten" to show him a copy before the unit left to start shooting in March 1926. Even if Chaplin had read it, he might have assumed, in light of *The Salvation Hunters* and the *Backwash* story for Pickford, that von Sternberg would automatically adopt a naturalistic, earthy style.

Von Sternberg used cameraman Eddie Gheller from *The Salvation Hunters*, but for the interiors he brought in Paul Ivano, who had worked on *Greed*. George Sims, as "Peter Ruric," signed on as assistant director, as did Riza Royce, von Sternberg's first verifiable mistress and eventual wife. For the interiors, shot at the Chaplin studios, Chaplin's longtime designer Charles D. "Danny" Hall, borrowed from Universal to work on *The Circus*, provided the sets. Aside from Purviance, the performers, though optimistically described as "discoveries," were all experienced character actors for whom this film represented a career best. Eve Southern, who played the hot-eyed Magdalen (and had debuted as a near-naked temple dancer in Griffith's *Intolerance*), never progressed beyond supporting roles, some of them in von Sternberg's films. She played one of Gary Cooper's lovers in *Morocco* and a gypsy fortune-teller in *The King Steps Out*. Gayne Whitman had his greatest success after sound, when his theatrical voice put him in demand for voice-overs and narrations.

Everything started smoothly enough. The fifty or so still photographs—all that remain of the film, aside from some notebooks kept by Ivano and a list of intertitles—show a film in von Sternberg's heightened visual style. There is even a shot in which Peter drapes one of his signature fishing nets over Joan in a symbolic attempt to keep her at home. On June 19, 1926, the *Los Angeles Times* noted completion of the film, which had by then been renamed *The Woman Who Loved Once*—a move that the journalist, in the first sign of hostility toward the production, labeled "conventionalism." Von Sternberg quickly reverted to the original title.

As soon as shooting ended, Purviance left Los Angeles on a three-month trip through the Pacific Northwest and Canada. According to Robert Florey, von Sternberg wanted to reshoot some sequences, but Chaplin felt he had already spent too much money. As to what Chaplin thought of the film, we have only the evidence of Grierson, who was invited to watch it with him. Chaplin, he says, was astonished at how little it reflected his Dickensian aspirations. At the first sight of Purviance as Joan, he exclaimed, "That's not a fisherman's wife!" Chaplin returned the film to von Sternberg, described how he thought the story should have been interpreted, and told him to reshoot parts of it. Von Sternberg did so, according to Grierson, but Chaplin was still unsatisfied and declined to release it. Chaplin's studio records show no retakes, however, which would have been difficult to do, since Purviance wasn't available. Nor does von Sternberg mention reshooting. But Florey writes of seeing "two versions" of the film.[3] Florey and Grierson also agree that von Sternberg defied Chaplin's ban on public screenings and invited a number of friends and reviewers to see it in a Beverly Hills theater. "This put Chaplin into a fury," says Florey, "particularly when the critics confirmed his opinion."[4] It was never shown again in public. In 1933 Chaplin destroyed all prints, clearing the way for *A Woman of the Sea* to be written off as a total loss for tax purposes. In 1991, in another exercise in tax reduction, his widow authorized the destruction of the last printed materials.

Chaplin never adequately explained the reasons for his dissatisfaction with the film. Maybe, as Grierson claims, he simply expected a very different version. Alternatively, it could have been pique at von Sternberg's holding a screening. A more plausible explanation emerged in a 1966 Chaplin interview. *A Woman of the Sea*, he said, "depressed" him. Anything to do with Purviance had that effect. In 1947 he gave her a walk-on in *Monsieur Verdoux*. "She . . . was not bad," he wrote, "but all the while her presence affected me with a depressing nostalgia, for she was associated with my early success—those days when everything was the future." Von Sternberg too blamed Purviance, but more directly. "She . . . had become unbelievably timid," he wrote, "and unable to act in even the simplest scene without great difficulty, When the camera turned, [she] trembled like the leaf of an aspen. The only remedy for this condition was alcohol, which had caused it, and this was unsuitable. I called for kettledrums, and the timpani distracted her long enough for her to play a part."

Was Purviance so obviously an alcoholic that her performance made the film unreleasable? Von Sternberg is the only person to suggest so, but the film's shot lists provide some corroboration. As David Robinson notes in his biography of Chaplin, "For the most part [von Sternberg] was shooting with considerable economy, generally printing the second or third take of a shot. Scenes that demanded work of the slightest complication from Edna, however, seem often to have required nine, ten or more takes."[5] More than ten years later, on *I, Claudius,* von Sternberg fell into an identical pattern of brief takes for most performers but dozens for scenes featuring the fractious and finally undirectable Charles Laughton.

After Chaplin destroyed the film, Grierson became both the primary source of information and the least reliable. Since documentary—and, in particular, Soviet agitprop—celebrated the nobility of labor, a film that exploited fishermen in a story of what Noël Coward called "high life and low loins" may have offended his political beliefs. In 1929, when Grierson made his only film as a director, *Drifters,* he chose a portrait of North Sea herring fishermen that might almost be, in its bleak rejection of pictorialism, a repudiation of *A Woman of the Sea.* In 1932, surveying Hollywood cinema, he attacked the film again, accusing von Sternberg of emphasizing "net patterns, sea patterns, and hair in the wind" and playing "with the symbolism of the sea until the fishermen and fish were forgotten."[6] He called it "the most beautiful picture ever produced in Hollywood, and the least human."[7]

Von Sternberg insists that he didn't resent the suppression of his work and that he and Chaplin remained friendly. He claims they "spent many idle hours with each other, before, during, and after the making of this film, but not once was this work of mine discussed, nor have I ever broached the subject of its fate to him." Sergei Eisenstein, however, claims that Chaplin confided to him of von Sternberg, "I've never met a more disagreeable layabout in all my life."[8]

The Ascent of Paramount

American husbands are the best in the world; no other
husbands are so generous to their wives, or can be so easily
divorced.

—Elinor Glyn

OF *A WOMAN OF THE SEA,* von Sternberg wrote that it "nearly
ended" his career. Offers of directing work dried up. Following the
double debacle of the aborted MGM contract and the shelved Chaplin
project, nobody would trust him with a film of his own.

On July 6, 1926, Riza Royce phoned her friend Frederica Sagor
and asked, "How would you like to stand up for me today? Von Sternberg and I are getting married."[1]

Sagor, who had never met the groom and barely knew his name,
joined the couple at the West Hollywood sheriff's office—"a dirty, tiny
store with two roll-top desks and two swivel chairs—one for the sheriff
and the other for the only working judge [in the district]. A toilet in
the back was in plain view. The only other furnishings were a battered
broom and a large cardboard box serving as a wastebasket."[2]

Sagor thought von Sternberg and Royce "mentally, spiritually, and
physically unsuited" and called their union "a curious, if temporary
alliance—a marriage convenient for both participants. It lent an aura
of security and respectability to an up-and-coming director who felt
himself in an atmosphere he did not fully understand or belong in, but

61

in which he was determined to be noticed. For the bride, it was an immediate and happy solution to her financial situation and a heaven-made opportunity to reach her ambition, to achieve stardom, with a talented young husband to further her career."[3]

Immediately after the wedding, von Sternberg took his new wife on a three-month honeymoon to Europe. As described to Sagor by Riza, it was no idyll. "On the train trip from LA to New York," wrote Sagor, "the honeymooners did not splurge on a compartment, but had separate beds. Von Sternberg ordered his bride to the upper berth, while he slumbered below. In New York, to keep expenses down, they stayed in the small Bronx apartment of his mother, sleeping on a broken-down sofa-bed in the living room."[4]

Before they sailed, von Sternberg asked Riza to give her winter coat to his mother, promising to buy her another in Europe. Riza complained that he never did, and she shivered across Austria and Germany, but since it was high summer, this seems exaggerated. In Vienna, two weeks after arriving, von Sternberg gave an interview to reporter Georg Herzberg, explaining expansively, "I want to show my young wife Europe and—civilization." He claimed to be "in negotiation with a big German company," which Herzberg assumed to be the near-monopolistic Universum Film Aktiengesellschaft, Europe's largest studio, sited at Neubabelsberg in Potsdam, outside Berlin, and known everywhere as UFA.

In Berlin, Riza discovered the true reason for their visit to Germany. After seeing *The Salvation Hunters,* Max Reinhardt had suggested that he might find von Sternberg some work in Berlin or even make him director of a theater company. Reinhardt's innovative production of Luigi Pirandello's *Six Characters in Search of an Author* had been hugely successful on tour, so von Sternberg proposed that they film it, with him directing and Reinhardt playing the key part of the producer. Although Reinhardt and Vollmoeller were cordial, von Sternberg soon realized it had only been talk. He did make some useful contacts, however, including actor Emil Jannings, but after a few weeks of what a colleague called "sniffing around," he and Riza returned to Los Angeles. There, according to Sagor, von Sternberg took out his disappointment on his wife, losing no opportunity to belittle and berate her. "Riza was made to understand her inferiority, ignorance, and stupidity," Sagor wrote. "[Von Sternberg] did not believe she had film possibilities, and would do nothing to advance her career."[5]

The couple moved into a small Spanish-style house at 6252 Drexel, off Fairfax. Sagor claims that Riza was expected to feed them, and even to hold dinner parties, on a budget of $10 a week. This doesn't square with the 1930 census, which shows the couple maintaining a live-in housekeeper. Nor does it explain a later newspaper report that the house on Drexel was new and built to their specifications. But Sagor clearly hated von Sternberg and resented the relationship. She was also far from impartial on the question of money. Once Riza married, Sagor presented von Sternberg with a bill for his wife's room and board during her time as Sagor's houseguest. He refused to pay, igniting a feud that smoldered for decades.

Fortunately for von Sternberg's career, Adeline "Ad" Schulberg was an admirer. Wife of B. P. Schulberg, West Coast production head of Famous Players–Lasky (FPL), and sister of the studio's production manager, Sam Jaffe, Adeline had been lobbying her husband to hire von Sternberg ever since *The Salvation Hunters*. Now Schulberg acquiesced—though only in part. His cable offered work only as an assistant director. Chastened, von Sternberg bent his neck and took the job.

Ben Schulberg wasn't a typical executive. A British visitor described "a strong-looking relaxed man, who resembled an amiable efficient crocodile smoking a large cigar."[6] In his early thirties, Schulberg was aligned with East Coast leftist culture rather than the gold-rush mentality of California. FPL/Paramount introduced von Sternberg to the pleasures of studio filmmaking. He even accumulated a retinue, beginning with a pretty script girl, Alice White. "After two weeks," recalled White, "he told me I was an excellent script girl, but that I didn't have the temperament for this business. For $18 a week, he wanted temperament! So I got temperamental!" She left to work for Chaplin, then went to First National, where she started acting and became a famous "jazz baby."

FPL/Paramount ran two studios—one in Los Angeles, managed by Schulberg, and another in Astoria, Queens, where Walter Wanger was in charge. Paramount enjoyed none of MGM's prestige, although it was eager to acquire some. In hiring Schulberg, Jesse Lasky and Adolph Zukor hoped for an equivalent of MGM's Irving Thalberg—someone able to conceive an entire slate of films, not just a single production, and manage a regiment of egotistical, chronically misbehaving creative people.

Toward the end of the 1920s, studios started developing distinctive individual styles. MGM, under head designer Cedric Gibbons, aimed for a hard-edged gleam, typified by its Scandinavian and American roster of talent. At Paramount, the influence was German and Austrian, with technicians recruited from UFA in Berlin and Sascha-Film in Vienna. Instead of high gloss, its films opted for soft focus and the new styles of performance and design pioneered by Reinhardt at the Kammerspiele in Vienna, which had no proscenium and no curtain. Effects were achieved with light alone, or by hanging translucent scrims onto which shadow effects were projected. Von Sternberg came under the influence of senior art director Hans Dreier, imported from UFA in 1923. Although von Sternberg liked to say he "dictated" the look of his films, dictation is not creation. He needed talented individuals to realize his conceptions, and none was more gifted than Dreier, who worked on all von Sternberg's Paramount productions. Dreier weaned him from the realism of von Stroheim and replaced it with the veiled sensuality typified by *The Docks of New York*. His contribution to the von Sternberg style was crucial. (It goes without saying that he receives no mention in *Fun in a Chinese Laundry*.)

Before taking over at FPL, Schulberg had his own company, Preferred. Its most precious asset was Clara Bow, whom he had discovered, put under personal contract, and made both a star and his mistress before bringing her to FPL in 1925. Bow was a petite five feet three inches tall, pinchably plump, and flagrantly sexual. With her brunette curls reddened with henna, she embodied the "flapper," the liberated modern woman typified by novels such as *Flaming Youth* and F. Scott Fitzgerald's *The Beautiful and Damned*. Her first Paramount film was *It*, inspired, remotely, by Elinor Glyn's sensational book that suggested only the elusive "It"—shorthand for sex appeal—conferred satisfaction and happiness. When director Clarence Badger became ill during production, someone was needed to cover for him, and although von

Sternberg always denied that he worked on *It,* he almost certainly shot a day or two. It was his first job at Paramount, and the fact that there were no tantrums, from either him or the stars, reassured Schulberg.

Riza continued to fret over her failure as an actress. Increasingly she listened to Sagor and Blanca Holmes (wife of Stuart Holmes), who became a celebrated astrologer and counseled everyone from Maria Montez to Marilyn Monroe. Holmes decreed that Riza's problems would be solved by a nose job. In October, without consulting her husband, she had it surgically straightened. Furious, he refused to pay for the operation and ordered her out of the house. Fleeing to the Dupont Hotel, Riza, still bandaged from her surgery, wasted no time in informing the *Los Angeles Times* that she would divorce him.[7]

At this moment, paradoxically, Schulberg asked von Sternberg to work on a film of Owen Johnson's novel *Children of Divorce.* Set on the French Riviera, it follows two cousins, Kitty and Jean, who clash over Ted, heir to a fortune—all three of them children of divorce. This sets the stage for a melodrama of love and renunciation.

During the shooting of *It,* Clara Bow spotted lanky newcomer Gary Cooper. He became both her lover and her costar in *Children of Divorce,* with Esther Ralston as the third participant in the love triangle. Shooting began in November 1926 under Victor Fleming, who had shared Bow's bed before Cooper. They had even planned marriage, but Bow knew her limitations. "I couldn't live up to his subtlety," she said.[8] Cooper made fewer intellectual demands. "He's hung like a horse," Clara confided to another young actress, Hedda Hopper, "and can go all night!"[9]

Furious at the Cooper-Bow romance, Fleming quit *Children of Divorce* and consoled himself with Alice White. The film passed to veteran director Frank Lloyd, who was unable to discipline the two flagrantly lustful stars. Also, Pasadena and Del Monte in rainy midwinter hardly resembled the Côte d'Azur. Viewing the result after Christmas, Schulberg decided the film needed some European sophistication, and he turned to von Sternberg. Suppressing his memory of how Louis and Hope Lighton had connived to butcher *The Exquisite Sinner,* he worked with them to rewrite and restage *Children of Divorce.* The actors, having gone on to new films, were available only at night, so shooting took place after hours. As all the sets had already been struck, von Sternberg and cinematographer Victor Milner filmed everything in a tent, timing shots between rainstorms. This gave von Sternberg complete command of lighting, particularly during Bow's death scene (suicide by poison) in Ralston's arms. Shadows and texture imposed a poignant atmosphere not present in Bow's acting. "She was dying," recalled Ralston, "and I was kneeling beside her, weeping. She was chewing gum. She had this great wad of gum in her face when they said, 'All right, Clara, get the gum out. We're going to shoot the scene.' She took the gum out, put it back of her ear, and died. Well, that struck me as so funny, I howled, and they had to wait for me to stop laughing before I could cry again."[10]

Children of Divorce showed that von Sternberg could be a company man and work as part of a team. He was rewarded by Schulberg with the film that would launch his reputation. He also reconciled with Riza, who withdrew her divorce petition, propping up the troubled marriage for at least one more year.

The City of Dreadful Night

And they tell me you are crooked and I answer: Yes, it is
true I have seen the gunman kill and go free to kill again.

—Carl Sandburg, *Chicago*

ONCE THE 1920 VOLSTEAD Act made it illegal to sell alcohol in
the United States, criminals amalgamated into gangs to manufacture,
smuggle, and distribute liquor. By 1927 they effectively ruled many cities, particularly Chicago, thumbing their noses at the forces of law and
order—which, Ben Hecht wrote, "did not advance on the villains with
drawn guns, but with their palms out, like bellboys." Hecht came to
Hollywood in 1927, encouraged by Herman Mankiewicz, who sent him
a now-legendary telegram that concluded, "Millions are to be grabbed
out here and your only competition is idiots. . . . Dont let this get
around." Once he arrived, "Manky" briefed Hecht on the "rules." "In
a novel," wrote Hecht, "a hero can lay ten girls and marry a virgin for a
finish. In a movie this is not allowed. The hero, as well as the heroine,
has to be a virgin. The villain can lay anybody he wants, have as much
fun as he wants, cheating and stealing, getting rich and whipping the
servants. But you have to shoot him in the end."[1]

Gloomily pondering these clichés, Hecht had an idea. "The thing
to do was to skip the heroes and heroines, and to write a movie containing only villains and bawds. I would not have to tell any lies then." In
public, Paramount crowed about the result, an eighteen-page treatment

called *Underworld*. Privately, studio executives wondered what to do with a document—dismissed by von Sternberg as "some almost illegible notes"[2]—that was less film outline than a prose poem in imitation of Carl Sandburg, laureate of Hecht's home city, Chicago. The first intertitle typified what Hecht conceded were its "moody Sandburgian sentences": "A great city in the dead of night . . . streets lonely . . . moon clouded . . . buildings as empty as the cave dwellings of a forgotten age."

Though Hecht and others called *Underworld* the first gangster film, the film has no real gangs. It ignores Prohibition and the $100 million-a-year bootlegging industry. The leading character, "Bull" Weed (George Bancroft), is, in Leo Goldsmith's phrase, "a boisterous but loveable psychopath" who works alone, looting banks and jewelry stores as much for the pleasure of it as for profit. The eternal scofflaw, he even leaves a calling card in the form of a silver dollar, which he bends in half, a metaphor of his contempt for society. Weed would be at home in any era, from antiquity to the American frontier. His educated friend "Rolls Royce" compares him to "Attila, the Hun, at the gates of Rome," and believes he was "born two thousand years too late."

Afterward, Hecht took sole credit for *Underworld,* which he described as "grounded in the truth [that] nice people—the audience—loved criminals, [and] doted on reading about their love problems as well as their sadism. . . . There were no lies in it—except for a half-dozen sentimental touches introduced by its director, Joe von Sternberg." In reality, various directors and writers struggled to find a film in Hecht's outline, and failed. Schulberg initially assigned the treatment to Art Rosson, who was working on a script with Robert N. Lee when a young producer, Howard Hawks, suggested that von Sternberg might be useful in creating the visual impression of a great city in the dead of night. On January 6, 1927, the *Los Angeles Times* announced that von Sternberg would work on *Underworld*—not as director, but as cinematographer.

"So here's what happened," director Monte Brice told Kevin Brownlow. "They're working on the script. Von Sternberg is hanging around; he's going to be on the picture, but nothing has been decided. He's sitting around reading a book *that* thick. It's got nothing to do with a picture—it's just a book. Every once in a while someone would come up and he'd lift his head and give them an answer. And it was usually a pretty good answer, to a problem that was going on over the other side of the room. All of a sudden this big switch. Art Rosson is out entirely, and von Sternberg is the director."[3]

Rosson was out, according to Hawks, because "he went up to San Francisco . . . to go to the prison there, and unfortunately got tight, so they had to fire him."[4] Rosson's drinking wasn't unjustified, since his wife Lu had become Hawks's lover. The teetotal von Sternberg inherited *Underworld,* with Henry Hathaway as his assistant. He took instant charge not only of directing but also of script, lighting, design, and even costumes; behavior that trampled Hollywood's collaborative production style—"the genius of the system."

Scorning Hecht's poetic text, he ordered a new screenplay from Jules Furthman, who had recently joined Paramount. As the son of a Chicago judge, Furthman was at least as qualified as Hecht to write about crime in that city. Moreover, he had been composing screen stories since 1918 and had even directed three features in the early 1920s. He would go on to cowrite *Mutiny on the Bounty, Only Angels Have Wings,* and *The Big Sleep,* as well as almost every von Sternberg film. For *Underworld,* however, he ceded credit for the adaptation to his brother Charles, perhaps as a means of squeezing an additional payment out of Paramount. Lee shared screen credit for the work he did before Rosson's departure.

Jules Furthman, who became von Sternberg's most consistent collaborator, never worked alone. He invariably came on board to adapt an existing novel or screen story or rescue an ailing script. Frank Capra called him "Hollywood's most sought after story 'doctor,' . . . in demand not for his inventive originality, but for his encyclopedic memory of past authors and their story plots. Filmmakers would tell him their story hang-ups; nine times out of ten, without recourse to research, Furthman would say: 'Oh, that plot was used by Shakespeare'—or Chekhov, De Maupassant, Sheridan, Goethe, Kipling, Stevenson, Conrad, Cooper, or one of a host of other authors."[5]

Furthman lived in then-remote Culver City, where he had moved with his wife when neighbors complained about the cries of their mentally handicapped son. In a community that barely read and had little interest in art, he amassed a library of rare books and collections of coins, orchids, and art. He owned works by Picasso, Matisse, and

Brancusi, and his seven greenhouses contained 48,000 orchid plants. When Furthman died in 1966, he was at the Bodleian Library in Oxford, researching a 1603 copy of Montaigne's *Essays* with annotations he believed to be in the hand of Shakespeare. As for his contribution to *Underworld*, naming a criminal "Buck Mulligan" for a character in James Joyce's *Ulysses*, still banned in the United States at the time, was surely a bibliophile's private joke.

Hawks's biographer Todd McCarthy calls Furthman "one of the nastiest, most cantankerous characters to carve out a place for himself in Hollywood. As the years went on, fewer and fewer employers would tolerate him, despite his undeniable talent." Hawks, some of whose best films Furthman scripted, agreed that the writer was mean, bright, and short, adding, "He'd say 'You stupid guy!' to somebody who wasn't as smart as him. He needed help [in writing a script], but when he got help he was awful good."[6] With Furthman's abruptness went a contrasting servility, not unlike that displayed by von Sternberg when someone with a stronger personality called his bluff. Lauren Bacall described to Peter Bogdanovich how, in her starlet days, Hawks had sent Furthman to her as, in effect, a pimp, urging her to call the director for the purpose of arranging a sexual assignation. Furthman was also more than ready to do menial jobs for von Sternberg. Sam Ornitz, who wrote the story Furthman adapted as *The Case of Lena Smith*, dismissed him as the director's "continuity man," a tame scribe retained to turn grandiose conceptions into workable screenplays. Sam Lauren, who worked with Furthman on *Blonde Venus*, called him, for unclear reasons, "that racketeer" and claimed that he drank and gambled so heavily that Paramount ensured his continuing availability by advancing him money, keeping him permanently in debt. More likely, however, any such income went to feed his various collections.

Despite dismissing Furthman in his memoirs as "a friend whom I trained to become a prominent screenwriter," von Sternberg appeared to enjoy Furthman's company. They shared tastes in art and traveled together around the Caribbean in 1932. Furthman remained loyal to von Sternberg well into the 1950s, persuading Howard Hughes to let him direct *Jet Pilot* and *Macao*. The script for his last film as screenwriter, Hawks's *Rio Bravo*, included two elements from *Underworld*—the act of money being thrown into a spittoon, and a heroine called "Feathers." A tip of the hat to an old friend, or some provident recycling? We'll never know.

Hecht, seeing his credit on *Underworld* watered down to "original story," wired von Sternberg, "You poor ham[,] take my name off the film." Paramount ignored him. And Hecht did not repudiate the film when it won the first Academy Award for Best Original Story. He never ceased to scorn the director, however, as just another intellectual wiseacre with a European accent. "There are thousands like that guy, playing chess on Avenue A," he sneered. But von Sternberg understood cinema far better than Hecht, who, as a screenwriter, proved erratic. Although Schulberg signed him to a year's contract at $300 a week, Hecht failed to produce a single filmable idea, and it wasn't until the mid-1930s that he made a reputation with films such as *Nothing Sacred*. He always regarded movies as beneath his intelligence—a prejudice shared, as it happens, by von Sternberg.

Nobody has unraveled the various contributions to the screenplay of *Underworld*. If Hecht or even Furthman were the primary author, one would expect more authentic detail. Real Chicago gangsters lived in hotels, spent lavishly, and surrounded themselves with henchmen and whores. In contrast, Weed has a modest apartment and hangs out at a low-class basement bar, the improbably named Dreamland Café. His only companions are his mistress Feathers (Evelyn Brent), who, in one of von Sternberg's many additions to the script, is always festooned in plumes, and "Slippy" Lewis (comic Larry Semon), a dapper and fastidious sidekick, presumably gay, who patronizes the café's most incongruous fixture—a coin-operated perfume dispenser. The film correctly shows the weapon of choice for both criminals and police as the Thompson submachine gun, and Weed's archenemy Buck Mulligan (Fred Kohler) runs a flower shop, like the real-life Dion O'Bannion, boss of the Chicago North Side mob, who was murdered in his own establishment by Johnny Torrio's gang in 1922. Otherwise, it's von Sternberg we see writ large in the characters and situations, some of which turn up in his later work.

Underworld's key relationship is the friendship between Bull Weed and disgraced, down-and-out attorney "Rolls Royce" Wensel (Clive

Brook), with whom Weed almost collides as he bolts from a bank he has just looted. "The great Bull Weed closes another bank account," jeers Wensel, and rather than leave a witness behind, Weed bundles him into his car. "You'd better keep quiet about this," he threatens. "Don't worry," says Wensel, "I'm a Rolls Royce for silence," and the amused Weed assigns him that nickname. They meet again in the Dreamland, where Wensel sweeps floors. Buck Mulligan tips him $10 but tosses it into a spittoon. As Wensel considers whether to retrieve it, Weed quixotically intervenes, adopts the derelict, and installs him in an old hideout. Cleaned up and sober, Wensel inevitably falls for Feathers.

Allocating *Underworld* to the untried von Sternberg came at a cost to the production. The budget dropped to that of a B movie, and the announced star, Austrian-born Jacob Krantz (renamed "Ricardo Cortez" to capitalize on the vogue for Rudolph Valentinoesque Latin lovers), abruptly left the cast. The man who eventually played Weed, burly, cheerful George Bancroft, had acted mainly in westerns and initially resisted the change in character, agreeing to take the part only if he could show a soft side to the brute. When director and star worked together again on *The Docks of New York,* two English visitors, Jan and Cora Gordon, noted that Bancroft "had his well-known rough and careless good-fellowship to maintain; his public demanded that of him. So, no matter what the character in the actual cast might be, he had to hold on to this rough good-fellowship to the last. . . . Hence the muted duel [between director and actor]. To be cast for such very sordid characters was trial enough, but to be forbidden to relieve that sordidness by the sweet pathos of a suggested innocence or by rude good nature might mean catastrophe."[7]

The studio assigned Evelyn Brent, married to staff producer Bernie Fineman, to play Feathers McCoy. Von Sternberg auditioned Gary Cooper for Wensel, but, says Cooper, the director "decided that I didn't look capable of carrying a gun and murdering people on the streets." This was apparently a pretext not to cast Cooper, because Wensel does neither. Instead, von Sternberg chose Clive Brook, whom he had met in Britain. Brook had been in Hollywood since 1924 but was relatively new to Paramount. Some directors found him too stiff, but his reticence acted as a foil to Bancroft's bluster. Larry Semon likewise was a cheap choice for the role of Slippy Lewis. The once-popular comic, bankrupt after some disastrous attempts at production and reduced to gag writing, hoped that drama would reverse his fortunes. It didn't, and he died in 1928 under mysterious circumstances.

In the fantasy crime community of *Underworld*, the criminals call an annual truce for a ball at which their mistresses compete to be named queen. "You gotta go," Weed tells Wensel, "Everyone with a jail record will be there!" The idea is as absurd as Brent and her plumes (extending, apparently, to feathers in her underwear), but carnivals are a von Sternberg signature, and he attacks this one with gusto. From the first moment, as Bull, Feathers, and Rolls plunge through the crowd at the ball, he fills the screen with movement and light. Black-suited men and brightly dressed women weave among the decorations; Rolls slumps over a drink, framed by dangling streamers, and looks around with distaste at the company he's forced to keep. As an intertitle puts it, "Everywhere the night deepened in silence and rest. But here the brutal din of cheap music—booze—hate—lust—made a devil's carnival." To underline the point, von Sternberg barrages us with faces—drunken, depraved, mad.

Except for Weed, the characters of *Underworld* are drawn perfunctorily. Brent's placid charm, mean rosebud mouth, and heavily made-up eyes give Feathers only a fraction of the mystery embodied in Marlene Dietrich. Clive Brook is even more wooden as Wensel than he is as "Doc" Harvey of *Shanghai Express*. Much that is interesting in their playing comes from the use of props: the ostrich plume that drifts down onto the unshaven Wensel when he first sees Feathers; the sexual byplay with books when they are left alone while Weed robs the jewelry store. The same is true of action scenes, in particular the aforementioned robbery, which takes place in a brisk montage: clock face shattered by a bullet, clerk backing away, gems snatched up, flower dropped to the carpet (incriminating an innocent Buck Mulligan). Then, as a crowd gathers, Weed arrogantly bends a silver dollar between his huge hands and drops it into the hat of a legless beggar, who looks up idly at this demonic apparition.

Underworld is a virtuoso apprentice work, but its histrionic and decorative style is unconvincing, and the plot is episodic. An authentic vision of a criminal subculture wasn't depicted on the screen until Howard Hawks's *Scarface,* where the same events, partly scripted by Hecht, offer a fascinating glimpse into the mechanics of power. But one need only view *The Salvation Hunters* again to see von Sternberg's progress. That first film lives in the shadow of von Stroheim; *Underworld* suggests a personal style.

Finished in a record five weeks, *Underworld* impressed Schulberg, although he was unsure of its public appeal. Some executives, startled by its break with formula, urged him to shelve it. Robert Florey dined with von Sternberg and Riza on the night of the Los Angeles premiere, then drove them to the screening at the West Lake Park Theatre. After giving detailed instructions to the orchestra leader and choosing the pieces to be played with the film, von Sternberg handed his tickets to Florey and asked him to watch the show with Riza. He preferred to walk in what is now Macarthur Park until it was over. There was no need to worry; released in August 1927, *Underworld* was an instant success. Although Paramount sneaked it into New York in a single minor theater, it soon became so popular that all-night screenings were held to cope with the crowds.

Having come to California with nothing, it now seemed to von Sternberg that there was nothing he could not achieve. He betrayed this sense in an interview with journalist B. G. Braver-Mann. Pausing in front of his house on the hills above Los Angeles, he stretched out his arms "as if offering a benediction." "Oh, Hollywood," he exclaimed, "my beloved Hollywood."[8]

A Great Man

It is dreadful to imagine what von Sternberg, who was all of thirty-four, must already have suffered to stage humiliation with such piercing discernment.

—Richard Brody on *The Last Command*[1]

UNTIL *UNDERWORLD* WAS RELEASED, von Sternberg remained, as far as Paramount was concerned, a negligible talent, fit only for standard studio products. In June, *Variety* announced that he would replace Dorothy Arzner as director of *The Glory Girl,* with Esther Ralston. Once *Underworld* hit, however, the company was ready to give him anything he wanted—beginning with a new contract that doubled his salary to $20,000 a week. He also received a $10,000 bonus and a gold medal.

Von Sternberg chose to regard this success as an endorsement of his autocratic methods. Having imposed absolute silence on his sets and a ban on eating, he now barred all visitors. If someone from the front office invaded his fiefdom, he was likely to stop shooting for the day and blame the interloper. This wasn't unique. John Ford habitually invited his producer onto the set for the first day of shooting, introduced him to the cast, and then announced that they would not be seeing him again. William Wellman also refused to shoot while Paramount production manager Sam Jaffe was watching. In the interests of getting films finished on time, Schulberg ordered his subordinates to humor directors and stay away. Actors had no such option, and von Sternberg was merciless in breaking down what he saw as "pretension." Having known him the longest, Clive Brook regarded him as almost a friend. On *Underworld,* after working for twenty-four hours on a complex scene with a large crowd of extras, he headed for his dressing room "to perform one of two functions," he told the director, "neither of which I will attempt to explain." When von Sternberg forbade him to leave, Brook responded with a pointed insult, at which the director announced there would be no more shooting that night, shut down the set, and sent all the extras home. The next day Brook was called to the office of producer Hector Turnbull. But instead of reprimanding him, Turnbull said, "Splendid. He's had that coming for a long time."[2]

Perhaps motivated by the cynical European philosophy holding that "it's not enough to succeed—your best friend must fail," von Sternberg also agreed to oblige Schulberg by carving a releasable film out of Erich von Stroheim's *The Wedding March,* which, after seven months of shooting, $1,125,000 spent, and 200,000 feet of film in the can, was still incomplete. On January 30, 1927, original producer Pat Powers, money and patience exhausted, sold the project to Paramount. Von Stroheim stopped shooting and started cutting, a laborious process that continued for most of the year. In the fall Schulberg learned that even the edited version ran eleven hours and that von Stroheim was secretly contemplating shaping the story into two films, with the remaining footage becoming the basis of a third section, *The Honeymoon,* that would run another three or four hours. On October 8, 1927, Schulberg gave the first two parts of the film to von Sternberg, with instructions to reduce them to about two hours; he gave *The Honeymoon* to Julian Johnson. Von Sternberg's cut of *The Wedding March* went on to be released, but *The Honeymoon* played only in Europe. Von Sternberg claimed that the task was completed with professional courtesy on both sides, but he and von Stroheim never spoke again. This rift echoed another in von Sternberg's life, since he and Riza had separated. On September 28 she was granted a divorce on the grounds of "cruelty."

Under the "ParUfaMet" agreement of 1925, Paramount, Universal, and MGM injected capital into the floundering UFA in return for the right to distribute German versions of its films through UFA cinemas, shoot in its studios, and import some of its performers and technicians.

These included Erich Pommer, a famously tough and ruthless young producer who had been fired as UFA's production manager following the cost overruns of Fritz Lang's *Metropolis*. Schulberg gave him a year's contract to supervise the importation and use of European talent. Pommer, with some help from Karl Vollmoeller, negotiated a three-year contract with Paramount for Emil Jannings, who, since Murnau's *The Last Laugh* in 1923, had been the most popular foreign star with U.S. audiences. *Janningsfilme*—in which an aging man is humiliated and degraded and dies of a broken heart—constituted an entire subgenre of German movie melodrama. European filmgoers had become weary of his outdated style, with its elaborate makeup and exaggerated use of eyes and eyebrows, but U.S. audiences remained enthusiastic. In their eyes, fidelity to character mattered less than an actor's ability to render himself unrecognizable.

Jannings and Pommer sailed for New York on October 4, 1926, and then took the train to California. Rather than alight with run-of-the-mill passengers at Union Station in downtown Los Angeles, Jannings got off at Pasadena, where a banner announced "American Film Guild Welcomes Emil Jannings, Screen's Foremost Dramatic Artist." To make him appear less alien, Paramount disguised his actual birthplace of Rorschach, Switzerland, and announced that he had been born in Brooklyn and taken to Europe as a baby. (For good measure, his birth date was also brought forward two years.)

Installed in an ersatz southern mansion on Hollywood Boulevard, Jannings lived on a medieval scale, eating, entertaining, and fornicating massively. In two years his weight swelled to 300 pounds. He would enthuse over enormous meals, greeting favorite dishes with, "This is what Emil likes. This is good for Emil." Von Sternberg was among the fellow expatriates who frequented the house, which also teemed with barking chow dogs, squawking parrots, and a flock of chickens named for rival stars—Garbo, Negri, Valentino, Gilbert. Having seen the German mark decline in value under the Weimar Republic, Jannings insisted on payment in cash and slept with $200,000 in a strongbox under his bed.

As his first project, Paramount proposed *The Way of All Flesh*—not Samuel Butler's autobiographical novel but a made-to-measure *Janningsfilme* adapted by a succession of hands, including Lajos Biro and

Jules Furthman, and directed by Victor Fleming. Jannings plays August Schiller, a cashier from predominantly Germanic Milwaukee who is entrusted with delivering some bonds to Chicago. On the train he's seduced and robbed by an attractive thief. In the film's most poignant scene, Schiller, now a derelict, creeps up to the window of his old home at Christmas, where his family is decorating the tree, and sees his own photograph, framed in black, in a place of honor. Rather than destroy their illusions, he trudges off into the snow.

Schulberg didn't misjudge U.S. audiences. *The Way of All Flesh* was a hit, making it more important than ever that Jannings's second film be equally successful. Disliking the scripts he was offered, Jannings appealed to von Sternberg, who suggested an original story, *Street of Sin*, that may have been in his bottom drawer since his days in England. Reminiscent of Griffith, it cast Jannings as "Basher Bill," a burglar in London's Soho. Reformed by Salvation Army girl Fay Wray, he's murdered by his gang after rescuing children from a burning orphanage. A succession of expatriates worked on the film, which Paramount didn't release until 1928, when it was generally panned, particularly in Britain. "Vaguely reminiscent of a *Limehouse Nights* adventure," sniffed one London critic, "but written by somebody not thoroughly cognisant of the people or the atmosphere."[3]

For his third Hollywood film, Jannings pinned his hopes on an original screenplay called *The General*. The central character is a czarist general reduced to working as an extra in a Hollywood movie based on a battle in which he had fought and directed by a Bolshevik who had been his prisoner. The story originated with Ernst Lubitsch and had been suggested by a meeting with Theodore Lodijensky, a former commander in the czarist army who, as "Theodore Lodi," had served as technical adviser and played a small role in John Gilbert's *The Cossacks*. Realizing that Lodijensky's story was a *Janningsfilme* in real life, Lubitsch recounted the tale to the actor. Some weeks later Lubitsch met Hungarian screenwriter Lajos Biro on the set and was surprised to hear him praise Jannings as not only a great actor but also a brilliant storyteller. Biro then proceeded to recount the Lodijensky saga, which Jannings had passed off as his own invention.

Biro wrote a treatment, which John S. Goodrich worked up into a screenplay. In his version, the general, called Dolguricki, is a popular World War I army commander who enjoys the trappings of power, including good living, beautiful women, and, in particular, the uniform. When the general catches his valet trying on his fur-lined coat, he's so incensed that he orders him shot, relenting only after the firing squad has already assembled. Dolguricki captures two revolutionaries, Karlovitch and his female companion Natacha. Karlovitch goes to jail, but Dolguricki, attracted to Natacha, keeps her at headquarters. A string of pearls fails to conquer her virtue, and the general is planning a new assault when revolution breaks out. After heroically commanding his men in a battle, Dolguricki escapes from Russia and, obsessed with Natacha, follows her to the United States. Arriving in Hollywood, he finds Karlovitch, now a film director, making a movie based on his final exploit. Believing Natacha is dead, Dolguricki loses his mind, leads the charge in Karlovitch's movie, and dies at the climax. An assistant remarks, "He was a great actor." Karlovitch, having learned from Natacha of his bravery and patriotism, replies, "He was more than that. He was a great man."

Jannings refused the film's first assigned director, Victor Fleming, because of an incident that occurred during *The Way of All Flesh*. For a scene in which Schiller gets drunk, Jannings insisted on downing four or five large whiskies "to get into character," after which he passed out. To the actor's fury, Fleming simply left him on the set to sleep it off—in some versions, for a few hours; in others, all night. Fleming happily relinquished *The General* to von Sternberg, who retitled it *The Last Command*.

As with all his films, von Sternberg claimed authorship of the script, which was credited to John S. Goodrich from a Biro story. In his memoirs, von Sternberg, probably still smarting from the debacle of *I, Claudius,* which Biro coscripted, dismisses Biro's credit, which, he says, appeared only as a favor to Schulberg, who "plead[ed] that Mr. Biro had been carried on the payroll for years and that this somehow had to be justified." This maligns Biro, who had, after all, cowritten *The Way of All Flesh*. However, the original Goodrich-Biro screenplay has survived,[4] and we can see that von Sternberg's claim of authorship isn't entirely unjustified, since his alterations to the original, both in structure and in tone, are fundamental.

First and most crucially, rather than developing chronologically, the film opens with the general already a broken old man. Now called Sergius Alexander, he's a pathetic recluse living in a rented room in Hollywood. By chance, his former prisoner Karlovitch, renamed Andreyev (William Powell), recognizes him from a photograph. "Have him report tomorrow," he says coldly, "and put him in a general's uniform." The scenes that follow show studio life as von Sternberg knew it, from the viewpoint of a director's yes-man. When Andreyev takes out a cigarette, a dozen assistants offer lights—a scene he repeats in *The Shanghai Gesture*. Their sycophancy contrasts with the arrogance of the costume men as they process the extras clustering outside the gates in what an intertitle calls "the bread-line of Hollywood." As the actors hustle and shoulder one another, bored functionaries pelt them with bundled uniforms, shouting, "One corporal . . . One general." In a further irony, Lodijensky, in a backhanded acknowledgment of having inspired the story, was given a small role.

Reflecting von Sternberg's preoccupation with clothing, the film repeatedly makes the point that you are what you wear. Through each rewrite, the general's coat remains a key prop. When his valet is caught trying it on, Alexander orders an aide, "If this happens again, remove the coat and shoot the contents." Later, Alexander almost cows the revolutionary mob with the help of the coat, until his valet yanks it from his shoulders, and with it his authority. Medals too assume talismanic significance. As a final touch to his movie uniform, Alexander tremblingly attaches a medal given to him by the czar. Other extras mock him, and the assistant director moves one of the decorations to an incorrect position on the uniform, bragging that he's done plenty of Russian movies and knows where it should go. When Alexander faces Andreyev, the director automatically puts the medal back where it belongs, a tacit acknowledgment of their shared values.

A flashback to 1917 is triggered by the medal. No longer a wreck, Alexander is arrogant, elegant, and feared. Evelyn Brent has to work hard as Natacha to convince us that a revolutionary who is ready to sacrifice her life would succumb to the charm of an enemy, particularly the portly, strutting Alexander. Patriotism, not pearls, proves to be the key. Ordered by the czar's aide to enliven an imperial visit to the front with "a little offensive in the morning—not too early," Alexander shocks even Natacha by refusing the order, despite its implications of almost divine authority. "I would take any risk to prevent a useless sacrifice," he explains. "I would gladly die tonight if it would help Russia."

"Before you die," she says tremulously, "come and have coffee—in my room."

The subsequent scene flirts with Lubitsch-like sex comedy. Listening at the door, one of the officers remarks to the other eavesdroppers, "These things are best handled *after* caviar." Although Natacha still plans to kill Sergius, his lèse-majesté has shaken her resolve. The moment when Alexander sees her pistol hidden under a cushion on the couch—von Sternberg interjects a quick dissolve and close-up of the gun as a visual exclamation mark—is almost gleeful, but her explanation for not shooting him—"I couldn't kill anybody who loves Russia as much as you do"—is classically von Sternbergian. Not for the last time in his films, a woman abdicates her power over a man to the greater force of love.

The most inventive sequence in *The Last Command* doesn't appear in the original screenplay. As the general's train speeds toward Petrograd, Alexander and his staff, Natacha included, party in his private car, unaware that revolution has broken out. A mob halts the train and drags out the passengers, ready to murder them, until a defiant Alexander descends. At his glare, the crowd edges back warily—until his valet breaks the spell by snatching off the coveted coat. The revolutionaries surge forward and engulf him, then spit him out, shocked and bleeding, against a wall with its tiny symbol of sanctuary—a plaster saint in a niche.

In the midst of this anarchy, Natacha takes charge. Wrapping herself in the Bolshevik flag, she exhorts the mob to advance on Petrograd in the captured train and force Alexander to stoke the engine, a punishment that she calculates will at least save his life. As they approach Petrograd, Alexander leaps to safety, leaving Natacha alone on the footplate as the train plunges into a frozen river. Although this audacious addition to the story provides a motivation for Alexander's head-shaking twitch, it also leads to a slip in the dialogue. If Natacha dies before she can describe his patriotism, Andreyev can't know that he was "a great man." Von Sternberg later claimed that the observation was based on the old man's remarkable behavior on the set, but the justification is shaky.

Shooting took five weeks—plenty of time for the director to alienate many of the cast and crew. According to Gary Cooper, William Powell walked off the set and demanded a salary hike—"danger money," in his words.[5] Powell stipulated in his next contract that he never again be required to work for von Sternberg, but he couldn't evade one more encounter, on *The Drag Net*. Once executives saw *The Last Command*, they worried that its attacks on Hollywood cynicism might cause offense. In addition, there were complaints of distortion in its handling of the revolution and even talk of shelving the film entirely, until financier Otto Kahn, a patron of the arts and a major stockholder, saw it and was impressed. Paramount released it, to remarkable critical success. The film received Academy Award nominations for Best Picture and Best Original Story, and Jannings was given the first Oscar for Best Performance of the year in both *The Way of All Flesh* and *The Last Command*. In von Sternberg's eyes, he had taken on the studio and won, although the victory would prove to be a hollow one, not least because an obscure author claimed, with convincing proof, that the story had been plagiarized. Looking for a scapegoat, the studio tried to blame Lubitsch, who shrewdly pointed out that since Jannings, Biro, and von Sternberg had denied him credit, he was not about to accept it now. Paramount grudgingly settled with the writer and put another black mark beside von Sternberg's name.

He was somewhat mollified by an unexpected reconciliation with his ex-wife Riza. While he was researching *The Docks of New York*, Riza arrived back from Europe, and they met in New York. "A short chat, and the reconciliation was completed," reported the *Los Angeles Times*. Von Sternberg told the reporter, "I'm just one of those old-fashioned people that wants to stay married. It was just a spat that caused our separation. Now we're happy again together. All's well that ends well."[6] Riza stayed in New York until his research was complete, and when they returned to Los Angeles she applied to set aside the interlocutory decree of September 1927. It has been suggested that the couple remarried after the offer from UFA to make *The Blue Angel* in Berlin, because Riza would not have been able to accompany von Sternberg otherwise; however, UFA had shown no interest in von Sternberg at this point. The relationship between Jo and Riza, though troubled, was passionate enough to resist repeated attacks of temperament. Their desire to stay together would survive for at least another year, until it encountered the irresistible force of Marlene Dietrich.

Came the Dawn

You ain't heard nuthin' yet!
—Al Jolson in *The Jazz Singer*

GIVEN THE SUCCESS OF *Underworld*, it appears astonishing that
when von Sternberg sailed for Germany in 1929 to make *The Blue Angel,* Hollywood regarded his career as almost over. Although his many
clashes with management contributed, his fall was mostly due to the im-
pact of talking pictures. Sound swept through Hollywood like a plague
to which the poorly educated and foreign-born possessed no immunity.
Actors such as Clara Bow and Vilma Banky, once gold plated, revealed
their underlying brass in the form of working-class accents or, worse,
the tones of Europe. Despite winning an Academy Award, Emil Jannings preferred to rush back to Germany before it was even announced.
His return was negotiated by Erich Pommer, who hoped that by luring
Jannings back to Germany, he could ride on his coattails, as he had in
Hollywood.

Von Sternberg's decline began with *The Last Command,* which
won favorable reviews but little profit. The four films that followed,
The Drag Net, The Docks of New York, The Case of Lena Smith, and
Thunderbolt, also died at the box office, for reasons mostly beyond his
control. *Docks,* for instance, had the singular bad fortune to be previewed for critics in the same week as *The Jazz Singer.*

With *The Drag Net,* Paramount tried to squeeze some extra

money out of *Underworld,* which it resembles to an embarrassing degree. The publicity department had no doubt about the comparison.
"BANCROFT Has the Town on Edge Again," it told cinema owners.
"If you are one of those who thought *Underworld* just about the last
word in crook melodramas, don't let this one catch you napping." In
the film, Captain Timothy "Two Gun" Nolan (Bancroft) is appointed
head of the New York detective force, and his first act is to round up
every criminal in town—the "drag net" of the title. Gang boss "Dapper" Frank Trent (William Powell) stands bail for all of them, including
"The Magpie" (Evelyn Brent), an independent minor gang leader who
affects tight caps of black-and-white feathers and is attended by her own
gunmen bodyguards. Setting out to get Trent, Nolan moves in on the
gangster's hideout assisted by his friend "Shakespeare" Donovan (Leslie
Fenton), who is killed. Blaming himself, Nolan resigns his commission
and becomes a drunk. Found unconscious by Trent, he is offered as the
pièce de résistance at a gangland banquet. The film concludes with a
machine-gun duel in a steel-shuttered apartment—a virtual repetition
of the conclusion of *Underworld.*

Since playing Bull Weed, Bancroft had not become any less self-
important. For a scene in which he's shot, von Sternberg instructed him
to walk up the stairs and, at the shout of "Bang!" turn and fall. But the
actor didn't respond to the first "Bang!" "*One* shot can't stop Bancroft,"
he scoffed.[1] The *New York Times* disparaged the film. "Notwithstanding George Bancroft's derisive laugh, Evelyn Brent's striking plumed
headgear and Josef von Sternberg's generous display of slaughter, *The
Drag Net* is an emphatically mediocre effort."[2] No copy of the film
survives that would allow us to corroborate this opinion.

Von Sternberg showed no alarm at his two consecutive failures,
even boasting to visitors on the set of his next film, *The Docks of New
York,* that his prestige remained as high as ever. This was whistling
in the dark. If Schulberg had known how badly *The Drag Net* would
do, he might never have approved *The Docks of New York.* Also, von
Sternberg's many enemies were lying in wait. Had *Docks* been a hit, it
might have silenced them, but by the time it reached cinemas, nobody
was interested in anything but talkies.

Despite its title, *Docks* is not a grimy picture of vice among longshoremen but a romance of moral rebirth. Bancroft, as stoker Bill Roberts, gives an impressively shaded performance, modulating from an amiable but mindless shoveler of coal to the lover of prostitute Mae (Betty Compson), whom he rescues after a suicide attempt and, quixotically, marries. For von Sternberg, the tone of *Docks of New York* is uncharacteristically gentle, almost feminine. Even the violence is handled playfully. Bill invites the label "gentle giant," with his habit of lifting people bodily from their chairs and clearing clients from a bar as casually as he might push aside a curtain. If someone becomes troublesome, he shoves them one-handed across the room, but always with an amused grin and a sense of enormous force held in reserve. After he's refreshed himself by holding a cask of beer over his head and guzzling the contents, he inquires amiably of the protesting owner, "Are you goin' to let me have a good time in my own quiet way—or must I take this place apart?"

Once he accepts responsibility for Mae, Bill bulldozes everything in his path, shoving aside the crowd of gawkers to carry her to her room, acquiring new clothes for her by smashing down the door of a pawnshop, and then taking her to the bar for coffee, a sandwich, and, almost as a second thought, a proposal of marriage. That these actions, however well meant, have consequences for people who, unlike himself, can't solve every problem with brute force, confronts him with moral choices and responsibilities for which he is ill-equipped.

As Kevin Brownlow remarks, *Docks* is the first film in which von Sternberg "achieves a feeling of warmth and humanity [and] seems to care about his characters instead of using them . . . to form patterns of light and shade."[3] The only downright villain is Andy (Mitchell Lewis), the bullying third mate. But even he is humanized when, walking into the saloon at the end of a long voyage, he finds Lou (Olga Baclanova), the wife he deserted three years earlier, greedily enjoying herself in the arms of another man. Lewis is sufficiently expressive an actor to respond to this unexpected encounter with surprise and pleasure, followed by embarrassment at the memory of his delinquency and resentment that he has been supplanted by someone else. The couple settle down to a rueful rapprochement that ends when Andy makes a pass at Mae, and

Lou, furious at herself for imagining that any reconciliation was possible, shoots him.

Although the film begins with contemporary exteriors of the Manhattan skyline, the sets—of clapboard rooming houses overhanging the docks, picturesque wharves draped with fishing nets, and a noisy saloon called The Sandbar—all belong to the world of W. W. Jacobs and Thomas Burke's *Limehouse Nights* rather than Eugene O'Neill. Film historian and archivist James Card, largely responsible for preserving this and other silents, wrote, "The entire film, save for the ending, immerses the viewer in a poetic idealization of the kind of place the New York waterfront ought to be but certainly is not. The docks, fog-shrouded at night, and in daytime glistening in softened sunlight, are just what one might dream of finding where the big ships come into the great port of New York Harbor. The nights are moonwashed with mystery, and not even the daylight dispels von Sternberg's pictorial magic."[4] As an intertitle acknowledges, modern ships are fired by oil, not coal. One could almost believe that the outdated setting was retained as a pretext for one of the film's most touching scenes: Chalked on a bulkhead of the boiler room are reminders of the pleasures awaiting them on shore—nude bodies, women's names, the word "beer." About to climb back into daylight for the first time in weeks, Bill pauses to ruminate on this crude gallery. One by one, the other stokers join him in mute anticipation.

In *The Docks of New York,* von Sternberg demonstrates for the first time the sophisticated manipulation of space that distinguishes his best sound films. His handling of scenes in The Sandbar, culminating in the wedding, is remarkable for its bravura. Divided by nets and railings, the set allows him to isolate significant action in the middle distance, with the bar in the foreground and the rest of the frame filled with brawling drinkers. Mae's indifference to whether she lives or dies, combined with an appealing and self-contained eroticism, makes her one of his noblest great heroines. Married to director James Cruze, Betty Compson chose her roles carefully and initially resisted playing Mae because, though not averse to taking the part of a whore, she disliked being cast as a cheap one. Her sense of shopworn lassitude adds immeasurably to the film, particularly when Mae, recognizing that Bill regrets their marriage and is about to leave her, still offers to sew up his shirt pocket, torn by the jealous Steve. A subjective camera shows the needle and cotton blurring with tears as Mae tries to thread them, playing Bill's shame and affection against her acceptance of inevitable loss.

In December, Max Reinhardt arrived in Hollywood, ready to direct his first U.S. film. Von Sternberg was at the station to meet him, along with Ernst Lubitsch, Joseph Schildkraut, Conrad Veidt, and other members of the German community. Also present were Douglas Fairbanks and Joe Schenck of United Artists, who had succeeded in luring the impresario to direct Lillian Gish in *The Miracle Girl*, a film about Theresa Neumann, an Austrian whose hands displayed the stigmata—the bleeding wounds of Christ. But a pall was cast over the event by the release a month earlier of Victor Sjostrom's morbid *The Wind*, in which Gish plays a fragile woman from Virginia, stranded in desolate west Texas and driven crazy by the incessant sandstorms. Even a tacked-on happy ending couldn't redeem it with audiences. Moreover, it was silent. At Reinhardt's press conference, almost every question dealt with talkies. Did he welcome the new medium? Would he film *The Miracle Girl* with sound? Ignorant and feeling ambushed, he was evasive.[5] This panicked Gish, and United Artists backed off. Shooting, scheduled to start immediately, was postponed and then canceled.

In the wake of *Underworld*, Paramount recognized the commercial value of taking stories from real life—the more sordid the better. This lesson would soon be put into practice by Warner Brothers, whose screenplays came straight from the headlines. *The Case of Lena Smith* was such a story. Paramount bought it for $3,000 as a vehicle for Esther Ralston. The writer, newcomer Sam Ornitz, was a committed socialist who had rejected the business world of his family to work with the New York Prison Association and the Brooklyn Society for the Prevention of Cruelty to Children. In the 1940s he would be persecuted by the House Un-American Activities Committee and, as one of the "Hollywood Ten," would serve nine months in prison for refusing to testify to Congress about his political affiliations.

Ornitz set his story in a small town—called in one draft "Mixed Pickles, NY." A Polish immigrant and unmarried mother, Leonie

Stepack, is abandoned by her criminal lover following his murder of a policeman, and her son is placed in a foundlings' home. For the rest of the story she struggles to get him back. "A simple bit of life," Ornitz explained to friends. "But it is somewhat different from the ordinary movie plot, I think."[6] Paramount agreed, to the extent that Ornitz was persuaded to amplify the story. His rewrite turned the heroine, renamed Lena Smith, into a prostitute who supports her lover and son. When busybodies protest, the boy is taken from her. She abandons prostitution, begins to take in washing, bullies her lover into finding a job, and, by rescuing someone else's child, so charms the townspeople that they intercede with the judge to restore her boy to her care.

At this point, von Sternberg became interested. The locale was moved to Vienna at the time of his childhood. Lena became a servant girl, newly arrived from Hungary. She visits the Prater with her boyfriend, Stefan, and is attracted by a young officer, Franz Hofrat. Four years later, Lena is a maid in the Hofrat house. She and Franz are secretly married and have a son, but because Franz fears the reaction of his overbearing father, their boy lives with Stefan's sister. Herr Hofrat finds out anyway, assumes the child is illegitimate, dismisses Lena, and has the boy put in an orphanage. Stefan offers his life savings to get him back, but only if Lena leaves Vienna, returns to Hungary, and marries him. The money is less than they need, so Lena gives it to Franz, who promises to increase it by gambling. Instead, he loses it and kills himself in remorse. Hofrat, blaming Lena for Franz's death, places her in the workhouse. She manages to escape and recovers her boy, then makes her way to her old village and Stefan.

Ornitz felt betrayed by the changes in his story. "They are going to set it in Vienna—1850," he complained, "and they are going to open the story with a carnival. Hell! What have I to do with a carnival in 1850? Then they say, 'You know, old man, this unmarried mother stuff won't go with the great American public, so we'll have to make it seem like she was seduced by the young man of the house; then he gets killed by accident, or something, and she has lost her secret marriage license. But in the end, after she has worked up and got the child back, he turns up and proves that she was married to him after all.'"[7] Von Sternberg was unsympathetic. The alterations brought the story in line with his own experience, not only in its Viennese setting but also in the plight of his own mother, who was unmarried when he was born and disapproved of by her future in-laws. Any political resonances were irrelevant.

The Case of Lena Smith opens in a Hungarian village in 1914, on the eve of World War I. Stefan (Fred Kohler—*Underworld*'s Buck Mulligan) and his wife Lena (Esther Ralston) plead with the military tribunal not to draft Franz, her son by an earlier marriage. When the panel demands a reason, we flash back twenty years. Lena, young and flighty, is leaving for Vienna, despite Stefan's offer of marriage. On her first night in the city she visits the Prater; is dazzled by its shows, particularly a magician; and falls in love with Franz Hofrat (James Hall). Together they enter the Magic Grotto, a "tunnel of love" that reminds us where von Sternberg's father worked at Coney Island.

Four years later, Lena is a laundry maid in the home of Franz's father (Gustav von Seyffertitz). The scenes of Lena and the other maids hanging the washing up to dry remind us of the girls who dried linen on the floor above the Sternberg house in Vienna. We learn that Franz and Lena are secretly married and that she sneaks out at night to see her child. While taking him on a nostalgic visit to the Prater and the Magic Grotto, she's spotted by a neighbor, who reports her to Herr Hofrat. Lena is dismissed, and her child is seized by the Bureau of Morals and Domestic Relations. As in the first draft, Stefan offers money, and Franz loses it and kills himself, but in the filmed version, Hofrat has Lena sentenced to six months in the workhouse, where she is whipped and locked in a cell. After escaping, she steals her child from the orphanage and struggles to get back to her village. Back in the present, the tribunal hears Lena out but refuses exemption, and she watches her boy march away. As an intertitle points out, "All her struggles, all her sufferings, all her hopes, have been for nothing. She has lost her son, after all."

All that survives of *The Case of Lena Smith* is four minutes showing Lena in the Prater, watching the magician. However, a script, stills, and a few of Hans Dreier's design sketches convey some of the film's intensity, particularly in the second half, during which Lena climbs a barbed-wire fence, is shot at, and immerses herself in a flooded trench, all to retrieve her child. As in the original version of *Blonde Venus,* the mother suffers in vain, losing her child at the end. Perhaps that is how von Sternberg saw himself—a boy whose mother was brutalized by his father and fled, leaving him to fend for himself.

Though miscast, Esther Ralston regarded *The Case of Lena Smith* as one of her proudest experiences and called von Sternberg "marvelous":

> Nobody had ever given me the chance to do anything but light comedy and so on. And, I was so impressed with him, and he brought out the best of me. . . . They took buckets of mud and poured it all over me, and I had to climb a barbed wire fence with the blood supposedly dripping from my hands. All of this was fascinating to me. I had never done anything like that, you know. And, they showed me in my old age with the wrinkles and the gray hair. And my son, who is now grown, is going off to war, and I'm to lose him again. That was the whole story.[8]

The Case of Lena Smith did only mediocre business. "If I ever looked for an Academy Award," Ralston said in 1992, "that film would be the one. But it came out the same time the talkies did, which is why it never got the showing it might have."[9] The title also misled many people into expecting a crime story. (In Austria it was released as *A Night in the Prater;* in France, as *The Calvary of Lena X.*) Only a few critics sensed how much the film reflected von Sternberg's early life. Mordaunt Hall in the *New York Times* noted "passages in this film that appear to be something on the order of childhood reminiscences, but . . . not set forth with any suggestion of whimsicality." Otherwise, he found it "drenched in agony" and "extravagantly harsh."[10]

In 1929 von Sternberg directed *Thunderbolt,* his first sound film. Superficially another gangster melodrama with George Bancroft, it was shot simultaneously as a silent and released as such in some places, particularly in Europe, where fewer cinemas were equipped for sound. Bancroft plays mobster Jim Lang, nicknamed "Thunderbolt" for his lethal punch, and Fay Wray is his girlfriend Ritzy, reputedly "the most decent kid in the rackets." We have to take her criminality on trust, however, since we see no evidence of it. The film begins with her promising her old boyfriend Bob Morgan (Richard Arlen), a bank clerk, that she'll abandon the criminal life. Learning of her liaison with Morgan,

Thunderbolt schemes to murder his rival. He's arrested before he can do so, but his gang succeeds in framing Morgan for a bank robbery that ends in murder, and both men find themselves on death row, where the rest of the story takes place.

Anxious to show off the superiority of films in which the sound was recorded on the film itself as a sound track, rather than on discs, Paramount, with von Sternberg's agreement, injected music and comedy into the film's second half. He boasted in his memoirs that *Thunderbolt* "put sound in its proper relation to the image"—a reference to its sound-on-film technology, but also a reminder of his belief that music and effects should provide dramatic emphasis, rather than being mere aural wallpaper. The prison scenes of *Thunderbolt* unfold in a cluster of cage-like cells, sufficiently open for the prisoners to argue with one another, banter, and even sing. The warden (Tully Marshall) has installed a piano on which a prisoner provides an impromptu obbligato to many scenes, including renditions of *Roll, Jordan, Roll* and *Broken-Hearted*. A barbershop quartet—or, rather, a trio, since one member has gone to a different kind of chair—harmonizes on *Sweet Adeline* and hopefully inquires if Thunderbolt happens to sing tenor. He's also allowed a dog in his cell, and the warden permits Morgan and Ritzy to marry, before a last-minute reprieve.

Because fixed microphones impeded a moving camera, von Sternberg shot these scenes in an uncharacteristic four-square style, framing the performers full length, usually facing one another across the image. Others walk from the back of the set to the foreground to deliver their lines, which emphasizes the sense of a filmed play. However, the inventive sound track of *Thunderbolt* doesn't excuse stagy performances and contrived action. Although Bancroft received an Academy Award nomination for his performance, that likely represented retrospective recognition of his work in *Underworld* and *The Docks of New York*. *Thunderbolt* established von Sternberg as an expert in the art of editing talkies. Paramount was in the process of converting its studios in the London suburb of Twickenham for the production of "quota quickies" to satisfy the British government's requirement that a percentage of films shown in British cinemas be locally made. Top editor Jack Harris was sent to Hollywood to learn about sound films, and he and von

Sternberg became friendly. Meanwhile, Emil Jannings, after concluding his Paramount contract with Lubitsch's Russian epic *The Patriot*, had returned to Germany, intending that his first sound film be made in Berlin and in his own language. Legend holds that *The Last Command* and his Oscar so pleased Jannings that he asked Erich Pommer, recalled to UFA in 1928, to hire von Sternberg as its director. The real story is very different.

The Lady with the Legs

> In my films, Marlene is not herself. *I* am Marlene. She
> knows that better than anyone.
>
> —Josef von Sternberg

TO MAKE A SOUND film in Berlin in 1929 was anything but simple.
Though Germany pioneered sound recording, as it had photography,
and companies such as Tobis-Klangfilm controlled major patents, others were held by the U.S. General Electric Company, which forbade the
use of its technology in German theaters. Not until June 1929 did a
U.S. sound-on-film talkie, *The Singing Fool,* play to German audiences,
and then only after legal wrangles had aborted earlier screenings. Up to
the last minute, it wasn't certain the film would open, and critics had to
fight for tickets with members of the public.

In September 1929, when UFA unveiled its *Tonkreuz* (Sound
Cross) complex, with four giant soundstages radiating from a central
hub, nobody was sure what films would be made there and whether they
would be suitable for export to countries using General Electric equipment. With this doubt went a growing hostility in Germany toward
Hollywood films, particularly if they featured local artists who had been
lured away by high U.S. salaries. For an actor like Emil Jannings to return and make a talking film in Germany was an act of social, political,
cultural, and financial significance.

Earlier in 1929, UFA, gambling that sound films would always need writing talent, hired Germany's most commercially successful scenarist, Robert Liebmann. As the studio's dramaturge—its resident screenwriter and adviser—he received 2,500 reichsmarks (US$500) a week, with an additional 10,000 reichsmarks (US$2,000) for five original screenplays. In May, popular playwright Carl Zuckmayer came on salary, with an agreement to provide three screenplays. Meanwhile, Erich Pommer had wormed his way back into UFA as an independent producer. While Jannings was still in the United States, the actor negotiated a new contract with UFA for his first sound film. It secured his services from November 1929 to February 1930 for $60,000. In a carefully timed arrival, Jannings returned to Berlin on May 15, the day before the Academy in Hollywood announced his Oscar win. At the same time, UFA revealed that he would make his sound debut at the end of the year in an original screenplay by Zuckmayer. On May 31 Jannings's next-to-last Hollywood film, the disappointing *Street of Sin,* based on von Sternberg's story, opened at one of Berlin's most prestigious cinemas, the Palast am Zoo. Three weeks later, on June 21, Karl Vollmoeller returned to Berlin. The creative team was in place that would bring von Sternberg's *The Blue Angel* to the screen—except that neither he nor that title had yet been mentioned. Instead, everyone favored a film about Rasputin, to be directed by Ernst Lubitsch. To maximize profits, it would be shot in both German and English.

In choosing as their subject the illiterate Russian monk who bamboozled the czar and his family, only to be murdered by resentful courtiers, Pommer and his colleagues were conscious of UFA's owner, the right-wing communications magnate Alfred Hugenberg. He had bought the bankrupt studio in 1927 and used it to produce cheerful musicals and stories of aristocratic heroism, suggesting a vision of what Germany had been before the onset of Weimar socialism. The royalist, conservative *Rasputin* looked certain to please him, since it would have followed a story line similar to that of *Rasputin and the Empress,* made by MGM in 1932. In that film, Rasputin is assassinated not for reasons of political expediency or court intrigue but because he raped Irina Yusupov, the wife of one of his killers.

Vollmoeller agreed to work on *Rasputin* for 23,000 reichsmarks (US$4,600), plus an additional 3,000 reichsmarks (US$600) to lease, for six months, his favorite summer retreat—two floors of Ca'Vendramin Calergi, the palazzo on Venice's Grand Canal where Richard Wagner had lived and died. To direct the film, the unanimous choice was Lubitsch. Ernst Correll, Pommer's replacement as production manager, was delegated to offer Lubitsch $60,000 to return to Berlin and be reunited with Jannings, whom he had directed in many of his early successes. But Lubitsch refused. Within the Paramount hierarchy, he was rising faster than he could ever hope to do in Germany. His career embodied a common gibe about Europeans in Hollywood: "If you begin a production with just one Hungarian, very quickly you have nothing but Hungarians. But if you start with all Germans, soon there is just one." Only when Lubitsch definitively declined did Pommer suggest von Sternberg—who, as well as being an acknowledged expert on sound film, would cost less. Jannings needed some persuasion to accept the substitution. He still smarted from something the director had said just before he left Hollywood. Asked what he thought of Lubitsch's Russian epic *The Patriot,* in which Jannings starred, von Sternberg dismissed it with a curt "*Scheisse*" (shit).

Nor was Jannings comfortable with the role of Rasputin, which he discussed with his wife, actress Gussi Holl, who enjoyed a veto on all his career decisions. In her eyes, Rasputin was nothing but a villain. Where, she demanded, was the downfall, the humiliation, the histrionics his fans expected? Moreover, this was dangerous ground, since the Yusupovs were still alive and socially prominent in Paris, with powerful friends. She was right to be cautious. Following MGM's film, the Yusupovs successfully sued for libel in both Britain and the United States. Scenes were cut or rewritten, and forever after, Hollywood productions carried a disclaimer that all characters were fictional and any resemblance to real people, living or dead, purely coincidental.

Either Jannings or Vollmoeller then suggested reviving a project the actor had discussed with G. W. Pabst. The novel *Professor Unrat, oder Das Ende eines Tyrannen* (Professor Garbage, or The End of a Tyrant), written by Heinrich Mann, elder brother of the more famous Thomas, dated back to 1905. Its main character is Immanuel Raat, a reclusive, widowed professor of English who lives in the Baltic port of Lubeck. He's nicknamed Unrat—garbage—by his students, one of whom is the precocious seventeen-year-old Lohmann, who hangs around Rosa Frohlich, a "barefoot dancer" appearing at a local dive. Raat visits the place, meaning to warn her off, but instead falls under her spell. After squandering all his money on her, he's dismissed from the school. He and Rosa marry and turn their home into a "club," where, under the guise of attending "lectures," clients can gamble and consort with whores. To Raat's perverse satisfaction, several former persecutors become clients and are ruined. But when Raat discovers Rosa in bed with Lohmann, he snaps, first trying to strangle his former student and then stealing his wallet. As he flees through the streets, people abuse and insult him. He's arrested and carted off in the municipal paddy wagon—like a load of garbage.

Von Sternberg bargained Pommer up to $40,000 from his first offer of $30,000. The deal also came with strings, attached by Paramount, to which von Sternberg remained under contract. For every week he spent in Germany past January 14, 1930, the price of his services rose. As the film didn't premiere until April 1, its cost soared to 2 million reichsmarks (US$400,000)—even more than *Metropolis,* whose overruns had led to Pommer's being fired from UFA.

When he and Riza stepped off the train at Berlin's Zoo station on August 16, 1929, and were greeted by Jannings and Pommer, von Sternberg felt he was entering a new and better world. He said as much to the assembled press. "It's as if I went to sleep in Hollywood and woke up in heaven." Despite its apparent spontaneity, their arrival, like that of Jannings on the eve of his Academy Award, had been stage-managed by Pommer. The couple had been in Europe for weeks. As soon as their boat berthed at Southampton, they traveled to London. Von Sternberg spent some weeks in the suburbs, working with editor Jack Harris to oversee the construction of Paramount's new sound studios. With Harris, he approved the building of the dubbing theater, the post-synch theater, and a sound transfer department and the conversion of the cutting rooms to sound.

After London, he and Riza spent some time in Vienna, then moved on to Saint Moritz in Switzerland, where Jannings was dieting off his Californian flab. Pommer, Zuckmayer, Vollmoeller, and Liebmann joined them. Von Sternberg confirmed his agreement to shoot the Mann story, which had already been discussed before he left Hollywood. He also proposed a new structure and a different title—not *Professor Unrat* but the name of the cabaret where his downfall begins—*The Blue Angel.* At his suggestion, enthusiastically seconded by Jannings, they would film only the first half of the book, concentrating on the degradation of Raat and exploiting the barroom setting that had served von Sternberg so well in *Docks of New York.* In the new version, Raat (renamed Rath) confiscates a postcard depicting Rosa Frohlich (now Lola-Lola) from a student, visits the Blue Angel, and is enchanted. He and Lola-Lola marry, but instead of staying in Lubeck, she continues touring with Rath, who plays the stooge in comedy skits and sells postcards of his wife to the punters who come to leer. After being humiliated when the show plays his hometown and he discovers that Lola-Lola has cuckolded him with a new lover (the strongman Mazeppa), Rath smashes her dressing room, flees to the school where he formerly taught, and dies clutching his old desk.

According to John Kahan, a young Berliner who worked for many years in Berlin and London as Pommer's assistant:

The first script was done by Heinrich Mann, but it was no good. He was a fine novelist but he didn't understand the medium. So they called in Carl Zuckmayer, who had just come out with *Der Frohlich Weinberg* [The Happy Vineyard, a popular stage comedy of 1926]. But his script was no good either—only some of the dialogue, about 70 percent of the dialogue. So Pommer said, "It is best if Robert Liebmann does it." . . . Liebmann used most of Zuckmayer's dialogue to write the final shooting script, and this was filmed. Von Sternberg of course revised certain scenes, but added only two or three.[1]

The record corroborates much of Kahan's account. Following his restructuring, von Sternberg appears to have added very little new material. Most people also agree that Liebmann wrote only dialogue and lyrics for some of the songs. In the German version, he's listed separately from the other writers and credited for only the *Drehbuch* (shooting script)—a lesser contribution. According to Zuckmayer, the acknowledgment to Vollmoeller was likewise a courtesy. "Vollmoeller wrote not a line," he said. "He was our contact man with Hollywood. It was he who inspired von Sternberg to come to Berlin, and convinced UFA that von Sternberg was the only masterful director of our film. The end of the film, in which the professor is shown utterly defeated, and returns, a broken man, to his old schoolroom, was von Sternberg's own invention, but I introduced the character of Lola-Lola's lover Mazeppa to give a chance in movies to my old friend Hans Albers."[2]

Once all were agreed, UFA closed the deal with Mann for a mere 25,000 reichsmarks (US$5,000), with an additional 10,000 (US$2,000) when the English version opened in New York. The terms were announced on August 23, only a week after von Sternberg arrived in Berlin—a clear indication that negotiations had been continuing for some time.

The von Sternbergs stayed for a few weeks at the Adlon, Berlin's best hotel. Manager Louis Adlon even claimed a part in the casting of *The Blue Angel*. Supposedly, Emil Jannings frequented its bar and mentioned the search for an actress to play Lola-Lola. In Adon's version, uncorroborated by Jannings or von Sternberg, the hotelier suggested Marlene Dietrich, who lived nearby and ate there often with her mother. As the pace of production quickened, the von Sternbergs rented the apartment of theater director Erwin Piscator, who was making a film in Moscow. Riza got a taste of the German capital's eccentricities when, rearranging cushions on a couch, she discovered a hypodermic syringe. Paramount delayed the German release of von Sternberg's most recent films pending his arrival there. When *The Drag Net* (in German, *Politzei)* premiered at the UFA Palast, he made a short speech. However, Herbert Ihering of the *Berliner Borsen-Courier* articulated the general opinion when he dismissed it as "tear-jerking, hypocritical nonsense." Reviewers were kinder to *The Docks of New York* on September 20, praising its manipulation of lighting and décor, which was possible only in a big studio. Rudolf Arnheim, the ranking intellectual among film critics, rated it "another big step in cinema's progress away from reporting and towards a world of its own."

This encouraged von Sternberg, since *The Blue Angel* existed entirely in such a synthetic world, remote from the political and social ferment of Germany in the summer of 1929. The Weimar Republic, hothouse of so much progress in society and the arts, was crumbling, and with it the security of the Jewish-socialist elite on which its artistic community depended. Two years before, the Nazis had staged their first Nuremberg rally. Even so, Berlin clung to its position as the center of theater and cinema. Only a few people sensed that all this would soon be swept away. One was Max Reinhardt. After the parties that ended the annual Salzburg festivals, which he directed, he invited a few friends to stay until dawn. Zuckmayer recalled, "Once, at a late hour, I heard Reinhardt say almost with satisfaction. 'The nicest part of these festival summers is that each one may be the last.' After a pause, he added, 'You can feel the taste of transitoriness on your tongue.'"[3]

With Pommer confined to bed with a broken ankle, the choice of an actress to play Lola-Lola fell to von Sternberg. It proved more difficult than anticipated. Some had good voices but thick legs. Others spoke fine German but bad English. Most troublingly, many could not sing. As long as *The Blue Angel* had been a drama and Lola-Lola a dancer, nobody had given much thought to the songs. But because this was a sound film, she had to be a singer, and that changed everything.

To play piano for the auditions, Pommer hired Friedrich Hollander. He had worked with Reinhardt at the *Schall und Rauch* and was well-known around Berlin cabarets as a songwriter and leader of the jazz group Weintraub's Syncopators. Von Sternberg's first choice for Lola-Lola was Brigitte Helm, the slinky femme fatale of *Alraune, L'Atlantide,* and *L'Or,* as well as the embodiment of the robot woman in *Metropolis,* but she was too busy and expensive. Hollander suggested Lucie Mannheim, an accomplished singer in operetta who was fluent in English; she later played the murdered spy Annabella Smith in Alfred Hitchcock's *The 39 Steps.* Riza proposed Hollywood actress Phyllis Haver, but von Sternberg still resented her: she had once dismissed him with a sneer as "Big Brain." Nor could she speak German, which likewise eliminated two other candidates, Louise Brooks and Gloria Swanson. Pommer told *New York Times* film reviewer Bosley Crowther that he favored an actress named Greta Massine, of whom nothing is known. (He may have meant Greta Nissen, the Norwegian ex–Ziegfeld dancer who lost out to Jean Harlow in *Hell's Angels* because of her heavy accent.) Subsequently, he supported Heinrich Mann's recommendation of his own mistress, Trude Hesterberg, another graduate of *Schall und Rauch* who was known for her comic songs delivered in a playful soprano. Widely assumed to have inspired the character of Rosa Frohlich, she was the first candidate von Sternberg interviewed—and ignominiously rejected, describing her, sarcastically, as a "stately and dignified elderly German lady." (She was either thirty-two or thirty-eight, depending on which biography one believes, and admittedly a little plump. Also, her comic singing style didn't fit his conception of Lola-Lola.) Rumors circulated that Mann resented how readily von Sternberg had discarded Hesterberg. He supposedly claimed that "Miss Dietrich's naked thighs" dominated the film. Stung by this, Dietrich, years later, penned a long comment on the endpapers of her own copy of the novel. It described the author as "a sad man living in the shadow of his famous, highly talented brother. He had a rare stream of contentment when his book . . . was chosen by Mr. von Sternberg. . . . He felt very honored and grateful to Mr. von Sternberg and gave him *plein pouvoir* [full power] to make all the changes he wanted to make. Character and story changes. . . . I heard he was not the least upset regarding the drastic changes his book suffered in the version that made the film a classic."[4]

With the deadline pressing, Pommer insisted that a decision on an actress be made. Kahan claims that, at this point, the moderately well-known Kathe Haack was signed. Haack had high cheekbones and large, expressive eyes, and her stage training gave her a strong voice. The official record doesn't refer to her, nor does von Sternberg, but he mentions none of the other candidates by name either.

On September 5, six weeks before shooting began, the von Sternbergs saw a musical comedy by Mischa Spoliansky and Georg Kaiser, *Zwei Krawatten* (Two Bow Ties). Typical of the 1920s, it shuffled together international high society, jazz, sex, crime, and a fantasy United States. Jean, waiter at a ball in Berlin, accepts money to exchange his uniform, including a black bow tie, for the white tie and tails of a fleeing gangster. In the pocket is a raffle ticket, and the prize is a cruise to the United States. Jean wins, allowing him to pursue American heiress Mabel, with whom he's infatuated.

The show featured two performers already cast for *The Blue Angel:* Hans Albers as Jean, and Rosa Valetti as Mabel's rich aunt, Mrs. Robinson. (In the film, they play Mazeppa and Frau Kiepert, wife of impresario Kurt Gerron.) Seats in the front row offered ample opportunity to appreciate both. However, according to legend, von Sternberg had eyes only for Marlene Dietrich, who played Mabel. "The 'Leonardo da Vinci of the camera' scrutinised the programme with his eagle eye," she wrote, "found my name, stood up and left the theatre. . . . From that moment on, von Sternberg had only one idea in his head: to take me away from the stage and make a movie actress out of me, to 'Pygmalionize' me."[5] Riza's account is slightly different; according to her, they went backstage after the show, where von Sternberg told Dietrich to contact him the next day at UFA.

Dietrich denies the story of them coming backstage, and there are persistent and credible indications from a number of sources that when von Sternberg saw *Zwei Krawatten,* he had already decided on Dietrich as Lola-Lola. He had certainly seen her before, in a photograph sent by her agent, Max Pick. Among the scores of head shots from hopefuls, hers intrigued him enough to ask Kahan about her. "*Der popo ist nicht schlecht,*" Kahan replied, "*aber brauchen wir nicht auch ein Gesicht?*" (The ass isn't bad, but won't we also need a face?)[6]

It's also likely that he saw her most recent film, and first starring role, opposite Fritz Kortner in Kurt Bernhardt's *Die Frau, nach der man sich sehnt* (The Woman We All Desire). Released the previous April, the film has surprising resonance with von Sternberg's work. Bernhardt frequently fills the frame with choreographed groups of extras moving in counterpoint, a von Sternberg signature technique. The cutting among three or four parallel series of actions at the New Year's Eve party, and the use of decorative elements such as streamers, recalls *Underworld* and prefigures *Dishonored.* Dietrich, though overweight, brunette, and burdened with ridiculously busy costumes, brings something of her von Sternberg persona to the film. Makeup accentuates her eyes and eyebrows, which Bernhardt uses to effect in a series of yearning close-ups—one of them through the veil of a cloche. Whether he had seen the film or not, the actress had sufficiently impressed von Sternberg for him to mention her to a new friend, Leni Riefenstahl, as a possible Lola-

Lola. Riefenstahl later claimed to have been a candidate for the role herself, but she was never seriously considered—though not for want of trying. In her version of events, she bluffed her way into von Sternberg's office and charmed him by praising *The Docks of New York*. He agreed to have dinner with her at the Hotel Bristol—where, over roast beef, he extolled Dietrich, with whom he was obviously smitten.

Screenwriter Walter Reisch also believes that von Sternberg knew Dietrich before *Zwei Krawatten*. They met, he said, when, en route to the script conference in Saint Moritz, the von Sternbergs stopped at Salzburg for the end-of-festival party in Max Reinhardt's Schloss Leopoldskron. (This could have happened: the festival took place in August, just before they arrived in Berlin.) According to Reisch, Dietrich was also present and, with considerable forethought, had brought her musical saw, the gift of another lover, Igo Sym. To play it, one bent the saw against one thigh and coaxed a tune with a violin bow—a pretext for displaying the player's legs, as Dietrich well knew. In Reisch's story, she performed Enrico Toselli's *Serenata,* beguiling von Sternberg.

Other plausible indicators point to Karl Vollmoeller's influence on her casting. Middle-aged, with round wire spectacles and a small moustache, the playwright didn't look like a famous womanizer and the host of the most outrageous parties in Berlin. It helped that he was hugely rich. "Vollmoeller liked always to have nice girls around him," said Kahan. "He was a millionaire, because his family owned [Vollmoeller Textil AG], one of the biggest factories making winter underwear for men."[7] Gottfried Reinhardt, son of Max, penned a sneering portrait of the playboy playwright:

[He] was so adept at arriving in the right place at the right time that, one day, as he drove his car through the side of the Brandenburg Gate leading from Berlin's center to the West End for a party, he saw himself driving through the opposite side leading from the West End to his lavish apartments in Berlin's Pariser Platz for one of his exclusive after-dinner orgies. . . . There were always swarms of young female careerists dancing attendance on him, setting their hopes on his constant rendezvous and transactions with the powers-that-be in the theatre, films and the *haute volee*.[8]

Vollmoeller, who spent part of each year in Hollywood, was instrumental in bringing German artists to the United States and finding work for American performers in Europe. Jannings owed his Hollywood contract partly to Vollmoeller. Lubitsch, William Dieterle, and cinematographer-director Karl Freund were hired at Vollmoeller's urging. He also helped attractive and exotic African American and Asian artists such as Josephine Baker, Katherine Dunham, and Anna May Wong find work in Germany, and exacted the customary sexual tribute.

His role in Dietrich's casting for Lola-Lola is corroborated by Ruth "Rut" Yorck, his sometime lover. A well-connected writer, actress, socialite, and confidante of almost everyone in the arts, Yorck knew von Sternberg as well as Dietrich, with whom she had acted in Vienna. Vollmoeller asked her to recommend Dietrich for some minor role in *The Blue Angel,* and he also wrote a letter of introduction to Pommer. Kahan confirms his involvement. "Von Sternberg did not first go to see *Zwei Krawatten*—that was later. One day, Liebmann, Pommer, von Sternberg and myself were discussing certain things, when suddenly from the reception a man came in and said, 'There is a young lady. She has a letter from Dr. Vollmoeller for Mr. Pommer.' Vollmoeller had given Marlene a letter of introduction, asking Pommer to give her some small part in the picture. And when Marlene entered the door, von Sternberg jumped up and said 'Erich, this is Lola!' He smelt it, instinctively; this was how his mind worked."[9]

In real life, Marlene Dietrich, then twenty-eight, could have been taken for a modernized version of Mann's heroine. Though she and her husband, Rudolf Sieber, a lowly stage manager for actor Harry Piel, had a small daughter, their marriage was designed to accommodate and exploit the opportunities and temptations of Berlin show business. Sieber had his own longtime mistress, Tamara "Tami" Matul, and ignored his wife's numerous liaisons with actors such as Willy Forst, since it was through these that she found work. Dietrich took little pleasure in sex. "I'm not interested in it," she confided in later life to journalist Leo Lerman, "but if men want it, why should I refuse?"[10] Two of her most famous lovers, Maurice Chevalier and novelist Erich Maria Remarque, were impotent. According to Lerman, she found the greatest satisfaction in nurturing those she admired. Lerman wrote, "Marlene, overcome by admiration, devastated by charm, undone by enthusiasm, felt she had only one tribute to offer; the remarkable gift of her beauty. She gave it unstintingly."[11]

Dietrich was a fixture at the late-night parties thrown by wealthy businessmen like Vollmoeller and members of the decayed aristocracy. She sometimes wore male evening clothes to these soirees, complete with her father's old monocle, and would dance with some other attractive girl, the two fondling and kissing on the dance floor while their friends whooped and applauded. She took lovers of both sexes, including gravel-voiced cabaret singer Claire Waldoff, who taught her to make something of her breathy contralto. Copying Waldoff and the equally mannish-sounding Zarah Leander, she developed the voice that would later make her famous.

Conscious of her pretty legs, she showed them off at parties, doing high kicks that revealed she wore no underwear. In such matters, she was quite unself-conscious. Leni Riefenstahl described an incident in which Dietrich, drinking in a café with actress friends, demanded, "Why does a woman always have to have beautiful breasts? Her bosom can sag a little, can't it?" She then lifted out one of her breasts for their startled inspection.[12] She was already attracting legends. One rumor claimed that Alfred Hugenberg, head of UFA, invited her to an extremely private party at Berlin's Olympic Club and presented her to Adolf Hitler, who became an instant admirer. Another anecdote, slightly more credible, involved Count Alexander "Sascha" Kolowrat-Krakowský, founder of Sascha-Film, UFA's Viennese subsidiary. The count, enormously obese, barely survived the production of *Café Elektric,* destined to be his last film. In December 1927, on his deathbed at a clinic in Semmering, outside Vienna, he asked his friend, director Karl Hartl, to gratify a dying wish—to enjoy one last look at Marlene's famous thighs. She obligingly presented herself at his bedside, hiked up her skirt, flashed, twirled, and left him to die happy.

Erich Pommer's wife Gertrude Levy was part of the same social scene as Dietrich, and she recounted the juicier scandals to her husband. So it's hardly surprising that, when she appeared at UFA, Pommer shouted, "Not that whore!" Taking their cue from Pommer, everyone on the team found reasons to reject her: her Berlin accent and barely adequate English; a singing voice that hovered between a growl and a purr, with no upper register; an awkwardly shaped nose; and at least ten kilos overweight. (Louise Brooks, hearing that Marlene was a candidate for the role, called her "a galloping cow.") A more rational man would have bowed to the logic of these objections, but the more Pommer argued against using Dietrich, the more angry von Sternberg became, blustering, "If that's how things are, I'll go back to the United States!"

Changing tack, Pommer said, "But Jo, what about the contract with Kathe Haack? She could sue."

"Talk to her, pay her off," von Sternberg said. "It will be worth it."

"So Pommer," said Kahan, "rang Kathe Haack, who was a very nice, decent girl. She didn't sue; she resigned and accepted her fee."[13]

Reluctantly, Pommer set up a screen test for Dietrich, but he took the precaution of filming one with Lucie Mannheim on the same day. In each case, Hollander accompanied them. (Dietrich rejects as "ridiculous" the story that American comic Buster Keaton was present during the auditions, although he may have visited the set later.)

Dietrich's test has survived, revealing that little of her later mystery and appeal was immediately evident. At the start, von Sternberg tells her, off camera and in German, "Go slowly, take your time." After turning her face left and right to show both profiles, Marlene, with a lighted cigarette in hand and leaning on the end of an upright piano, sings repeatedly, in her approximate English, the verse of a recent hit, "You're the Cream in My Coffee." As she does so, she continues smoking and argues in German with the unseen Hollander. After a couple of repetitions, she tells him, "This is supposed to be music, right?" (It has been suggested that she was genuinely angry and that Hollander didn't know the song—which hardly seems likely, given his accomplishment as a composer and the simplicity of the tune.) After more byplay with the cigarette, she snaps at Hollander, "You call that piano playing? I'm supposed to sing that junk?" Later, she thumps a fist on the piano and says, "Good God, it doesn't go that way! Don't you get it?" Following this, she climbs up on the piano, crosses her legs, adjusts her skirt to show them off, and sings in German "Why Cry?" a torch song by another popular Berlin composer, Peter Kreuder. The lyrics include the following: "Why cry when you leave someone? / There's someone else waiting at the next corner." Once the song ends, she asks the off-camera director, "Did you get it all?"

The next day the production office unanimously judged Mannheim the obvious choice. Only von Sternberg disagreed. In the end, it was not he nor even Pommer who made the decision, but Jannings and Hugenberg. Paradoxically, Jannings welcomed the casting of an un-known—moreover, one with a bad reputation and no beauty besides. It gave him more space to shine. As for Hugenberg, he belatedly realized that the author of *Professor Unrat* was not the great Thomas Mann but his less eminent brother. Unable to halt the production, he insisted that the film should in no way represent Rath as successful or emblematic of German values. Fortunately, the revised story removed the book's political message. Rath, instead of turning the tables on his tormentors, remained pathetic to the end, a victim of sexual obsession, for which society could hardly be blamed. As for the object of Rath's lust, in Hu-genberg's eyes, the trashier she was, the better.

In October UFA signed Dietrich to a one-picture contract for a perfunctory 20,000 reichsmarks (US$4,000), increasing to 25,000 (US$5,000) if the film proved good enough for U.S. release. It's hard to say who was more surprised—Dietrich or her friends on the party circuit. The night she signed, she's reputed to have visited two theatrical hangouts—the Silhouette, patronized by male cross-dressers, and the bar of the Hotel Eden Am Zoo—and bragged to everyone, "You've always said I couldn't act." Unconvinced, the assembled drag queens responded, "You *still* can't!"

With Lola-Lola now reconceived as a singer, Friedrich Hollander was hired to provide her songs, and Peter Kreuder became his orchestra-tor. In the film itself, Hollander leads Weintraub's Syncopators as the Blue Angel's house band, and he can also be seen playing piano at the wedding of Rath and Lola-Lola. Von Sternberg and his editor S. K. "Sam" Winston coached Dietrich in English. Winston's contribution to von Sternberg's career deserves to be better appreciated. In addition to editing both the German and English versions of *The Blue Angel,* he cut *Morocco;* worked at UFA from 1930 to 1933, supervising the dubbing of Paramount's films into German; then returned to Hollywood to edit *The Scarlet Empress, The Devil Is a Woman,* and *The Shanghai Gesture.*

George Grosz watched the two men at work on *The Blue Angel*. "Both of them wore berets and thick woollen scarves around their necks, as if they were cold,"[14] which, being used to California, they probably were. He compared them to a sorcerer and his apprentice in a fable by Grimm, "since they communicated by means of incomprehensible whistles, as if they were birds."[15] Grosz even suggests, whimsically, that perhaps Winston was descended from a canary. For all we know of this shadowy but important figure, he might well have been. Not surprisingly, he receives no mention in von Sternberg's memoirs.

Falling in Love Again

> Wars will wash over us . . . bombs will fall . . . all civiliza-
> tion will crumble . . . but not yet, please . . . wait, wait . . .
> what's the hurry? Let us be happy . . . give us our moment.
>
> —Billy Wilder, Charles Brackett, and Walter Reisch, screenplay
> for *Ninotchka*

ON OCTOBER 29, 1929, the U.S. stock market crashed and the Great
Depression began. By December, Nazi Party membership swelled to
178,000. If von Sternberg or Dietrich noticed, neither said so. Something more important was taking place. One was falling in love, and the
other was letting him.

Although her husband would disappear for long periods, Riza
didn't immediately notice. She was busy enjoying her own small celebrity, being interviewed and photographed for fashion spreads in
magazines such as *Die Dame*. Once she realized the extent of his infatu-
ation, the arguments began. During one of them, she asked why he
didn't divorce her and marry his "discovery." Von Sternberg replied,
unexpectedly, "I'd as soon share a telephone booth with a cobra."[1] His
hostility and Marlene's passive acceptance of it fueled their relationship.
To adore a woman and to have her, in return, admire him and cater
to his every sexual whim, yet feel no love, gratified his most profound
masochistic desires. Von Sternberg could bully, manipulate, humiliate,
or insult her, but she never fought back. Frederica Sagor, no friend of

either, shrewdly assessed their attraction. "Von Sternberg's sexual weakness was something that she, in her sophistication and worldly outlook on life, could handily take care of. And she did. To Dietrich, it did not matter if the attraction was man or woman. She was cognizant of all the ways of making love and enjoying sex. . . . She worked hard to achieve her stardom. She was no accident. She had what it takes."[2]

In the first flush of their affair, the lovers, according to Riza, fornicated on a tiger skin in a bedroom with a mirrored ceiling. The image flirts with writer Elinor Glyn's sensationalism, yet who is to say they didn't? Von Sternberg was a closet masochist and role player; Dietrich was a promiscuous bisexual with a flair for cross-dressing and a taste for figures of authority. Sex between them was always going to be what the surrealists called "convulsive"—"as beautiful," in Lautremont's phrase, "as the chance encounter of a sewing machine and an umbrella on a dissecting table." Complementary freaks, they would transit the cinema landscape for the next decade, leaving in their wake a succession of enigmatically gorgeous but discarded objects—stillborn children of a marriage solemnized at the very moment the world came crashing down, a love affair consummated in Armageddon.

Nobody grasped the extent of the global catastrophe that would follow the Wall Street crash, but von Sternberg tried to insulate Dietrich from its effects by urging Schulberg to offer her a long-term deal and bring her to the United States. She could, he suggested, be the answer to Greta Garbo that Paramount had long been seeking. "While the filming of *The Blue Angel* was in full swing," wrote Dietrich in her memoirs, "von Sternberg brought an American to the studio—B. P. Schulberg, the general manager of Paramount Studios."[3] Schulberg did come to Berlin on October 20, but he had more on his mind than meeting an unknown, untried actress. When the stock market crashed, all German loans were canceled, destroying Hollywood's financial arrangement with UFA. *The Blue Angel* would be one of the last productions released as "A ParUfaMet Film." With the sound patent conflict not yet resolved, influential people in the German film business were actively resisting the release of U.S. films, including many Paramount productions. George Bancroft had been sent to Berlin on a charm offensive. He attracted approving press coverage with his habit of sluicing down a few pints of beer for breakfast. Seizing the opportunity, a brewery hired Bancroft and Jannings for an advertising film, some of which was directed, improbably, by Sergei Eisenstein. The Soviet government had cautiously let its most famous filmmaker off the leash, allowing him to tour Europe and the United States with his companion Grigori Alexandrov and cinematographer Eduard Tisse, ostensibly to study techniques of sound film.

According to Dietrich, Schulberg "offered me a seven-year contract in Hollywood. 'I wouldn't like to go away,' I answered very politely. 'I would like to stay here with my family.' He was just as polite and then disappeared again. Von Sternberg had made him come over from America to show him some scenes from the film."[4] Schulberg did visit the set, as did Bancroft (where he chided von Sternberg for not being at the railway station to greet him), and all attended a special screening of *Underworld* on November 2. But Schulberg could not have viewed scenes from *The Blue Angel,* since shooting had begun only two days after he arrived. He might have seen Dietrich's mediocre screen test, but until von Sternberg proved he could work some magic with this unpromising unknown, there would be no contract.

Driving von Sternberg to UFA's Potsdam studios on his first day, Pommer asked what he planned to shoot. When the director said he wasn't sure, the producer demanded to be informed each morning of the exact schedule. What might have seemed a shrewd strategy, given von Sternberg's history of multiple takes, backfired when he announced that, if this was the case, Pommer could turn the car around and return him to his apartment. Pommer capitulated. It was an idiotic argument. Since von Sternberg filmed chronologically, he spent the first days shooting the models of Lubeck with which the film opens. But he liked to goad, and Pommer, fretting at the threat of overruns, was a perfect victim.

In creating *The Blue Angel,* von Sternberg ignored contemporary Germany. No automobiles appear, no radios or cinemas; the lamps that hang in almost every shot burn oil or gas. Except for Rath peeling leaves from a calendar that begins at 1923 and ends with 1929, it reflects the Europe von Sternberg grew up in. In Rath, he skewers the teacher of Hebrew from the yeshiva his father forced him to attend. His attempts to make the student Ertzum pronounce the word "the" come straight from life.

Having never met a woman like Dietrich, he assembled her character from the work of writers and artists who had, in particular, playwright Frank Wedekind. Lola-Lola is derived from Lulu of *Wedekind's Fruhlings Erwachen* (Spring's Awakening) and *Die Buchse der Pandora* (Pandora's Box). Like Lola-Lola, she's a dancer who so captivates an older man that he sacrifices his reputation for her. Past and future lovers surround her, and she even appears at a ball in male evening dress to tantalize a lesbian countess. Wedekind, like von Sternberg, visualized himself in his characters and sometimes acted in his own plays. One line of *Die Buchse der Pandora* applies particularly to von Sternberg's relationship with Dietrich. "I've noticed," the young author says to Lulu, "a curious affinity between sensuality and artistic creation. I can either exploit you artistically, or I can love you."[5] And he immediately begins to make love to her.

For Dietrich's "look," von Sternberg also returned to the nineteenth century. Lola-Lola's trashy costumes are sometimes attributed to Tihamer Varady and the unknown Karl-Ludwig Holub, but neither receives screen credit, and it's evident that their work closely followed von Sternberg's ideas. "Seen from the front," he told Dietrich, "you should bring to mind Félicien Rops; from the rear, Toulouse-Lautrec." Belgian eroticist Rops enjoyed a vogue in France and Germany in the 1880s, but in 1930 he was known mainly to connoisseurs, so von Sternberg felt free to plunder. In particular he adopted Rops's figure of a small-breasted woman, naked except for black stockings, fancy garters, and an elaborate head-dress, sometimes incorporating a male hat. Salacious cherubs often surround his women. In *The Blue Angel,* one such creature clasps Lola's leg in the poster used to advertise the show. A line of grotesque cardboard cherubs also hangs over her head as she sings, while others decorate the edge of the stage. It's they who give the bar its name.

From one of the film's first shots—of a shop girl admiring a poster of Lola-Lola stuck to the window, then imitating her arrogant hands-on-hips pose—we're encouraged to think of Dietrich as two-dimensional, a moving photograph, our private dirty picture, or, in von Sternberg's own words, "a pictorial aphrodisiac." For earlier films, he had glued pinups to walls, scribbled messages in chalk or greasepaint, and filled sets with streamers, nets, or veils. Now he indulged himself like a toddler with a box of crayons. Every flat surface is textured, decorated, *busy*. He encrusts Lola's dressing room with old posters, clutters the bar and the poky rooms backstage with screens, hanging costumes, stacked chairs, nets, and mirrors. None of these details appear in the original set drawings by Otto Hunte; they are entirely the director's additions.

British critic Raymond Durgnat delighted in those additions, which captured the authentic squalor of cheap bars. "If the film abounds in objects," he wrote, "they are not so much symbols (i.e., a code for something else) as carriers of atmosphere. The cabaret is blotched and scabrous, the air a quagmire of heat, smoke, beer fumes and powder, the music hoarse and scrannel. Streaks of muggy light ooze through cobweb-like curtains. Only Marlene could survive the hideous dress in which she sings her first number. The dresses of the fat cows behind her are not so much spangled as blotched like toadskin. The whole film is in the key of dirt."[6]

The Blue Angel is the first film in which von Sternberg conceives the screen image as a diorama. What he calls the "dead space" between camera and subject, and between subject and background, comes alive. People and objects pass before our eyes and under our noses while, behind the supposed subject of interest, others flow by, often in the opposite direction. In an early scene of a girl unloading geese in a market square, he places her in the middle distance, filling the foreground with shadowy baskets and bales, outlining her against a shimmering background. Rath's entries into the cabaret are bravura exercises in technique, with Jannings ducking under low lintels, groping through nets, fumbling with doors, climbing stairs, emerging on a balcony, and perching there, flanked by proprietor Kiepert and a nude female torso. The other customers gawk up as he stares transfixed at Lola-Lola, isolated as on a slide between dangling props and the décor. Rath and Lola-Lola are filmed across a dressing table crowded with scent bottles or over the shoulders of their wedding guests. Though UFA's stages were no smaller than those of Paramount, von Sternberg rendered them as cramped, almost stifling. Yet we don't yearn to escape. Rather, we shove aside the crumpled underwear, slump into the chair, and snuggle down into its perfumed intimacy.

Few important characters in cinema are developed as perfunctorily as Lola-Lola. We know nothing about her, not even her real name or where she comes from—which, as with all whores, is the way we prefer it. Von Sternberg doesn't try our patience with the cliché, "What's a nice girl like you doing in a place like this?" She isn't nice, and she's exactly where she belongs. Who can imagine Lola-Lola outside the boudoir? In discarding the second half of Mann's book, he frees us of the necessity to try. We see and share what he sees in Dietrich—his own lusts, reflected back from that prostitute's face, which tells us, "Anything's possible, *liebchen,* if the money is right." And the face is all the more alluring for our knowledge that nothing she does will mark it. At the end of the film we retain only the fantasy—a puff of cheap face powder, the memory of a crushed pair of panties on the floor, and a few songs, raucous or huskily provocative, that survive more in echo than expression. One final glimpse of Lola-Lola astride a chair, half singing, half speaking *"und sonst gar nichts"* (and nothing more), is an irrevocable curtain, with no hope of an encore. At that moment, our time is up, and for us, she ceases to exist, as we cease to exist for her.

Cinematographer Lee Garmes takes credit for creating "the Dietrich face" on her first American film, *Morocco,*[7] but in *The Blue Angel* we can already see it emerging, an evolution from what Maurice Tourneur taught von Sternberg—that light should appear to fall from a single source. By placing a lamp close to her face and above it, cameraman Gunther Rittau forces the cheekbones out of her chubbiness and deepens her eyes. A second lamp, at a distance but at eye level, spotlights the face, isolating it from the cluttered décor, defining her as the center of every shot. To minimize the tip-tilt of her nose, he adds another lamp, letting the three discs of light overlap in the center of her face, overexposing the nose and blurring it with light.

Shooting began on November 4, 1929. As well as working chronologically, von Sternberg insisted on keeping all sets standing in case he needed to reshoot—a system he used again on *I, Claudius,* with just as much inconvenience to the studio. Dietrich claims in her memoirs that four cameras ran simultaneously, but this can hardly be true. In Hollywood, directors of silent films often shot with two cameras, side by side, to provide an identical negative for the film's European version. This was impractical on a sound film. The camera was heavily "blimped" to mute the sound of its motor, and space had to be found for the recordist in his insulated booth, the size of two telephone kiosks. For shots without sound, he may have used two cameras occasionally, but for sound sequences, he rolled only one and shot the English and German versions on alternate days—an added complication for the technicians and for Pommer, but a boon for the actors, who often fluffed their English lines.

The need for two versions posed special problems. Not all the actors spoke English, and among those who did, their fluency varied. Several shots were deleted or altered on this account: the English version, which often differs in terms of camera angle and action, is also twelve minutes shorter than the German. To further complicate things, von Sternberg decided that, even in the English version, the use of English, like his use of sound, should be realistic. Thus, most characters speak English only when the plot dictates. Jannings lectures his students in English, but otherwise they speak German. Von Sternberg could imagine only one reason for Lola-Lola to speak English: it's her native tongue. When Rath addresses her in German, she says in English, "You must talk to me in my own language."

When Dietrich struggled with a word, von Sternberg reassured her that, if necessary, Riza could stand off-camera and speak the English dialogue while she mimed it—a technique Alfred Hitchcock used on *Blackmail,* where Joan Barry's voice replaced that of the heavily accented Anny Ondra. (Von Sternberg had seen its effectiveness on September 9, when both silent and sound versions of *Blackmail* screened at UFA.) In the event, Riza was never needed. Some biographies weave stories around Dietrich's supposed inability to pronounce the word *moths* in the English lyrics of "Falling in Love Again," but it's clear from the film that she does so easily. If a line did give her trouble, von Sternberg changed it or dropped it altogether, telling her, as he often told performers in his films, "Oh, just say something more or less the same."

Following her claim that she had suggested Dietrich for the part of

Lola-Lola, Leni Riefenstahl elaborated on her involvement in the shooting. By the time she got around to writing her memoirs, she had, in her own imagination, taken center stage. "Von Sternberg brought me to the studio every day," she claimed, "until it got too much for Marlene. . . . She started behaving very crudely to try and make me leave in disgust. Von Sternberg noticed and stepped in, but she said she'd leave the film if I came to the studio again."[8] Nobody else ever remarked on this incident, and we can almost certainly attribute it to Riefenstahl's tireless capacity for reinvention.

Max Reinhardt visited the set. So did Eisenstein, for whom von Sternberg screened some rushes. "He took each scene about twenty times," said the Russian, no slouch himself at multiple takes.[9] Amiable, even fawning in his presence, Eisenstein was privately scathing about his colleague. In his diaries he claimed that von Sternberg shared his own homosexual inclinations. "He has a predilection for well-built males," he alleged, "and even stayed at the Hercules Hotel"—a reference to the Hotel Herkules-Haus, adjacent to the Herkulesbrücke (Hercules Bridge) near Nollendorfplatz, then, as now, the center of Berlin's gay scene. (Christopher Isherwood lived at Nollendorfstrasse 17 while he wrote the *Berlin Stories,* which became the basis of the musical *Cabaret.*) Although Eisenstein scholar Ronald Bergan agrees that "this curious statement . . . seems to be completely unfounded," he doesn't exclude the possibility that von Sternberg may have been tempted to experiment by "the heady atmosphere of the last days of the Weimar Republic [which] was penetrating everybody's psyche."[10]

Other visitors to the set included an attractive Russian émigré, sculptor Dora Gordine, who became a friend in Hollywood, and the artist George Grosz. He and von Sternberg had already met in the studio of Rudolf Belling, who was sculpting a portrait head of the director, later cast in bronze. Shortly after, Belling, Grosz, and von Sternberg were guests at dinner with dealer Alfred Flechtheim. When Belling asked if film directing was lucrative, von Sternberg replied, "I don't really earn a great deal; not quite three times as much as the President of the United States."[11] Grosz was less impressed by the sum than by the fact that, as von Sternberg dropped his bombshell, he didn't even look up to see the effect. Suddenly this quiet-spoken little man became interesting, inspiring Grosz to devote part of his memoirs to "Svengali Joe," as a Berlin journalist had christened him. (Nor did he exaggerate. Until 1949, the president received $75,000 a year. Von Sternberg, at $20,000 a week, was substantially better recompensed.)

The day before shooting ended on January 22, 1930, Sidney Kent, Paramount distribution chief, viewed a rough cut of *The Blue Angel* in Berlin and cabled Jesse Lasky about Dietrich: "She's sensational. Sign her up." This was an order, not a recommendation. Kent, shortly to become general manager of Paramount Publix, effectively ran the company. On January 29, Schulberg cabled Dietrich with an offer that reflected his resentment at being dictated to: "Have pleasure to invite you to join brilliant roster of players at Paramount Publix stop Offer you seven year contract beginning at five hundred dollars per week escalating to three thousand five hundred per week in seventh year Congratulations."

This was the standard studio contract, demanding virtual slavery. All the same, von Sternberg urged her to accept. The sum of $500 was paltry, but such deals were renegotiated as a matter of course. Dietrich temporized. She resented the self-satisfied tone of "brilliant roster of players" and the assumption of acceptance implied in "Congratulations." She also had other commitments—to UFA, to the theater company that produced *Zwei Krawatten,* and to her husband and child. (It was also rumored that she procrastinated intentionally, hoping to be cast in G. W. Pabst's *Buchse der Pandora.* One anecdote places her in Pabst's office, ready to sign, when the call came confirming Louise Brooks. It's a nice story, but impossible; *Buchse der Pandora* was shot before *The Blue Angel* and opened on January 30, 1930, while the latter was still filming.) A compromise evolved. Paramount would import Dietrich for two films only, but at $1,250 a week, and for the moment, Rudy and their little girl Heidede would remain behind in Berlin.

Though *The Blue Angel* would delight the public, it infuriated three of the people most involved in making it. Jannings, as expected, reacted badly to the von Sternberg–Dietrich affair. During production, he did all he could to rupture their rapport, throwing tantrums and threatening to walk out (although it's probably not true, as suggested by some, that he tried to strangle her during a fight scene). He was particularly incensed by von Sternberg's handling of the scene in which Rath, crazed with jealousy, wrecks Lola's dressing room: the director lingered on the expressions of those who watched, ignoring Jannings completely. A similar scene in *Variete,* in which he destroyed a café upon hearing of his wife's infidelity, had been that film's high point, and the actor felt robbed of a great moment. Thereafter, he insisted on approving the final cut of his films, with disastrous results. Alfred Hugenberg also found the film distasteful. Suspecting that the character of Rath satirized him, he raged at Pommer for creating a parody of the German bourgeoisie, although the cost of the production made it impossible to delay its release. Angriest of all was Riza von Sternberg, who sailed for the United States and sued for divorce.

Although Lola-Lola's songs became one of the film's most memorable features, they were almost an afterthought, dashed off in a few days by Friedrich Hollander, who skillfully exploited the deficiencies of Dietrich's voice, basing the songs on her two best notes, with many words in a husky *sprechgesang*—half spoken, half sung. This also suited primitive recording systems, which favored a low, even tone. The theatrical setting made *The Blue Angel* ideal to demonstrate von Sternberg's belief that music should arise naturally from the action. He accompanied each opening of the door to Lola's dressing room with a burst of music from the show going on outside, and found other pretexts to introduce it as well. Throughout the film, he cut to an elaborate clock with a set of figures that emerge when it strikes. As the statuettes pass in procession, the chimes play *Ub immer Treu und Redlichkeit,* an old tune praising loyalty and honesty. It's the first piece of music in the film, and at the end, as the camera lingers on the dead Rath, we hear it again.

Hollander embraced von Sternberg's methods, preferring them to the tradition of operetta, in which all action stops when the cast bursts into song. He also enjoyed working to a deadline. "The musical collaborator in a film should be constantly present during its shooting," he wrote just after working on *The Blue Angel.* "Collaboration at speed means that a suggestion is sketched out on the piano, gets the director's approval, making sure that image and sound harmonize; the instrumentation is sketched out too, then tried out with the orchestra and recorded on the sound-track—all this in half a day." A forgetful eccentric, given to wearing mismatched socks and odd shoes, Hollander worked best on the lavatory, with music paper pinned to the back of the door. This technique produced his most famous composition, the song known in English as "Falling in Love Again." No such song was originally included, as von Sternberg felt that the raucous *Ich bin die fesche Lola* (They Call Me Naughty Lola) would be enough to beguile the vulnerable Rath. Once his view of her softened, however, he demanded something more tender. Challenged to compose a love song for a woman who didn't believe in love, Hollander retired *zum klo* (to the lavatory) and emerged with a rueful waltz, writing not only the music but also the lyrics, celebrating the satisfactions of uncomplicated lust.

> *Ich bin von Kopf bis Fuß*
> *Auf Liebe eingestellt,*
> *Denn das ist meine Welt.*
> *Und sonst gar nichts.*
> *Das ist, was soll ich machen,*
> *Meine Natur,*
> *Ich kann halt lieben nur*
> *Und sonst gar nichts.*

Literally translated, this means:

> From head to foot,
> I'm made for love [sex]
> Because this is my world.
> Otherwise, there's nothing.
> This is what I must do—my nature.
> I can only have love.
> Otherwise, there's nothing.

As she sings *von Kopf bis Fuß*, Lola-Lola makes a gesture with her hand that takes in her whole body, offering it to anyone confident or rich enough to claim it. Her frankness leaches all sentiment from the song. Like another poignant ballad of prostitution, Cole Porter's "Love for Sale," it leaves no room for romance.

Disappointingly, the English lyrics give a different impression. Hurriedly composed by Sammy Lerner, a Romanian best known for the theme to the cartoon series *Popeye, The Sailor Man,* they neutralize Hollander's Dionysian statement. As the first song Rath hears from Lola-Lola, they should implicitly warn him and the rest of us what to expect from her. In English, however, they become apologetic:

> Falling in love again
> Never wanted to.
> What am I to do?
> Can't help it.

Both Dietrich and Hollander detested the sweetening of its Berlin astringency. But the damage was done, and for the rest of her career, she'd be shackled to lyrics that said precisely the opposite of what the song intended.

Der Blaue Engel premiered on April 1 at Berlin's Gloriapalast. Von Sternberg wasn't present. With each week costing UFA a fortune in penalties, he left as soon as shooting ended. Sam Winston completed the editing and mixed the sound. Even though the *Bremen* sailed the next day, Dietrich had no intention of missing her premiere. In his memoirs, Peter Kreuder claims that von Sternberg hired a claque of fifty people to attend the premiere and applaud following "Falling in Love Again," and to allow for it, ordered fifteen seconds of black leader spliced in after the song to avoid interrupting the film. Kreuder's reminiscences are unreliable and repudiated almost entirely by Dietrich (herself no more reliable). However, the opera claque was an institution. Members hired themselves out to provide applause for any event from an automobile *concours d'elegance* to a fashion show, and the blank-film trick resembles the practice of "forcing an encore," in which the claque rushed the stage at the end of an aria and threw small bouquets, distracting the conductor long enough for a "spontaneous" ovation.

The demand for seats was so great on the first day of screening that the film played four times, with the stars making personal appearances at the afternoon press show and the gala evening premiere. While waiting to go on, they remained backstage in the greenroom. Kreuder arrived halfway through the press show and was instantly attacked by Jannings about the black film. When he refused to remove it, Jannings, he claimed, knocked him down. But no amount of violence could arrest Dietrich's progress. Addressing the audience that night in her white evening gown and fur stole, she looked every inch a star. "I don't leave Berlin lightly," she told them. "First, because Berlin is my home. Second, because Berlin is . . . Berlin. Though I shouldn't say it, I am a little afraid of Hollywood." She had no reason to fear the reaction that night. "It was such a powerful stark tragedy," one critic wrote, "that several seconds elapsed before the audience broke into enthusiastic applause."[12] As for her Hollywood debut, she revealed in her speech that it would be in *Amy Jolly, Die Frau au Marrakesch,* an obscure autobiographical novel by Benno Vigny, onetime Foreign Legionnaire.

Since she was going straight from the theater to the boat train, a truck loaded with her luggage—thirty-six pieces, according to Kreuder —stood at the stage door. It had to push through the mobs around the cinema, but it strains credulity that Kreuder, as he claims, played an upright piano on the back of the truck while Marlene and Willy Forst danced the Charleston and tossed champagne glasses to the crowd. Forst and another handsome admirer, the actor Francis Lederer, did accompany her on the train to Bremerhaven, along with Resi, her dresser from *The Blue Angel,* who would become her maid. Although nobody else mentions it, her husband was apparently present as well, since Dietrich wrote in her personal copy of one biography, "und Rudi?"[13] But the failure to note his presence is understandable. From that moment, Marlene Dietrich was entirely her own woman.

The Woman All Women Want to See

What is most beautiful in virile men is something feminine; what is most beautiful in feminine women is something masculine.

—Susan Sontag, "Notes on 'Camp'"[1]

DIETRICH'S ARRIVAL IN NEW YORK had elements of farce. She later retailed the story to Leo Lerman in a tone of just-between-us-girls *fausse naivete:*

> In those days, maids were always seasick. Everyone was sitting together in first class and worrying about their maids. But Resi was not only seasick; she lost her teeth—and was the reason I was late for the first interview. Resi, she wouldn't come out from her cabin until I promised to take her to a dentist immediately.
>
> All the American [passengers] had black dresses and pearls and mink coats and the orchids, ropes of orchids, they had been saving in the ice box all through the voyage. I had on what any German wore when traveling—a grey flannel suit and a slouch hat, very manly, and gloves. A man came aboard from . . . a tug boat, he took one look at me and said, "Oh, no. . . . I can't let America see you like that. They'll think you're a lesbian." So my trunk had to be brought up again, and I had to get dressed all over. . . . I left Resi and went to the interview and was an hour late.[1]

Dietrich chose not to remember that she wasn't simply an hour late but an entire day late, and her wardrobe was not the only problem. As she stepped off the *Bremen*, an attorney representing Riza von Sternberg served her notice of two lawsuits. One, a $100,000 libel suit, related to an interview in Vienna's *Neues Wiener Journal,* in which Marlene had called Riza an "undutiful wife" and claimed that von Sternberg planned to divorce her, if she didn't divorce him first. The other, for $500,000, was for alienation of his affections. Paramount delayed the press reception twenty-four hours while lawyers negotiated. In return for keeping her suits out of the papers, they promised Riza generous treatment when the divorce came to court.

Jesse Lasky officially unveiled Dietrich the following day at a press lunch. The press conference "was all men," she complained. "Not a woman. Paramount arranged it that way."[2] The following day, studio publicists, anticipating a call for head shots of the new star, had her photographed by fashionable portraitist Irving Chidnoff.

In Beverly Hills a house awaited, chosen by von Sternberg. Instantly, the Hollywood machine pounced. A dietitian helped her lose thirty pounds, and voice coaches worked on her English. For the moment, her hair remained brunette, but von Sternberg decreed it should be cut short and brushed back to accentuate her brow and cheekbones. After that, Marlene was placed in the hands of Dorothy Ponedel, the first woman to be admitted to the Makeup Artists' Guild. Ponedel plucked her eyebrows and redrew them into high-arching lines that became her trademark. To accommodate von Sternberg's preferred high-key lighting, with a lamp shining down directly from above, she accentuated Dietrich's cheekbones by shading under them with her own improvised eye shadow made from burned match heads mixed with baby oil. Not only the area around the eyes but also the eyelids themselves were darkened. A white stroke under the eyes increased their apparent size, drawing attention from her nose, which was further diminished by a line of silver down the bridge.

Used to the melodramatic Pola Negri and the secretive Greta Garbo, Paramount's publicity department was nonplussed by Dietrich's hausfrau manner and mannish wardrobe, as well as being nervous about Riza's lawsuits. The studio rationed her public appearances, since Dietrich on the arm of von Sternberg tended to steal the show. One such event was a pre-wedding party at the Beverly Wilshire Hotel for Irene Mayer, Louis's daughter, and producer David O. Selznick. Dietrich made "a spectacular entrance," wrote the bride-to-be, "followed by Josef von Sternberg. She strode across the full length of the enormous dance floor. The silence was broken by applause. . . . She practically seemed the guest of honor."

Chidnoff's New York portraits arrived. Although the photographer had a reputation for realism, these saccharine images showed a simpering Dietrich, still darkly brunette and hilariously mumsie in a fur-collared bed jacket, as if ready to curl up with a cup of cocoa and an Agatha Christie novel. Horrified, von Sternberg suppressed them and ordered that no film or photograph of Dietrich leave the studio without his approval. He became the only director to supervise the still photography sessions of his star. He dressed the sets, arranged the lighting, then stood behind the photographer, directing every shot. As he refined her persona, the stills became more sophisticated. He frequently placed a veil of *mousseline de soie* in front of the lens, diffusing the light so that she appeared to glow.

Dietrich claimed that she had read *Amy Jolly* when she met its author while vacationing on the North Sea island of Sylt, and had included a copy with her parting gifts when von Sternberg sailed for the United States earlier that month. However, he must have already read it and sent a copy ahead to Schulberg, since the rights were not free but belonged to German producers Hermann Fellner and Josef Somlo. They had planned it as a vehicle for Lily Damita, possibly as a stage play, until the incendiary actress frustrated their plans by embarking for Hollywood and marrying Errol Flynn. An English-language script already existed, written by playwright Vincent Lawrence. Although Lawrence receives no screen credit, Jules Furthman's screenplay for *Morocco* is described as "based on the play *Amy Jolly*."

The film begins with a contingent of the Foreign Legion marching into Mogador (today's Essaouira). Traditionally, the Legion accepted anyone tough enough to defend the various hellholes of France's Asian and African colonies from resentful indigenes. It became a refuge for men trying to forget or to be forgotten. Gary Cooper plays such a person, with a colorless, obviously invented name (Tom Brown), no past to which he's prepared to own up, and no future. Until he meets Amy, his existence has contracted to one of fighting and fornicating. Movies could still get away with a great deal of innuendo in 1931, and Furthman missed few chances. Glimpsing Tom bargaining in gestures with a prostitute as the troops wait to be dismissed, his sergeant demands, "What are you doing with those fingers?"

"Nothing—yet," he replies insolently.

That night, Amy stands on the deck of a steamer about to dock. She'll later associate herself with Brown by calling herself one of the "foreign legion of women." Also like them, her name is false: *aimee jolie* in French means "beloved and pretty." Sophisticated and at one time a star—Brown notices that in old photos she's wearing sables—she has been reduced to playing seedy shows in remote outposts like this North African backwater. An officer on the boat calls such women "suicide passengers—one-way tickets—they never return." Amy's character needed laundering to make her acceptable even in pre–Production Code Hollywood. In the novel, she's an unrepentant prostitute and a drug addict besides. Also, in Vigny's conclusion, she doesn't follow Brown into the desert (as in the film) but leaves Morocco entirely, heading for Buenos Aires.

Cooper, who received top billing, initially regarded the film as his own—an impression von Sternberg didn't contradict. "As I was by then well-known to audiences from *The Virginian*," Cooper said, "[it was thought] I would be the sort of partner who would make Marlene, as it were, popular by association. Von Sternberg told me that he had something in mind like the co-starring of Garbo with John Gilbert—the very American with the very European."[3] Once Cooper signed, however, William Powell called to warn him about von Sternberg, whom he called "arrogant, callous, and quite unable to motivate an actor, let alone respect him."[4] By then it was too late; the director had already pulled the rug from under the feet of the unsuspecting young star.

As Amy arrives in Mogador, another passenger, the wealthy artist La Bèssiere, volunteers his assistance, but she declines. His character was originally English and named "Kennington," a role earmarked for

125

British-born character actor Holmes Herbert, but von Sternberg, without consulting Schulberg, hired Adolphe Menjou. The suave character actor had spent the last few years working in France and was having some difficulty reestablishing himself in Hollywood. He had even contacted Irving Thalberg and offered to take a 50 percent salary cut to rejoin MGM. Menjou was thus understandably startled to get the role of La Bèssiere, for which von Sternberg uncomplainingly paid his pre-talkie rate of $20,000. Cooper received only $1,500 a week, for a total of $6,750 for the four- to five-week shoot, and Dietrich received $5,625. The entire production cost about $450,000.

Filming began on July 15. On July 17, von Sternberg, working in sequence as usual, shot Dietrich's first scene: "Exterior. Ship deck—Sequence A." Amy is standing at the rail of the night steamer when La Bèssiere makes his discreet pass. Her first line, "I don't need any help," conveyed nothing on the page. But von Sternberg knew that the way she delivered it would set a pattern for the rest of her career. Garbo's first words in her sound debut, *Anna Christie*—"Gif me a visky, ginger ale on the side, and don' be stingy, baby"—unapologetically exposed her European roots. By refusing to disguise her accent, she reconfirmed herself with her public as sui generis. Von Sternberg decided that Dietrich should do the opposite. Her first line must betray nothing of her nationality—which, as in the real Foreign Legion, disappeared in the act of enlisting. Though it took ninety-one takes to efface her accent, in particular her pronunciation of *help*, the woman who rejects La Bèssiere's advances comes from both nowhere and everywhere. Rather than playing Garbo at her own game, Dietrich inaugurated a new style. If there was to be imitation, let them imitate her.

For Amy's first night at the cabaret of the fussy LoTinto (played by Paul Porcasi, archetypal movie headwaiter and café owner), La Bèssiere joins the Legion adjutant, Caesar (Ullrich Haupt), and Caesar's wife, played by Eve Southern from *The Sea Gull*. Another of Tom's lovers, she waves to him where he's sitting in the pit, accompanied by the prostitute with whom he had bargained earlier in the day.

Among those watching the shooting of this scene was Sergei Eisenstein, whom the U.S. government had tentatively allowed into the country, with encouragement from Ernst Lubitsch and Ben Schulberg, to discuss a possible Paramount project. To neutralize Eisenstein's image as a dangerous Bolshevik, Lubitsch arranged visits with every celebrity from Walt Disney and Charlie Chaplin to "wonder dog" Rin-Tin-Tin and threw dinners at which Eisenstein sat down with other acquaintances from Berlin. His visit to the *Morocco* set was such a photo opportunity. The Russian played along but privately jeered at von Sternberg's pose as the great director—perhaps done for his benefit. "There was deathly silence," he wrote in his memoirs. "Von Sternberg was on a platform wearing a black velvet jacket. A hand supported his head. He was thinking. Everyone was silent, holding their breath. . . . Ten minutes. Fifteen. It didn't work."[5]

Eisenstein was wrong. Having announced his intention to "touch lightly on a Lesbian element," von Sternberg launched a sapphic show-piece that specifically referenced Dietrich's history of cross-dressing and gender-bending misbehavior. Ambling out in top hat and white tie and tails, she strolls among the tables, letting the audience get used to her as a man. Accepting champagne from one patron, she asks his pretty companion for a flower, kisses her full on the lips in return, then throws the flower to Tom. His girl is furious, even though all Tom does is companionably tip his cap, comrade to comrade. The kiss was always in the script, but Dietrich added the flower. That way, even if the studio executives thought the kiss too risqué, they couldn't cut it, since the explanation for the flower would disappear.

For her second number, "What Am I Bid for My Apples?" Amy changes into a revealing bare-legged outfit and sells apples from a basket —a covert way, LoTinto explains, of extracting tips from the audience. Von Sternberg again uses props to convey shades of meaning. Amy accepts too large a payment from La Bèssiere for his apple but offers one to Tom for free—an explicit proposal, which he accepts conditionally, taking the apple but borrowing money to pay for it. In return, Amy slips him the key to her house, flagrantly defying LoTinto's advice to take a lover in the officer class. With such scenes, von Sternberg widens *The Blue Angel*'s vision of love as a destroyer. The couple lavishes contempt on everyone, from LoTinto, with his clumsy attendance on his new star, through Caesar and his wife, down to La Bèssiere, who, looking and sounding like von Sternberg (no doubt his motive for insisting on Menjou), is persistently humiliated. Yet, like Rath, Bull Weed, and General Alexander, he connives in his own downfall.

Despite public assurances of mutual esteem, Cooper detested the director, claiming he received better guidance from Menjou. Von Sternberg disliked the young actor simply because of his height (six feet four inches), which emphasized his own shortness. Though gossip linked Dietrich and Cooper as offscreen lovers during *Morocco,* Cooper preferred Mexican actress Lupe Velez, who was so eager for him that she haunted the set. Knowing it would irritate his director and costar, Cooper cuddled her on his lap between takes. Dietrich and von Sternberg were more amused than offended, recognizing the gesture for what it was—the same pique felt by Emil Jannings at seeing the film stolen by an unknown.

"None of us had ever been to Morocco," said Cooper, "and I remember asking von Sternberg if he could point the country out to me on a map—and I don't believe he could."[6] Marrakech, where Vigny set the original, lies well inland, but von Sternberg preferred port and desert to be next to each other, so he casually amended geography. Second-unit director Henry Hathaway was in awe of his inventiveness. "He just had a rail and a piece of deck and a curtain and fog—and there you were, on board ship. He took an old Mexican street on the back lot and said 'Bring me some eucalyptus poles and palm leaves,' and then we had Mogador."[7] "We had lattice-work in the streets," Lee Garmes recalls. "We shot at his suggestion at high noon for some interesting rippling shadows. Quite a lot of the picture was done in natural sunlight, rare at the time."[8]

As the legionnaires march in, dust from their boots mingles with fretted sunlight under the roof of the casbah. Merchants drag their animals out of the road in advance of the soldiers, while improbably beautiful whores watch from their windows. Personal drama is subjugated to the realities of heat, death, and sex, summarized by the image of a girl leaning against a phallic pole surmounted by a skull. Enervating heat dominates the film, dramatized not only in the flaring shadows but also in the stirring of palm fans. The nightclub is alive with them, and they animate the image, just as the handkerchiefs waved in *Blonde Venus* during the boat farewell make the screen flutter with light. Amy covers her face and Brown's with a fan when they kiss for the first time, and when he enters her house, he automatically reaches out to a hook from which, to his surprise, the fan hung there by her predecessors (and, by implication, almost all his lovers) has been removed.

La Bèssiere offers Amy a diamond bracelet and proposes marriage. She refuses both, preferring Tom's promise to desert the Legion and flee with her to Europe. But before she can tell Tom of her decision, he sees the bracelet, notes the flowers with which his rival has filled her dressing room, and retreats, though not before writing on her mirror, "I changed my mind. Good Luck." Raymond Durgnat rightly notes that, in an inversion of *The Blue Angel, Morocco* is a film in which the woman is degraded and humiliated by her lover. Of Cooper, he writes memorably of "the lean, rude, tense contempt smouldering in his wiry features, in such contrast to Marlene's white, placid calm."[9]

The moment when Amy leaves Tom alone in her dressing room is one of the most vivid not only in *Morocco* but in the work of Dietrich and von Sternberg as a whole. She backs out, slowly pulling the door behind her, murmuring, "I'll be back. Wait for me." The door closing on her lost, tremulous face presages the poignancy that animates *Shanghai Express*. Once again, we owe the moment to von Sternberg's capacity for effect. According to Dietrich:

> Sternberg said "Walk to the door, turn, count to ten, say your line, and leave." So I did, and he got very angry. "If you're so stupid that you can't count slowly, then count to twenty-five." And we did it again. I think we did it forty times, until finally I was counting probably to fifty. And I didn't know why. I was annoyed. But at the premiere of *Morocco* at Grauman's Chinese Theatre, when this moment came and I paused and then said "Wait for me," the audience burst into applause. Sternberg knew they were waiting for this—and he made them wait, and they loved it.[10]

The incident inspired another von Sternberg–Dietrich legend. In the gossip-column version, he ordered Marlene to "count to six, then look at that light as if you can't live without it."

After von Sternberg showed her his rough cut, Dietrich slipped a note into his pocket on the drive home: "You—Only you—the Master

—the Giver—Reason for my existence—the Teacher—the Love my heart and brain must follow." Almost as flatteringly, Eisenstein, with no hint of his true contempt, wired, "Of your great directorial creations, *Morocco* is the most beautiful. Admiration and Love."

Before *Morocco* opened, talk in the trade labeled Dietrich as just the latest fly-by-night foreigner who, like Anna Sten, Tala Birrell, and Lily Damita, was doomed to break her neck against the icy north face of Garbo. Once the film was released, *Variety* reinforced that opinion. "*Morocco* is too lightweight a story to be counterbalanced by the big-time direction given it. . . . There's nothing to the picture, except what Josef von Sternberg gives it in direction. . . . The rest is apple sauce." French critics were even more scathing. Michel Vauclaire wrote, "Every year in the US, half a dozen novels are published about the Legion, in general very severe and all quite fantastic. It's obviously on this sort of fiction, so denuded of truth, that Sternberg has based his research. Perhaps the film reflects the American public's idea of legionnaires. In France, despite its dramatic pretensions, it will raise a laugh."[11]

Defying the critics, the public in both the United States and Europe loved *Morocco*. Dietrich, art director Hans Dreier, photographer Garmes, and von Sternberg were all nominated for Academy Awards. Hoping to cash in doubly, Paramount opened the English-language version of *The Blue Angel* in New York on December 5 and released recordings of Dietrich singing its songs. In January the film went on to general release but achieved only modest returns, since heavy accents and indifferent recording hampered the audience's understanding of the dialogue. It succeeded best in the United States in German, with English subtitles.

Schulberg, as predicted, tore up Dietrich's two-film contract and wrote a better one for three additional films teaming director and star. On June 5, 1930, just before shooting began on *Morocco*, the California Superior Court had granted Riza a divorce on the grounds of cruelty, after she testified that von Sternberg "was always looking for a fight, and cross as a bear." As Paramount had promised, the terms were so generous they surprised even the judge, who commented he had never seen a suit settled with so little haggling. In addition to $1,200-a-month alimony for five years, Riza would receive $25,000 within a year—provided, as privately understood, the other lawsuits were quietly dropped.

Riza, however, was stung by the news of von Sternberg's prosperity, and even more by the fact that Dietrich was now openly his lover. On August 9, just after *Morocco* finished shooting, she publicized the suits, on the pretext that von Sternberg had refused to pay the agreed alimony unless she definitively withdrew them. Dietrich's attorneys responded that "for four months she had resisted suggestions that publicity could be avoided if these suits could be settled." They described Riza's accusations as "absurd and unwarranted."[12] Rudy Sieber hurried from Paris to play the supportive husband. An exasperated judge fined von Sternberg a few hundred dollars for his late payment of alimony but charged, "the court cannot escape the conclusion that both parties to the action looked on the solemn order of this court as a mere instrument to be utilised as a pawn in litigation."[13]

While Rudy was in Los Angeles, Paramount threw parties to honor him and its new star. Jesse Lasky Jr. remembered one at Schulberg's beach house where Marlene was the center of attention:

Earthy, lusty, yet mysteriously sophisticated, the lady swaggered into the crowded room, flanked by the two disparate males, bringing a breath of continental bistros, exotic places. She had a certain sloe-eyed magnetism that years and time would never dim. From head to toe she was a star, loaded with that particular magic that stars exude, and when all eyes had filled themselves with her presence, the speculation began. Was one of these two men her lover, one her husband? If so, which was which? The golden-blonde, blue-eyed young Teutonic athlete who might have stepped out of a Wagnerian opera, brimming with vitality and bronzed from some Alpine ski slope, was her husband, Rudy Sieber. The caved-in, dishevelled, unkempt, gnome-like von Sternberg was her admirer and discoverer. A Hollywood cliché was shattered.[14]

As Lasky's sneering tone implies, the Hollywood establishment felt that von Sternberg was too full of himself to let it pass unpunished. Among the other guests at the party were Fay Wray and husband John

Monk Saunders, the slim, moody, and eventually suicidal ex-aviator on whom some thought von Sternberg based Tom Brown. In conversation, Saunders made a point of correcting von Sternberg's grammar, a slur he never forgave.

Once a new star stepped into the spotlight, inconvenient husbands or other reminders of an earlier career were expected to make themselves scarce. Those who did so were rewarded. Rudy Sieber became director of the Paramount dubbing studio in the Paris suburb of Joinville, which produced foreign-language versions of its films. Dietrich leased an apartment for him and girlfriend Tami. Heidede, rechristened Maria, remained in Hollywood, where she soon became accustomed to her mother's new playmates, starting with Maurice Chevalier. Nevertheless, for her daughter's benefit, Dietrich insisted on maintaining the pretext that she and von Sternberg were not sleeping together. Having left Dietrich's house by the back door, he would drive up shortly thereafter, dressed as if he had just come from a game of golf. Maria would always open the door for him, and he would solemnly enquire if both had slept well. Marlene enjoyed teasing him by claiming to have dreamed of Greta Garbo.

Dietrich's bisexuality, far from being disguised, became the engine of a publicity campaign at which she and von Sternberg connived. Paramount, equally complicit, fanned the perception that Dietrich could satisfy the lusts of every person—male, female, or undecided. For a party at the Schulbergs', she wore a navy blazer, white flannel trousers, and yachting cap. Von Sternberg photographed her in the outfit, and Paramount suggested circulating it as a postcard captioned, "The Woman Even Women Can Adore." The studio also billed *Morocco* with the slogan, "Marlene Dietrich, the Woman All Women Want to See," and her mannish suits and slacks set the fashion. She even dressed in male evening clothes for the premiere of *The Sign of the Cross,* a joke on the pietistic Cecil B. DeMille. Her behavior signaled to Hollywood's "Sewing Circle" of covert lesbians that a new player was in town. She became the favorite topic around Santa Monica's sapphic bars such as the Golden Bull and S.S. Friendship, and enjoyed liaisons with, among others, Mercedes de Acosta and actress Kay Francis.

As an adult, Maria Sieber accused von Sternberg of resenting her presence, a charge supported by the hostile children in *Blonde Venus* and *The Scarlet Empress*—played by Maria herself in the latter. More damaging psychologically was her mother's tendency to treat Maria as a coconspirator in her new role as serial seducer. In her memoir of her mother, Maria recalls eavesdropping on a conversation between her parents just before Rudy returned to Paris. They joked about Chevalier's teenage gonorrhea that had rendered him impotent, the priapism of von Sternberg, Marlene's taste in women, her disappointment at the quality of the partners on offer at Paramount (even closet lesbian Claudette Colbert), and her preference for the girls at MGM. Dietrich may not have particularly enjoyed sex, but she knew its power. *Ich bin von Kopf bis Fuß Auf Liebe eingestellt.*

Morocco provided one more surprise. In September 1932 Dietrich received a letter in French from Agadir, Morocco. It was signed "Amy Jolly." The writer claimed to have inspired the character in the novel and film, following an affair with Vigny fifteen years before. No longer able to earn a living playing the piano, said Jolly, she had opened a *pension de famille,* a family boardinghouse, to support her grandchildren. She explained that she had written to Vigny when the book was published, and "he answered by professing his pleasure at having heard from me," she told Dietrich. "What could he do for me, he asked? I responded that he could do just one thing; not let me end up in the gutter, now that I am old and poor. He made me thousands of promises but sent me only a few hundred francs. But as soon as the film was released, he apparently became frightened that I would protest, and the silence became complete." The letter to Dietrich ended, ominously, by saying that this should not be regarded as blackmail or begging but simply as a cry for help. Dietrich apparently sent money. She also asked a friend, the writer Charles Graves, who knew French Morocco, to investigate further. His brief report jolted her: "Well. I've now called on Amie Jolie. At her *bordel,* she hires out small girls of eight or nine years old to soldiers of the Foreign Legion, Maroccan *Tirailleurs* and Spahis—which makes me feel rather sick."[15]

Spies

The more you cheat, the more you lie, the more exciting
you become, X-27!
—Victor McLaglen in *Dishonored*

IN PUTTING DOWN ROOTS in California, von Sternberg was an
exception among emigrant filmmakers. Many who had arrived before
sound were now being shed as their accents proved a liability. Others,
like Jannings and Pommer, saw better prospects of success in Europe
than in a Hollywood struggling with the Depression. Among those
who departed was Alexander Korda. He had pursued a career in his
native Hungary, as well as in Vienna, Paris, and Berlin, where he had
directed Dietrich in a couple of films. Eventually he wound up in Hollywood, where he made four indifferent pictures before deciding in 1930
to extricate himself from a dead-end contract with Fox and return to
Europe. Von Sternberg was the only person to see him off on the Superchief. Neither could know that they would meet again in a few years on
the far side of the world, nor under what peculiar circumstances.

Those who succeeded in the Hollywood system worked hard
for their money. Once the von Sternberg–Dietrich duo became a hot
property, cinema owners badgered Paramount for more. Even before
Morocco was released, they completed *Dishonored,* a spy drama of the
First World War. It shows signs of haste: MGM was preparing *Mata*

Hari with Garbo, and Paramount saw a chance to set Dietrich against her in a similar role, mano a mano, letting the box office decide.

Garbo's film, although it earned money, embarrassed her admirers. It required her to perform a preposterous "erotic" dance and exercise her allure on the effete Ramon Novarro. Dietrich showed the female spy in a better light, not solely as a seductress but as an ingenious agent who was adept at disguise and could even transpose military secrets into music, then play them back on the piano—skills with which she out-smarted a succession of colossally obtuse men. Von Sternberg's story, originally titled *X-27,* was scripted by Daniel N. Rubin. It was renamed *Dishonored* by Paramount, a change the director resisted because the heroine is not, by her standards, dishonored. Although she betrays her country by letting an enemy escape, she does so honorably, for love. Gary Cooper, still smarting from *Morocco,* declined to play Kranau, head of the Russian secret service. Any number of personable romantic leads could have substituted, but the studio imposed Victor McLaglen—a baffling choice, since at six feet three inches, he towered over Dietrich. Moreover, he looked nothing like a Russian, was pushing fifty, and had played no romantic roles for years, preferring military bruisers. He was also under long-term contract to Fox. Possibly he was working off an old commitment to Paramount, but everyone was mute on the subject of his choice, including von Sternberg.

Dietrich plays Maria Kolverer, a war widow turned prostitute in World War I Vienna. As a suicide victim is carried out of her tenement, she remarks, "I am not afraid of life—although not of death either." The head of the Austrian secret service, played by Gustav von Seyffer-titz, just happens to be passing and overhears. He tests her patriotism by inviting her to spy for the enemy and, when she reports him to the police, recruits her as agent X-27. Sent to tempt General von Hindau (Warner Oland), she hooks him at another of von Sternberg's streamer-clogged masked balls. Von Hindau is the equivalent of La Bèssiere in *Morocco,* Ned Faraday in *Blonde Venus,* and Don Pasquale in *The Devil Is a Woman*—the bearded, impeccably dressed von Sternberg look-alike who grovels to the Dietrich character. He invites her home but offers a lift to a handicapped man in a clown costume, who passes the general a cigarette. Naturally, the clown is her rival H-14 (McLaglen), and the cigarette contains a message. Once she discovers the deception, X-27, impressed and intrigued, dismisses the general's wistful wish that they had met under different circumstances and permits him to avoid disgrace by putting a bullet in his brain.

At times, *Dishonored* is less spy story than Lubitsch-style sex comedy. Disguised as a peasant maid in dirndl, boots, and braids, X-27 fools the lecherous Colonel Korvin (Lew Cody) into revealing his secrets. The headquarters of Austrian Intelligence is worthy of a comic opera, with an enormous wall map and a jumble of chemical apparatuses—possibly for the manufacture of poison pills and other necessities of espionage; the secret service chief (von Seyffertitz) inaugurates a telephone conversation with von Hindau by announcing that he has a new recipe for invisible ink. The concluding scenes, of H-14 and X-27 making love in a prison cell, recall the conclusion of Lubitsch's *The Merry Widow*, where Maurice Chevalier and Jeanette MacDonald are reconciled in a dungeon. The full weight of the film's absurdity falls on the climax. Following H-14's capture, X-27 spends the night with him, then leaves her gun behind, allowing him to escape. Tried for treason, she doesn't deny the charges and is sentenced to be shot. As her last request, she asks, no less absurdly than anything Lubitsch ever invented, for a piano and the dress she wore as a prostitute—"I wish to die not in the uniform in which I served my country, but my countrymen." She is still pounding out *Donau Wellen* when the young officer arrives to take her to the firing squad.

Von Sternberg exploits the execution to the hilt. First, Dietrich asks for a mirror to adjust her veil, and the lieutenant offers the reflection in his gleaming sword. She scoops up her cat and accompanies him to the snow-blanketed courtyard. There she hands the cat to the officiating priest and takes her place against the wall. The lieutenant gives her a blindfold, but she uses it only to wipe away his tears. Hand on hip, smiling slightly, she waits while he joins the firing squad. The drum rolls and rolls—and he cracks, throwing down his sword and shouting, "I will not kill a woman! I will not kill any more men either. You call this patriotism? I call it butchery. You call this serving your country? I call it murder." As he's hustled away and his commanding officer takes his place, Dietrich uses the delay to adjust her stocking. The bullets send her reeling against the wall, but nobody delivers the traditional coup de grâce. Instead, von Seyffertitz casually salutes her corpse, glances without expression at a stone imperial eagle in a niche, and follows the soldiers back inside. Of *Dishonored,* one is tempted to say, like Marshal Pierre Bosquet of the charge of the Light Brigade, "It is magnificent, but it is not war."

Nobody in Hollywood appeared to find *Dishonored* ridiculous, but Luis Buñuel, then on short-term contract at MGM, saw a preview at the invitation of the producer and called Dietrich's demise "predictable." "What are you talking about?" expostulated the executive. "I'm telling you that's never been done before in the entire history of the cinema." To prove his point, Buñuel woke his housemate, Edouard Ugarte, and started outlining the plot. After a few sentences, Ugarte growled, "Don't bother with any more. They shoot her at the end," and returned to bed.

Von Sternberg claimed to have contributed to the music of *Dishonored,* the first time he did so. He later wrote a "Violin Composition" for *The Scarlet Empress* and boasted of not only conducting a symphony orchestra but also correcting the leader on a fine point of theory. In neither case was he awarded screen credit, and since he played no instrument nor had any musical training, one is bound to be skeptical.

After *Dishonored* finished shooting in November 1930, Dietrich left for Germany to spend Christmas with her family. The visit, augmented by appearances to promote *Morocco,* stretched into 1931. She didn't return until April 24, leading the press to speculate that she might remain in Europe. Edwin Schallert pointed out in the *Los Angeles Times* that Garbo now worked with directors other than Clarence Brown, responsible for many of her successes. "The most interesting event of the future," he concluded, "will be Marlene's declaration of independence—if it is ever declared."[1] The fan press speculated about the power von Sternberg exercised over Dietrich. Parallels were drawn with two recent films: *Svengali* and *The Mad Genius.* Both featured John Barrymore as a brooding, bearded Jew who manipulates a talented but impressionable gentile. Few writers grasped the reality—that Dietrich was the more powerful member of the duo.

Rather than appear to be waiting on her, von Sternberg agreed to take over a project that had gone sour—the film of Theodore Dreiser's *An American Tragedy.* Since the request came directly from Adolph Zukor, the most powerful man at Paramount, he could hardly refuse. Dreiser had been inspired by the 1906 murder case of Chester Gillette, who drowned his girlfriend in Big Moose Lake in upstate New York and went to the electric chair on March 30, 1908. The novel struck at the social basis of crime, suggesting how a young man, ill educated and lacking intelligence or strength of character, could find himself trapped by circumstances into believing that murder offered the only route to a better life.

His protagonist, Clyde Griffiths, is the son of street-corner evangelists who insist, to his humiliation, that he join their preaching. The resulting ostracism is subtly suggested when one of Clyde's benefactors inquires if his parents are "still doing their . . . er . . . *work?*" Fleeing from involvement in a hit-and-run car accident, he becomes a hotel bellboy and is taken up by rich cousins, who employ him in their shirt factory. Clyde seduces Roberta, a girl on the production line, but then meets the beautiful and rich Sondra. Just as Clyde and Sondra are about to marry, Roberta reveals that she's pregnant. Clyde takes her away to a mountain resort, and while they are canoeing on a lake, she drowns—whether by accident or design, even Clyde isn't sure. To the law, however, the case seems cut-and-dried, and Clyde goes to the electric chair.

Dreiser sold the novel to Paramount for $150,000 shortly after it was published in 1925, with the right to veto any screenplay. When sound arrived, Dreiser sued the company for having failed to make the film and demanded an additional fee for the talkie rights. Paramount offered $50,000, payable when the film was made, and, in a controversial move, hired Sergei Eisenstein to write and direct. Paramount put Eisenstein, Alexandrov, and Tisse on a six-month contract, and Eisenstein and Alexandrov, with help from British left-wing sympathizer Ivor Montagu, wrote a screenplay. Schulberg hoped for "a simple, tight whodunnit about murder." Instead, Eisenstein experimented with "inner monologue"—a stream-of-consciousness voice-over suggested by the work of James Joyce and Gertrude Stein, both of whom he had met in Paris. A typical scene between Sondra and Clyde read: "They stand up. Of a sudden, all his fears are reawakened. Realisation of what the morrow may bring floods back in full force. He stands cold, perplexed. . . . 'Darling,' says Sondra, and they embrace. . . . Clyde feels it is the last time he will ever kiss her."[2]

Conveying such complex states of mind was beyond the commercial cinema, let alone the kind of performers under contract to Paramount. As Howard Hawks succinctly put it, "if [a script] starts out saying 'He looks at her and the yearning of ten years shows in his eyes' . . . I've never found an actor who can do that."[3] All the same, Dreiser endorsed the screenplay and urged the company to produce it. His motivation was at least partly avarice. At the lunch where he and publisher Horace Liveright had negotiated the original deal, Jesse Lasky had opened the bidding at $90,000. When Liveright, as a bargaining tactic, refused the offer, Dreiser threw a cup of coffee in his face.

At Schulberg's request, producer David Selznick read the Eisenstein scenario. In October 1930 he called it "the most moving script I have ever read . . . positively torturing. When I finished it, I was so depressed that I wanted to reach for the bourbon bottle." He conceded that it was "a glorious experiment" but concluded, "as entertainment, I don't think it has one chance in a hundred." Paramount was relieved when the U.S. government rescinded the Russians' visas in December, and they moved to Mexico. With more than $200,000 invested in the project, Zukor asked von Sternberg to see what he could do with it. Though he later dismissed the film as "an assignment,"[4] the chance to supplant Eisenstein as he had von Stroheim in editing *The Wedding March* was too tempting to resist.

Anyone self-educated and upwardly mobile is likely to find Dreiser's novel redolent of a sense of "there, but for the grace of God. . . ." But von Sternberg, confident of the absolute rightness of all his actions, detected no such lessons. "I eliminated the sociological elements," he said, "which, in my opinion, were far from being responsible for the dramatic accident with which Dreiser had concerned himself." He claims he didn't read Eisenstein's screenplay. Instead, Schulberg assigned journalist and poet Samuel Hoffenstein, fresh from New York, to collaborate on a new one. Von Sternberg claimed, as usual, that Hoffenstein merely worked on the treatment and that the script, except for some of Dreiser's dialogue, was his own. But any adaptation, no matter who penned it, would have almost written itself, clinging to the formula of the crime film.

Dreiser loathed the early drafts and flew to Los Angeles to argue about them, without result. Although lawsuits were threatened, nobody was sure if the author's veto power extended to the sound version, so Schulberg put the film into production without informing him. On March 3, 1931, the day shooting started, the *New York Times* reported that Hoffenstein was meeting Dreiser in New Orleans to show him the final script for the first time. Most of this report was devoted to von Sternberg's vituperative attack on authors generally. A few days earlier, George Bernard Shaw had criticized U.S. films, suggesting that Hollywood could learn from British and European productions. "George Bernard Shaw is antiquated and old-fashioned," the director retorted. "He is operating, thinking, talking and writing in terms of the last century. He emptied himself twenty years ago, and that also applies to many of the so-called literary giants—in particular Theodore Dreiser." The newspaper remarked, "von Sternberg would offer no personal reasons for special mention of Dreiser."

As Clyde, the studio assigned Phillips Holmes, a young player with an apologetic, self-effacing style; the *New York Times* judged his performance "flabby." Frances Dee carried off the hauteur of Sondra, but Roberta, the unlucky factory girl, was oddly embodied by Sylvia Sidney. Schulberg had spotted her in a Broadway play and brought her to Hollywood, where, in more ways than one, she replaced Clara Bow, talking over some of Bow's roles and also becoming his mistress. Sidney defeated all von Sternberg's lighting skill. Able to turn any woman into a whore, he was less expert at conveying innocence. By emphasizing Sidney's pillowy lips and startled eyes, he made her look as if someone had just made an obscene suggestion, to which she was giving serious thought.

The credits play over a shimmering pond ruffled by breezes, foreshadowing Roberta's death on a lonely forest lake where, as singing, ukulele-strumming young people coast by in canoes and pines loom above the still water, her floating hat marks her grave. Shot with the same simplicity, *An American Tragedy* could have been as intensely emotional as *The Case of Lena Smith,* with which it has some resonance. However, this was an important novel, von Sternberg was an "A" director, and although the publicity department sold it as an unglamorous slice of life ("Drama That Happens Around You Every Day—When the Wild Life of Impetuous Youth Burns Away Age-old Barriers!"), custom demanded that it be given the full studio treatment. Because some significant moments took place in a shirt factory, Paramount decreed that it should be the best shirt factory money could buy. Von Sternberg, said a press release, "requested his technical staff to provide real machinery and people who knew how to operate it. Thousands of Hollywood extra girls were available, but none knew how to operate collar-making machines. The studio solved the problem by arranging with a big factory to rent out special machinery, install it in working order on the set, and furnish experienced operators."

Inevitably, this "authenticity" is wasted. What we notice is the flat, dusty light as Clyde, apparently supervising the sewing girls, furtively passes notes to Roberta, revealing that they have become lovers. The overkill extends to the courtroom scenes, which were shot like an inquisition, with shouting attorneys and leering spectators. The prosecutors even produce the incriminating boat and invite a sweating, wild-eyed Clyde to reenact Roberta's death. Lee Garmes also recalled the director's pride in the meticulously constructed garden seen beyond the couple as they sit on the windowsill of her room, and the care with which he simulated moonlight to show it off successfully. But in retrospect, it's an exercise—Escoffier boiling an egg.

Britain, South Africa, and Italy banned the film for its premarital pregnancy, which caused less comment in the United States. *Variety* dismissed it as "an ordinary program effort with an unhappy ending. . . . There is not a performance in the cast of any real interest."[5] Dreiser sued Paramount (unsuccessfully), claiming that the film "outraged" the book. The mother of Chester Gillette also sued for $150,000 over her son's unsympathetic depiction. Von Sternberg seldom referred to the film again. By the time it was released, Dietrich was back in Hollywood, and he set out to make for her his most intense visual poem.

Talk Like a Train

—sleep, death, desire
Close round one instant in one floating flower.
—Hart Crane, *Voyages*

HAD VON STERNBERG MADE only *Shanghai Express*, his position in the pantheon of filmmakers would be secure. Few films of any era are so integrated in décor and performance. Not until Stanley Kubrick would one get the sense of an inspired visual intelligence brought to bear on every image, every frame. Each element in *Shanghai Express* is subordinated to the intensification of "spiritual power." The flimsy plot, the measured delivery of its minimal dialogue, the larger-than-life characters, the stylized China in which the action takes place—all recall opera more than film. If (as Woodrow Wilson may—or may not—have said) *The Birth of a Nation* is "history seen by flashes of lighting," then *Shanghai Express* is passion lit by arc light—one definition of pure cinema.

"A single page by Harry Hervey" is credited as the source. Hervey, a Texan who spent his life knocking about Asia producing sensational novels such as *King Cobra, The Devil Dancer,* and *The Black Parrot,* was offhand about the incident that inspired him. "The Chinese revolution was in full swing and my train was held up by revolutionists, a common occurrence at that time," he said. "By adding a few characters and embellishing the drama . . . I had the story." Jules Furthman fleshed it out, creating a screenplay that resembled an opera libretto, existing mainly as a pretext for the arias. Ex-lovers, an English doctor and a courtesan of unknown origin (conceivably Russian), meet on a Chinese train that is halted by a warlord. He holds the doctor hostage in exchange for his own lieutenant, a prisoner. Once his man is returned, the general threatens to send the doctor back alive but blind. The courtesan prays for his safety, showing that she still loves him. Fortuitously, the warlord is killed and the lovers escape, to be reunited as the train reaches its destination.

To accommodate the fantasy, von Sternberg constructed what he called "a China built of *papier-mache*." He filled it with a thousand Asians, all speaking Cantonese; few of the waiters and domestics recruited as extras spoke the correct language, Mandarin. The Santa Fe Railroad closed off the San Bernardino and Chatsworth stations and rented him a train. Its carriages were painted, to his specifications (and sometimes by himself, physically), with Chinese characters and camouflage patterns. Miles of trackside country were scoured of every un-Chinese sign, building, or feature in preparation for a running battle between two trains that was never filmed. Even John Grierson, who despised Hollywood glamour, couldn't restrain his admiration. "Its photography is astonishing; its sets are expensive, and detailed to an ingenious and extravagant degree; its technique in dissolve and continuity is unique. The film might be seen for its good looks alone."[1] German critic Rudolf Arnheim, who scorned the story, also surrendered to its visual extravagance. "Once again we experience a primitive plot being used as an opportunity to create an enchanted sea of light, a supernatural magic world. We think we are seeing not likenesses of real objects but a painter's fantasies of blackness and lightness all run together. Shadows hang over the figures, over the locomotive; Marlene Dietrich's face is crosshatched by a black veil, and when the machine takes on water at the station, the mysterious black pipe between the clouds of steam resembles a ghost."

The film's structure rests on its design, executed by Hans Dreier and two of von Sternberg's protégés, Peter Ballbusch and Richard Kollorsz. Façades were hung with banners or decorated with ideographs, and sets of towns and stations were built so close to the line that in rehearsals, the locomotive tore them down. The credits, which include a huge gong being struck, smoke wreathing over lilies and dragons, and a hand brushing calligraphy on a page, alert us that décor bears vitally on the action and the characters.

The most effort, however, went into Dietrich's appearance, starting with the hat, garnished with curved black plumes, she wears when boarding the train. Despite claims by both, neither Dietrich nor studio costumer Travis Banton created the hats. Like Dietrich's veiled cloche in *Morocco,* they were the uncredited work of John Harburger, who, as "John Frederics," "John P. John," or "Mr. John," provided hats for numerous Hollywood films, as well as privately for their stars. Von Sternberg's attention to even so minor a detail signifies the degree to which costume and décor are the true stars of his films. As Drake Stutesman points out in an essay on Harburger, hats in *Shanghai Express* play an important role in characterization:

Lily is first seen in the crowded railway station. . . . She wears a rimless cloche made of black iridescent feathers which are set in swirls over her head, though the feathers are not initially obvious. Across her face, in a flat shape, is a diagonal lined veil, ending just above her lip. . . . Her cloche's shuttered, alluring veil and snug glistening skull-cap reveal sensual independence and tight-lipped call-girl secrets. . . . The hat's close veil continually alludes to self-protection but what seemed a stiff visor is later shown to be soft fabric, rippling in breezes. . . . The second hat appears once the journey begins, literally and metaphorically. Lily wears another cloche, made of plain mat fabric, an effect virtually dividing her oval face into white and black pieces. Now having met her lover, she is at odds with her old resolutions. Her emotions are beginning to show, mirrored in opposing white sweeps of thick willowy feathers, as long as twelve inches each, at the hat's right base.[2]

The search for just the right plumes occupied the entire costume department. According to Maria Riva, Travis Banton discarded dozens of others before finally settling on the tail feathers of Mexican fighting cocks, their black-green iridescence furnishing the perfect gleam and shimmer. Stutesman continues:

These horn shapes form a V, pointing toward the face, but also represent how her feelings for this man are spilling out of her, out of her control. Midway behind the hat, and upright, are white feathers, less distinct than those at the neck. Finally, and not instantly apparent, there is a veil, again diagonally crossing the face, very faint, ending below the lips, with strong black dots marking a line along its edge. Her veil appears and disappears to the viewer's eyes in much the way Lily's guard lowers and raises in the midst of her intense feelings. . . . Her control and strength are implicit in the hat's structure.[3]

Shanghai Express is literally a film of black on white. Lily dresses in no other shades: black plumes against a white face, white jeweled collar on a black dress, black lace over her pale body. Her luggage is black with narrow white stripes, her gloves black with white palms, her black handbag fastened with a white clasp. In her first meeting with her old lover, the banners that frame them in the window are, on his side, white and gray, but on her side they are black, boldly scrawled with white lettering. This effect succeeded so well that von Sternberg decided films shouldn't just be screened in tones of black, white, and gray, but shot that way as well. On *The Devil Is a Woman,* sets and costumes would be almost entirely monochrome, with even living props, such as a flock of geese, chosen for their lack of color.

The titles of *Shanghai Express* prefigure a second motif—of signs, printing, letters, and notes. Calligraphy weaves through the story, papers whirling metaphorically in the wind of the train's passing. We face a blizzard of newspapers, telegrams, passports, visas, and the omnipresent *hanzi* ideograms, spattered over almost every flat surface, cryptic and alien like the Chinese faces revealed as a station assistant cleans a window in the opening scenes. Even more effective is its sense of onward motion, subliminally suggesting the movement of the train and the *cafard* of the long journey. In a 1970 interview Clive Brook said, "I remember very clearly 'Von' telling us we were on a train, and he said that people on a train always talked in rhythm with the wheels. I was dashed if I could really see what he was driving at, but I do remember very well him bringing a metronome on the set, and saying 'Now, that's the rhythm of the wheels. Talk in time with that.' Darn difficult, you know."[4] Mocked as one of his more eccentric pronouncements, this was actually sensible advice at a time when primitive sound recording favored the monotone, and although his explanation may have been obscurely expressed, this type of dialogue management adds to the sense of unceasing, almost hypnotic movement.

The theme is repeated in cutting and shooting. Left-hand tracking shots are linked by dissolves, a contrast to the wipes that connect the more episodic *Blonde Venus*. To fill "dead space," most interiors are shot through windows and past blinds, which further preserves the subjective "longitudinality" of a train journey. Sequences within the dining car are shot in successive cuts, always from the same angle and along the axis of the train's motion. For Lily's night walk and the waking of the passengers when the bandits invade, he utilizes a corridor set that, whether in slatted sunlight or lit from within by a shifting handheld lantern, becomes a visual parallel of emotional claustrophobia as well as an evocative contribution to the illusion of travel. Even more delicately suggestive of motion are Lily's plumes and furs, always in faint, stirring movement, brushed by a draft, quivering with the train's vibration.

The story of *Shanghai Express* revolves around trust. Lily was discarded by Harvey five years earlier after a disastrous though unspecified test of his faith in her, and she has become an expensive whore— "Shanghai Lily, the notorious white flower of China." At their first reunion, she says, "You've heard of me." Then, turning Harvey's attention back to the doubt that divided them, as well as isolating the theme of the film, she continues, "and you always believe what you've heard." "I still do," Harvey replies—a challenge she can't ignore.

Some reviews wrongly categorized *Shanghai Express* as a variation of the omnibus film, typified by the same year's *Grand Hotel*, in which a number of parallel stories take place, having only a location in common. But the other passengers on the Shanghai Express are, as Rudolf Arnheim wrote, "born of the turmoil and disappear again into it." They exist only to remind us of the theme of belief at the heart of the relationship between Lily and Harvey (whom she calls "Doc"). Initially, we accept them at their own valuation: intolerant missionary Carmichael (Lawrence Grant); baffled, French-speaking Major Lenard (von

Sternberg's old mentor Emile Chautard); tetchy German businessman Baum (Gustav von Seyffertitz); Louise Closser Hale as Mrs. Haggerty, censorious keeper of a boardinghouse (*"What* kind of house did you say you kept?" enquires Lily, deadpan—a pre–Production Code pun on "bawdy house," or brothel); lovely Anna May Wong as Hui Fei, a prostitute about to retire into marriage; Sam Salt (Eugene Pallette), gambler and raconteur; and Warner Oland's Henry Chang, a haughty Eurasian whose cane is knobbed with a white bone hound's head and whose conversation has the arrogant and epigrammatic quality of von Sternberg's own. Though all suffer for their deceptions, only Chang dies for his. Given a choice, von Sternberg always cast himself as the victim.

All, it emerges, have something to hide. For Mrs. Haggerty it is nothing more sinister than smuggling her dog into the compartment. Later, at a midnight passport check, a Chinese passenger is exposed as a spy and led away. But when Chang drops his incognito to reveal that he's a general and announces his intention to ransom the passengers against his lieutenant's return, appearances that were indestructible in the artificial life of the dining car and the smoking room are shattered. Baum, secretly a dealer in opium, is branded by Chang as punishment. Lenard is revealed as a poseur, cashiered from the service. Sam Salt claims that his confiscated ruby ring and diamond pin are fakes, but we're not convinced.

Only Lily and Doc tell the truth. In the most significant encounter, they meet at night on the open balcony at the rear of the train. Gradually, painfully, Doc reveals how much he still loves her. Longing is as palpable as the breeze stirring her furs, memory as agonizingly present as the portrait of Lily that looks out, drowned in desire, from Harvey's watch. They kiss, Harvey drawn down to the upturned face, Lily taking his cap to allow the kiss to continue: an explosion of steam and noise from the engine's whistle, a snap cut of the train snatching a telegram from a loop on a post—then Dietrich, in another von Sternberg fetish, places the cap triumphantly atilt on her head. It remains only for Lily to crow over Harvey's defeat, and she does so with style.

"There's a lot of things I wouldn't have done if I had those five years to live over again," whines Harvey. (What does she *see* in this man?)

"There's only one thing I wouldn't have done, Doc," purrs Lily. "I wouldn't have bobbed my hair."

Another such moment begins as Lily presses her face and hand against the grimy window of Chang's headquarters, searching for some sign of Harvey. None forthcoming, she returns hopelessly to the train, where Carmichael recommends prayer. She returns to her carriage to wait for news, and in two remarkable shots, we see her forearms in the moonlight, hard shadows obscuring all but the hands stirring in her lap. A dissolve, and they fill the frame, not, as Carmichael assumes, locked in prayer, but turning, caressing, twin creatures cautiously exploring each other. They glow in the light, a symbol of anguish, caught in a private act of sacrifice, a Gethsemane of eroticism.

The moment in the penultimate reel when Lily and Harvey have to settle their personal feud is the most moving in the film. Restless in her compartment, lounging in a black negligee and smoking with the nervous savagery that other actresses later made a cliché of tortured womankind, she strolls at last along the eternal corridor to Harvey's room. Sleepy, sulky, carelessly provocative in black lace, she has a crushed fatigue that is hauntingly like the aftermath of sex. Nothing of any import is said; a light is exchanged, smoke wreathes into the narrow room, a cough accentuates the barely concealed desire. Slowly, painfully, Harvey yields a half-confession of belief in her story but, on the subliminal level, acknowledges his need for her, even at the price of emotional destruction. Lily returns to her compartment and closes the door. And as she leans back against it to draw one last time on her cigarette, the camera moves in to show the shocking tremor of her hands—a sign, perhaps, of the train's motion, but equally of her own excitement? Distress? Smoke drifts and gathers, her face turns up to the light—triumphant, fulfilled, alone.

By the time the train arrives at Shanghai, Lily has total control. After some hide-and-seek in jewelers' shops and among the reunions, she returns to Harvey with a watch she has purchased to replace another lost. Confident of her ownership now, arrogantly in command, she buckles it on and rips off the price tag, as if it is the man she has bought. She caresses the watch strap, the wide belt across his chest, his gloves. As he kisses her, Lily transfers his whip and gloves from his hand to hers, a gesture at once provocative and metaphoric: *You're mine now.*

As Stutesman points out, hats also contribute to this scene's subliminal language. "[Lily] gets off the train wearing the original cloche. Fearing her lover's loss forever (he still rejects her), the veil's lines have been intensified, as her self protection has redoubled, all the more obvious because, having been affected again by love, she must try harder to hold herself aloof. But, ultimately, her lover humbles himself before her and, united, they kiss. She retains her hat as does he (a colonel's, which she has worn once) but significantly she denudes him of his petty props—his *Falling in Love Again* riding crop and gloves. Their hats are all they need."[5]

So intricately choreographed are the key scenes in *Shanghai Express* that one doesn't immediately notice the underlying oddities of acting technique. Brook is stiff to the point of inertia, while Dietrich's eyes, particularly in their confrontation at the rear of the train, roam ceaselessly, looking at everything but him. Verisimilitude in performance interests the director not at all. Dietrich, though transformed into a beautiful object, is no better an actress in this film than she was in the screen test for *The Blue Angel,* but her deficiencies don't concern von Sternberg. First and foremost an artist, he cares only for his personages' "dramatic encounter with light."

Shanghai Express decisively launched the legend of von Sternberg the Tyrant. The atmosphere on his sets soon became notorious. "There is a tenseness about them," wrote one journalist uneasily, "a feeling of impending doom." The simplest distraction—a misplaced prop, an uninvited visitor—could trigger a tantrum. These were made worse by a technological advance introduced for the first time on this film. Visiting the set, Jesse Lasky Sr. noticed von Sternberg bawling into a megaphone to direct crowd scenes, and losing his voice in the process. He told studio manager Sam Jaffe (not to be confused with the actor) to procure him a microphone. "Von Sternberg had never used a public-address system," recalled Lasky, "and was as fascinated with it as a child with a new toy. . . . As I entered the stage where they were working, I couldn't even see the set at the far end, but I could hear the booming voice of the director reverberating through the enormous structure like a train announcer's in Grand Central Station. Von Sternberg was staging an intimate close-up of Marlene and Clive Brook, almost breathing in their faces as he gave them directions, but still using the microphone."[6] For someone who wore the clothes of larger men, a voice louder than life was equally appropriate.

The gesture didn't soften his hostility toward Jaffe. Henry Hathaway, von Sternberg's assistant from *Morocco,* describes how, as *Shanghai Express* neared completion, he was "sitting across the street in a restaurant having a cup of coffee and a guy sits down alongside me, and says, 'It's too bad about Sam Jaffe. . . . They fired him. He got in a fight with von Sternberg.' " Jaffe did leave Paramount in 1932, to become a successful independent producer. Von Sternberg may have speeded his departure, but it's just as likely that Jaffe was a victim of the same studio politics that would oust Ben Schulberg, his brother-in-law.

Shanghai Express was released in February 1932. Reportedly, the government of China protested at the depiction of its nationals as either prostitutes or homicidal warlords and demanded the film's suppression. As Japan had just occupied Shanghai, seized the port of Nanking, and would shortly occupy Harbin, the embattled Chinese had more to worry about than a film, and the threat came to nothing—fortunately for both Paramount and von Sternberg, since *Shanghai Express* was to make millions.

Lee Garmes's cinematography, for which von Sternberg was substantially responsible, won him an Academy Award. The film would also be nominated for Best Picture and Best Director but lose to *Grand Hotel* and to Frank Borzage for an obscure melodrama called *Bad Girl.* This snubbing surprised nobody. Voted on by fellow filmmakers, who in turn deferred to their studios, the awards were a popularity contest that von Sternberg was bound to lose.

Sergei Eisenstein had dismissed *An American Tragedy* after walking out halfway through. He called the film "very poor" and attacked von Sternberg's refusal to employ the technique of inner monologue on which his own version had relied. He was no more impressed with *Shanghai Express,* stigmatizing it as a "Kiddy Kar" version of a similar Soviet film. Its success was even more galling because Eisenstein's attempts to launch a film in Mexico with backing from novelist Upton Sinclair had ended in disaster. In March 1932, broke and stranded, Eisenstein and his friends were refused visas to reenter the United States, even if only in transit to Europe. Sympathizers circulated a petition to Mary Pickford, Charlie Chaplin, Frank Capra, Sam Goldwyn, Cecil B. DeMille, Ernst Lubitsch, and many others, asking them to sign a telegram protesting the decision. The only reply came from von Sternberg, who wired, "Will be glad to sign collective telegram petitioning secretary of labor to readmit Eisenstein." Reluctantly granted thirty-one-day tourist visas, the Russians sailed from New York in April 1932, never to return to the United States. Despite von Sternberg's support, Eisenstein continued to snipe at him and his work for the rest of his life.

Come Early, Stay Late

They called Hop's girl the Blonde Venus. Hop did not mind
because she was not his real girl.

—Ernest Hemingway, *Big Two Hearted River I*

WITH *SHANGHAI EXPRESS* COMPLETED and Riza's lawsuits no
longer news, von Sternberg proposed filming Émile Zola's novel *Nana*,
about a failed actress turned courtesan in Second Empire France, but
Samuel Goldwyn had beaten him to it with a version starring the latest
answer to Garbo—Russian actress Anna Sten. Paramount wasn't disap-
pointed. Some executives felt that Dietrich had already played too many
prostitutes, and a change of tone was advised. Also, notwithstanding
a 1926 film by Jean Renoir, *Nana* resisted movie treatment, as it contained nudity, lesbianism, an illegitimate child, and Nana's death from
"smallpox"—a euphemism for syphilis.

All the same, Paramount would not have protested any film the
couple chose to make, since *Shanghai Express* grossed $3.7 million at a
time when the studio's annual income had sagged from $25 million in
1930 to a mere $8.7 million in 1931. Because of Zukor's greed in snap-
ping up 500 cinemas at Depression prices in 1929–1930, Paramount
Publix was in receivership and would shortly be declared bankrupt.
Schulberg, chosen as scapegoat, was invited to "retire" by midyear. Von
Sternberg and Dietrich negotiated the deal on their next film during the

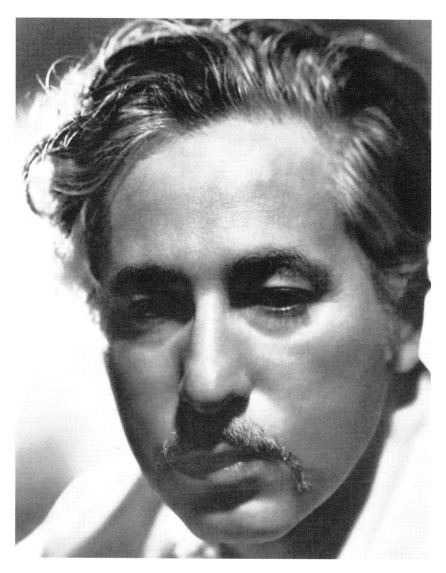

Josef von Sternberg at the height of his powers in the mid-1930s. He told Clive Brook, "The only way to succeed is to make people hate you. That way they remember you."

Von Sternberg's first feature, *The Salvation Hunters* (1925), stars Georgia Hale and George K. Arthur (above). Arthur and Hale are shown with Bruce Guerin and Otto Matiesen (below). Despite its debt to von Stroheim, the film shows the photographic and decorative flair for which von Sternberg became famous.

Von Sternberg appears awkward with Renée Adorée on the set of *The Exquisite Sinner* (1925), his first disastrous studio film. The cane is already a feature.

Von Sternberg demanded total silence on the set. Even watches were forbidden. In the posed shot with cinematographer Max Fabian and members of the cast of *The Exquisite Sinner*, the director is the only one not enjoying the joke.

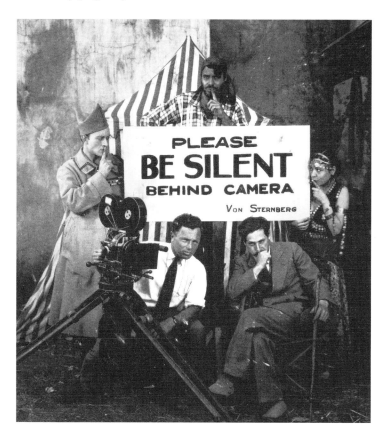

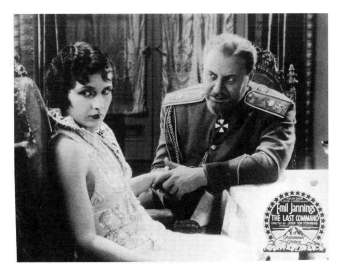

Evelyn Brent and Emil Jannings in *The Last Command* (1928).
Jannings's uniform, and particularly his medal, is an important
plot element, showing von Sternberg's flair for storytelling
through objects.

A prostitute (Betty Compson) and a ship's stoker (George Bancroft) are improbable lovers in
The Docks of New York (1929), the finest of von Sternberg's silents.

William Powell as "Dapper" Frank Trent and Evelyn Brent as "The Magpie," rival gang bosses in *The Drag Net* (1928). The feathers of Brent's cap and the streamers in the background are familiar von Sternberg motifs.

George Bancroft is restrained by the guards from attacking Richard Arlen in von Sternberg's first sound film, *Thunderbolt* (1929), as the warden (Tully Marshall, right) looks on.

Esther Ralston as the servant girl struggling to save her son in *The Case of Lena Smith* (1929), von Sternberg's last silent. The story has resonance with his own childhood, as he spent his early life brought up by a doting mother and an often absent father.

The chrysalis and the butterfly. Marlene Dietrich (left) in 1925, before von Sternberg, and (right) in *Shanghai Express* (1932).

Von Sternberg directs the vehicle of Marlene Dietrich's transformation, *The Blue Angel* (1930).

In *The Blue Angel* (1930), Lola-Lola (Marlene Dietrich) introduces her husband (Emil Jannings) to the man who will supplant him, the strongman Mazeppa (Hans Albers).

Marlene Plays Lead In Court Drama
As Trial Of Alienation Suit Nears

By BOBBIN COONS
HOLLYWOOD (AP)—The eyes of all Hollywood are turned to New York courts as the climax approaches in a legal contest involving the most intriguing triangle the screen city has known in years.

The principals are Marlene Dietrich, exotic German screen actress; Josef von Sternberg, the director who "discovered" her, and Mrs. Riza Royce von Sternberg, who has twice married and twice divorced the picturesque director.

On the sidelines in Europe, stands Rudolph Sieber, husband of Miss Dietrich and himself a film director abroad, affirming his faith in his wife and in his friend, Von Sternberg.

On October 5, in New York, hearings began on Mrs. Von Sternberg's damage suits against Miss Dietrich, one of which asks $500,000 for the alleged alienation of her former husband's affections. The other asks $100,000 for libelous remarks the actress is alleged to have made against the plaintiff.

Miss Dietrich, who was selected by Von Sternberg for "The Blue Angel," a picture to be made in Germany last year, and who subsequently came to Hollywood and became a star almost overnight, characterizes Mrs. Von Sternberg's allegations as ridiculous, unfair, and unjustified.

Her husband, Sieber, came to Hollywood recently, he said. "To testify by my presence and in any other way that I can testify that I know that these charges against her are utterly unfounded." Now he has been called back to his work in Europe.

In her alienation of affections action, Mrs. Von Sternberg charges that the director furnished an apartment for Miss Dietrich and allowed her to use his charge accounts.

In the libel suit she alleges that the actress, in an interview printed in a European newspaper, said Mrs. Von Sternberg was an "undutiful wife," and that the director had planned to divorce her if she, Mrs. Von Sternberg, had not divorced him first.

Hollywood has watched the drama brewing ever since Miss Dietrich arrived in this country, to continue in films under the tutelage of her discoverer, and to be seen with him constantly at the social functions. Hollywood regarded their companionship as merely an outgrowth of their professional connection as master and pupil, for Von Sternberg is admitted to have given Miss Dietrich the screen personality she possesses today.

They're the Cast of Characters

Suits filed by Mrs. Riza Royce von Sternberg (below) against Marlene Dietrich (left) alleging libel, and alienation of the affections of Josef von Sternberg (right), divorced husband of Mrs. von Sternberg, went to trial in New York October 5. Mrs. Von Sternberg seeks $600,000 from Miss Dietrich, who has risen to film stardom admittedly through the masterful direction of Von Sternberg.

Papers in the damage suits were served on Miss Dietrich last April when she returned from a visit with her husband, bringing her daughter, Maria Sieber, aged 5, to Hollywood with her. Existence of the suits, however, was not revealed until July.

Lola-Lola's last enigmatic stare at the end of *The Blue Angel*. Art intruded on real life when von Sternberg's wife, Riza Royce, sued Marlene Dietrich for libel and alienation of affections and demanded a divorce.

An exercise in damage control, Los Angeles, 1931. Marlene Dietrich and daughter pose with husband Rudy Sieber next to Dietrich's director and lover, von Sternberg.

(Left) Von Sternberg in costume with a less formally dressed Gary Cooper on the set of *Morocco* (1930). (Right) Paramount exploited Dietrich's bisexuality and cross-dressing, promoting her as "The Woman All Women Want to See." She wore a man's tuxedo to accompany Maurice Chevalier and Gary Cooper to the premiere of Cecil B. DeMille's *The Sign of the Cross*.

In *Morocco* (1930), Dietrich's burned-out cabaret singer rejects marriage to wealthy Adolphe Menjou, preferring subjugation to embittered Foreign Legionnaire Gary Cooper.

Dietrich's peasant-girl disguise as spy X-27 in *Dishonored* (1931) references von Sternberg's first love.

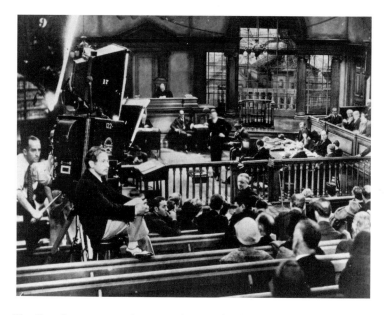

Von Sternberg appears dapper and uninvolved on the set of *An American Tragedy* (1931), a project he snatched from under the nose of Sergei Eisenstein and then dismissed as "just an assignment."

Sylvia Sidney about to be drowned in *An American Tragedy.*

Nobody carried off headgear like Dietrich. Her plumes in *Shanghai Express* (1932) (top left) came from the tails of Mexican fighting cocks, and her wig in *Blonde Venus* (1932) (top right) was dusted with real gold. Nothing, however, equaled her theft of Clive Brook's cap (below) in *Shanghai Express,* topped by her comment that, if given the last five years to live over, she would change only one thing—"I wouldn't have bobbed my hair."

Von Sternberg called *The Scarlet Empress* (1933) a "relentless excursion into style." Despite Travis Banton's astonishing costumes, the swaggering performance of John Lodge (right) as one of Catherine the Great's "regiment of lovers," and Sam Jaffe (below) as her daft, doll-loving husband, the film expired under the weight of its pretensions.

Von Sternberg directs *The Devil Is a Woman* (1935), which ended his partnership with Dietrich and, effectively, his career. Cesar Romero replaced Joel McCrea, who walked out after one day. The real star, as is so often the case with von Sternberg's films, is the décor and the costumes—in this scene, the hat.

Von Sternberg poses diffidently with Franchot Tone and Grace Moore on the set of *The King Steps Out* (1936). He's more genial and less soberly attired, in Javanese turban and jodhpurs, as he loiters with Merle Oberon and Charles Laughton, costars in the doomed *I, Claudius* (1937).

Von Sternberg replicated his tyrannical and violent father in the Wallace Beery character in *Sergeant Madden* (1939). Laraine Day and Tom Brown keep Beery and Alan Curtis apart.

In *The Shanghai Gesture* (1941), von Sternberg celebrated the synthetic China of cheap fiction, with Ona Munson as Mother Gin Sling, Gene Tierney as her corrupt daughter Poppy, and Victor Mature as Dr. Omar, the "thoroughbred mongrel" and "Doctor of Nothing." Boris Leven's designs for the gambling pit (below) earned an Academy Award nomination.

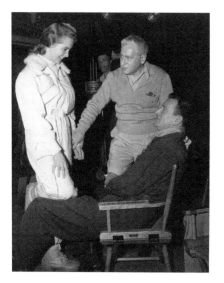

Von Sternberg "makes nice" with Janet Leigh and John Wayne on the set of *Jet Pilot* in 1950, but he's in a more somber mood at the 1967 Sydney Film Festival, with director David Stratton (left) and festival president Dugmore Merry. (Photograph of Stratton by Robert McFarlane, courtesy www.joseflebovicgallery.com)

With *The Saga of Anatahan* (1952), von Sternberg achieved his expressed ideal: a totally synthetic film shot on an entirely artificial setting, with all the characters embodying aspects of himself and actors who did exactly as they were told (since none of them spoke English). Akemi Negishi, the "Queen Bee" of the stranded men, defines his vision of woman as the alluring destroyer.

transfer of power to incoming studio boss Emmanuel "Manny" Cohen, formerly head of its newsreel division.

The duo's next film, *Blonde Venus*, began as an outline variously called "East River," "Song of Manhattan," and "Velvet." The last title seemed the most promising and survived the longest, but von Sternberg's reading of *Nana* may have reminded him that, in her brief stage career, Zola's heroine played a "blonde Venus." A character of the same name also appeared in Offenbach's operetta *La Belle Helene,* and Hemingway used it in a 1925 story.

In later years, von Sternberg shrugged off *Blonde Venus.* "There is little to be said about this film," he wrote, "except that I tried to leave the company before making it. But Miss Dietrich also left, refusing to work with anyone else, and I was forced to return, as we were both under contract." One wouldn't imagine from this offhand reference that this was his most personal film, with obvious autobiographical resonance. The Dietrich character, a German singer, leaves the stage to marry an American scientist. They move to New York and have a son. During his experiments the husband is poisoned and, in a well-worn cliché, finds that the only doctor who can cure him is in Germany. To raise money for his treatment, the singer goes back to work and, hiding the fact that she's married with a child, becomes the mistress of a wealthy but crooked politician. The husband is cured, returns unexpectedly, discovers her infidelity, and throws her out. Taking their child, she goes on the run. The husband hires detectives to find her and hits the bottle while he waits for news. Eventually, she's forced to surrender the boy and returns to show business, where she is again a sensation. The husband deteriorates, however, until she gives up her career to care for him, and the family is reunited.

Von Sternberg and Dietrich wrote the treatment jointly, offering it to Paramount for $25,000. When Schulberg pleaded hard times, they accepted $12,000. Looking for a pliable new writer who would obey orders, von Sternberg offered the task of scripting *Blonde Venus* to S. K. "Sam" Lauren, who had just joined Paramount after two flops as a Broadway dramatist. "I couldn't stand von Sternberg," Lauren recalled, "[but] he seemed to take to me." As the screenplay developed, the singer's husband, Ned Faraday, became much less concerned about the liaison between his wife, Helen, and politician Nick Townsend. In fact, the two characters are quite friendly, as were von Sternberg and Rudy Sieber. Ned acquires his own girlfriend, as did Sieber, and agrees to a divorce, after which Helen and Nick marry and raise her son. "When he gave me the plot," Lauren said, "I thought 'This guy's crazy.'" Nobody could doubt that Helen and Nick equated to Marlene and Jo, while Ned and his mistress stood for Rudy and Tami.

As Lauren finished each draft, von Sternberg passed it to Jules Furthman. Lauren didn't share Capra's enthusiasm for Furthman, calling him, for reasons not immediately clear, "that racketeer," while grudgingly admitting that the other did almost all the work. "Finally, I finished the treatment," Lauren continued. "Von Sternberg called me into his office, about three times the size of Hitler's, and, with one hand on the script, went into an interminable, impressive silence, which was enough to scare the bejeezus out of me. He brushed the script onto the floor. He said, very slowly, using the royal plural, 'We choose to overlook the presumption that this screenplay has ever been written.'" Lauren and Furthman continued to collaborate, fleeing at one point to Palm Springs in hopes of avoiding von Sternberg. According to Lauren, when they returned, Furthman handed in a scene set in a brothel. "I was amazed at the literacy of it," said Lauren. After Furthman read it out loud, Lauren told him, "Jules, that's a fine piece of writing." "It ought to be," interjected von Sternberg, "It was fine when Zola wrote it in *Nana*."

In March the script was submitted to Ben Schulberg, who, according to Lauren, described it as "the goddamndest piece of shit I've ever read in my life." More troubling than any artistic objections were the problems it presented with regard to Hollywood's newly formed self-censorship authority, the Motion Picture Producers and Distributors of America (MPPDA). *Blonde Venus* flouted two key rules of its Production Code: "Law, natural or human, shall not be ridiculed, nor shall any sympathy be created for its violation," and "The sanctity of the institution of marriage and the home should be upheld." The censor assigned to the project, Lamar Trotti, a screenwriter himself, particularly objected to Ned's infidelity and alcoholism. "It does not seem proper," he wrote, "to have [Helen's] affair justified in the minds of the audience by tearing down the character of the husband, who, up to this point, has been a decent man who was deceived by his wife."[1] Censors also expressed concern about how Helen makes the money to pay for Ned's treatment—in early drafts, simple prostitution—as well as the fact that she performs at the Magnolia Club in New York's Harlem. O'Connor, the club owner, is seen talking to two African American women, and the walls of his office are decorated with photographs of "young girls of all colors." By the time *Blonde Venus* reached the screen, African Americans had been relegated to menial roles as barmen, band leaders, and chorus girls, while audiences were entirely white—more or less the prevailing situation in real Harlem establishments such as the Cotton Club.

Asked to rewrite the story, von Sternberg refused. Paramount suspended him and, in April, threatened a $100,000 lawsuit for breach of contract. Expressing surprise at the low valuation placed on his intransigence, he left for a holiday in New York. Incoming studio head Manny Cohen was en route to Los Angeles, and their trains converged at Kansas City. The trade press published a report, never corroborated, that both men stepped off to stretch their legs and had a brief discussion on the platform. If so, they reached no agreement. On Cohen's arrival in Los Angeles, he ordered *Blonde Venus* reassigned to the pedestrian Richard Wallace. When Dietrich declined to act in it, Paramount, hoping to goad her into returning, circulated the rumor that she would be replaced by Tallulah Bankhead, who fanned the flames by announcing, "I always did want to get into Dietrich's pants." When von Sternberg arrived in New York, he told the press, "I will return to Hollywood and my profession in a few days. But it probably won't be at Paramount. Yes, they threaten eternal excommunication or something like that if I go elsewhere, but I don't think they can prevent it. I don't anticipate either of us will have any trouble."

This was brave talk for a man facing disaster. At the annual meeting of Paramount Publix, Cohen announced Schulberg's "retirement," removing the executive who had been von Sternberg's staunchest supporter. Paramount's lawyers also announced that both director and star would remain on unpaid suspension until the case came to court, perhaps a year hence. Von Sternberg returned to Los Angeles on May 2 and immediately became embroiled in some hard talking with Cohen and his new administration. The balance of power had shifted in favor of Dietrich and von Sternberg once *Shanghai Express* began racking up impressive grosses, and exhibitors wanted more of the same. Cohen should have caved in. Instead, a week later he announced that *Blonde Venus* would go into immediate production with a compromise screenplay that retained Helen's relationship with Nick but removed Ned's affair and drinking and concluded with Helen renouncing Nick and returning to Ned and their son. Von Sternberg and Dietrich offered no explanation for their climbdown. Cohen may have rationalized that neither wished to waste a year when Dietrich's box-office appeal was at its height. He didn't suspect that their acquiescence was a smoke screen. Secretly, they had decided to leave Paramount when their contracts ended and set up independent production in Europe. For the moment, however, they kept quiet and started work.

In Chicago, during the delay between the arrival of the Twentieth Century from New York and the departure of the Superchief for Los Angeles, von Sternberg visited an art gallery to purchase Georg Grosz's 1924 watercolor *Married Couple.* In what appears to be a hotel room, a nude woman washes herself with a cloth while a man, suspenders dangling, stands on a balcony with his back to her, smoking. That they have just had sex is clearly implied, and the mirror on the wall behind the woman, hanging crookedly, suggests that it was violent—or, more likely, tilted by them, the better to watch themselves. Few pictures are more emblematic of von Sternberg's sexuality or so singularly appropriate to the film he was about to make.

Almost every von Sternberg film takes place in a few claustrophobic locations. *Blonde Venus* is the exception. The story moves from Germany to New York, the Deep South, then Paris, and back to New York. Settings include a Brooklyn apartment, French and U.S. nightclubs, flophouses, cafés, bars, brothels, stations, and a pond in the Black Forest. Yet the atmosphere remains languid, an opium dream in which time stands still. Incidents flow into each other. Squalor dissolves. Anguish becomes pleasure.

From the opening credit sequence, of a willow-reflecting pool disturbed by nude bodies surging past just below the surface, this is a "blonde" film—silky, glistening with light and warmth, enveloping us in a perfumed cloud of hair. Mendelssohn's playful *Midsummer Night's Dream* overture complements the swimmers, who are softened into indistinctness behind foliage, evoking one of von Sternberg's early sexual experiences (stumbling upon a group of nude bathers in the *Alte Donau*). Dietrich and her friends are surprised by a band of hikers led by Ned Faraday (Herbert Marshall—puzzling casting, since he was British and had an artificial leg). With a brisk wipe, von Sternberg hurries us on to what really interests him in the film: its autobiographical element. Dietrich, transformed from *Rheinmàedchen* to housewife and mother, is bathing her son Johnny (Dickie Moore) in their Brooklyn apartment. From his first idle remark as he splashes in his bath—"there's an alligator in here"—Johnny embodies hostility and duplicity, reinforcing Maria Riva's contention that von Sternberg was resentful of her and regarded her as an impediment to his relationship with her mother. The boy plays with grotesque toys, snipes at a clockwork Mother Goose with his toy rifle, pettishly demands that his parents recount their first meeting in the form of a fairy tale, and pulls out the eye of his teddy bear to let it snap back into its face. Later still, as he and his mother go on the run, he wears a grotesque mask on the back of his head—literally two-faced.

Faraday, thoroughly identified with Rudy Sieber, is the apotheosis of wimphood. Visiting a doctor, who toys undiplomatically with a skull during their conversation, Ned explains his exposure to radiation and suggests that his colleague purchase his body as a medical curiosity. Offered a mere $50, he returns home and, glooming amid the retorts of his home chemistry lab, accepts with fatalism the necessity of abandoning his family and traveling to Germany for a cure. As he does so, Helen embroiders black birds on a sampler and impassively explains the necessity of her going back on the stage to finance his treatment.

In earlier versions of the screenplay, Helen became a street prostitute, but in rewrites she moved upmarket, employing the casting couch to win her way back into show business. How she does so is telegraphed in a single artfully staged scene at the office of casting agent Ben Smith

(Gene Morgan). In a reception room clogged with the dark shapes of those awaiting an appointment, one thing catches our attention: a single gleam of light off to one side—a corner of Dietrich's face. Thanks to artful lighting, it draws the eye like a gold coin half buried in earth. Smith, whisking her into his office past the statue of a nude woman, tells her she has got him "all heated up." He washes his hands in the corner basin, almost like a doctor preparing to make a gynecological examination—which perhaps, in a sense, he is. We never find out what takes place, nor do we need to; Helen has crossed the frontier between hausfrau and sex queen. With a new name, wardrobe, and morality, she is transformed.

"First Time Tonight. The Blonde Venus. Come Early, Stay Late." Another von Sternberg sign heralds the rebirth of Helen Faraday as Helen Jones, aka the Blonde Venus. As Dietrich applies her makeup in the cluttered dressing room, the headliner she has supplanted, "Taxi Belle" Hooper (Rita La Roy), speculates on her speedy promotion, but Helen's cool inquiry—"Taxi Belle, do you charge for the first mile?"—implies she's no better. Taxi flounces out to join elegant politician Nick Townsend (Cary Grant), sensually comfortable with the club's jungle décor.

Then "Hot Voodoo" begins—not Duke Ellington, but certainly his orchestration. Shamelessly, von Sternberg gives us the Cotton Club with both barrels; thumping tom-toms and whinnying wah-wah brass embellish a chugging two-four beat. A drumhead spattered with shadows heralds a shuffling chorus line of haughty, half-naked African American dancers, heads out of frame to make them a frieze of hips and thighs, tufted with plumes. The squatting gorilla they drag slashes ineffectually at the audience, slobbering, snarling among its captors. ("Is that a real animal?" somebody asks the black barman, and he stutters, "I . . . I . . . I . . . if that animal were real, I w . . . w . . . wouldn't be here.") More drums, and the ape, still swaying, takes one paw in the other and draws it off to reveal a glowing white hand, the jeweled wrist of von Sternberg's most audacious creation, an albino jungle creature whose drowned face is surrounded by disordered hair that becomes an exploding mop of gold, transfixed with arrows—an act that merely makes more fatally provocative this blend of beauty and beast. Body arrogantly clad in plumes and sequins, she croons, "All night long / I don't know right from wrong," thrusting forward her metallized breasts as if to impale the lover careless enough to approach.

In creating Dietrich's musical numbers, von Sternberg turned the customary methods on their head. Instead of choosing songs offered by studio contract composers, he summoned a number of resentful song-smiths to audition their new material. The fictional Helen behaves with similar autocracy. Far from the conventional chanteuse, singing of her need for a man and bewailing his absence or indifference, she appears as a frank predator, publishing her appetite for flesh. "Hot Voodoo" is explicit, but von Sternberg drives home the point in "You Little So and So," one of the numbers chosen by Dietrich at the auditions, in which Helen, dressed in black, prowls behind jungle palms, and the baroque extravagance of "I Couldn't Be Annoyed," her number in a Parisian nightclub (managed by old friend Émile Chautard). In white male evening clothes, lapels glittering with rhinestones, she reviews with lesbian arrogance a group of veiled beauties, strolling among leaning Gothic arches, crouching monsters, and nude female torsos, one of which is the background to her reunion with Townsend. To reemphasize the point that *she* calls the sexual shots, von Sternberg uses white greasepaint to scrawl on the mirror of her Paris dressing room, amid sketches of nude female bodies and gallows, the lines from Kipling's "The Ballad of East and West": "Down to Gehenna and up to the throne / He travels the fastest who travels alone."

Cured, Ned returns to Brooklyn two weeks early and discovers Helen's affair. Their confrontation is so limply played it would be a compliment to call it "perfunctory." While Marshall does his professional best, snarling with resentment, jealousy, and injured pride, Dietrich, meticulously lit as ever, stands immobile and expressionless. She mouths the standard responses without inflection, content simply to be beautiful. As Graham Greene said of her, "she consents to pose; . . . as for acting, that is merely the word for what goes on all round her; she leaves it to her servants."[2] One could hardly imagine a clearer indication of the contempt in which von Sternberg holds this conventional device of domestic drama, inflicted on him by the censors. He can't wait to get Helen on the train with Johnny and off on her protracted flight through rural America, into which he pours all his craft. His own hobo experiences are evident in these scenes, some of which also resemble descriptions of the vanished *The Case of Lena Smith*. The simplest incidents are handled with elaborate care: Helen's offer to wash dishes in return for a meal, and café owner Dewey Robinson's sneering, "You're gonna wash *my* dishes? See the chef!" have the ring of remembered humiliation; a hay-cart ride, golden straw shimmering in the sun; a plainly lesbian club owner (Cecil Cunningham) moving through a room of slumped girls and stacked chairs to warn Helen she must move on (and explaining, startlingly, "I've got a kid myself"); a flophouse with sagging bunks and a clientele of card-playing hags.

Each new degradation simply makes Helen more desirable. Drifting always farther south, she's arrested and tried in a court of blinding white, the walls given texture by side-lit shreds of peeling paint. Judge and clerk fan themselves in the slatted light while a stylized white eagle spreads its wings above the bench. Her New Orleans hideout glows like a Hollywood heaven, infested with pigeons and cooing doves, white shutters dissolving in the sunlight. Her tattered clothing; her implicit availability during her conversation with the detective (Sidney Toler) who clumsily tracks her down; her dismay when Faraday arrives to take Johnny, leaving her slumped under a pepper tree in the whirling debris of the departing train: immersed in a haze of heat and light, these lose their bitterness and become erotic images of another, heightened reality.

Among the tales about *Blonde Venus* spread by syndicated gossip columnists, one of the least likely was almost true. "Marlene Dietrich," claimed the columnist, "grinds a fifty-dollar gold piece into dust every day and sprinkles it in her hair." Before every take, makeup expert Max Factor did indeed dust the "Hot Voodoo" wig with real gold dust at $60 an ounce, to impart an authentic shimmer. Tallulah Bankhead, least apologetic of Hollywood's lesbians (and viewed contemptuously by Dietrich for her habit of seducing extras and secretaries), was working nearby on *The Devil and the Deep* (also with Cary Grant, and Gary Cooper as well). Notorious for not wearing underwear, she hikcd up her skirt one afternoon to display pubic hair speckled with gold and inquired of the goggling crew, "Guess who *I* had for lunch today?" However, she and Marlene were never more than polite enemies.

Dietrich expressed an equally low opinion of Cary Grant, who had only just arrived in Hollywood and was struggling to both make a living and create an image. The instant von Sternberg saw him, he told him, "You part your hair on the wrong side." Grant switched, permanently. Dietrich told Charles Higham that she had indicated to Grant she wouldn't be averse to having sex with him, but he declined, proving to her satisfaction that he was, as often rumored, predominantly homosexual. Thereafter she dismissed him as "that shirt seller," since, committed to a six-film contract on starvation wages, he was forced to moonlight at his old trade of haberdashery salesman to supplement his income. He had sold neckties on the streets of New York when he first came to the United States. Now he supplied shirts to the cast and crew of *Blonde Venus* as a source of extra cash.

Playing the lead in *The Devil and the Deep,* as a jealous submarine captain who sinks with his ship rather than see wife Bankhead run off with Cooper, was British actor Charles Laughton. He made a point of greeting von Sternberg in the commissary and praising his work. A closeted homosexual and masochist, Laughton loathed his ugliness and obesity and was often beaten up and robbed by the male whores he hired. Shortly after their first meeting, von Sternberg received an anguished call from Laughton at the Garden of Allah. He had been diagnosed with syphilis. Von Sternberg hurried to the hotel, talked him out of suicide, and remained with him for three days and nights until the diagnosis could be checked and proved false. This knowledge of Laughton's secret life may have influenced the way von Sternberg dealt with the actor when he directed him, later in the decade, in *I, Claudius.* The fact that Laughton would admit such a potentially damaging fact as his homosexuality also adds weight to Eisenstein's suggestion that von Sternberg was at least bisexual.

Postproduction on *Blonde Venus* ended in August. Von Sternberg's contract would expire in December, which left little time to start another film. He and Schulberg discussed a new deal, but von Sternberg, for obvious reasons, dragged his feet, still assuming that he and Dietrich would sever their connection with Paramount at the same time. The studio had bought Ernest Hemingway's *A Farewell to Arms,* and von

Sternberg proposed reuniting Gary Cooper as the Hemingway character, wounded on the Italian front in World War I, with Dietrich as the nurse with whom he falls in love but who dies in childbirth. The company agreed to Cooper but preferred Helen Hayes over Dietrich and the more reliable Frank Borzage to direct.

Just before *Blonde Venus* began shooting, Riza withdrew her lawsuits for libel and alienation of affection. In March, Paramount produced a statement from the Viennese journalist retracting the offending article, and the other suit was settled out of court. Rather than handing over cash, von Sternberg gave Riza some of his art collection. Having scrimped on the housekeeping so that he could buy paintings, she took satisfaction in using some of the lesser pieces to pay off creditors such as Frederica Sagor.

Von Sternberg, sufficiently wealthy by now to buy whatever he pleased, patronized the art dealers who serviced the Hollywood community and also attended local shows. Since the artwork was often controversial, these shows took place in private homes or in bookshops, in particular those of Jake Zeitlin and Stanley Rose. *Los Angeles Times* art critic Arthur Millier called von Sternberg "an omnivorous collector of the most violent modern art."[3] Sergei Eisenstein, predictably, caviled. "He collected leftist art," he conceded. "But it was not quite the thing. The names weren't 'right,' the pictures were of the wrong periods."[4] He may have had a point, to the extent that the works by Matisse, Gauguin, and Léger that von Sternberg bought in the 1930s were minor. He was on firmer ground with living artists such as the Mexicans and Dix, Grosz, and Belling, whose German or Austrian background he shared. Billy Wilder, himself a major collector, said, "The three greatest art collections in Hollywood were Edward G. Robinson, Josef von Sternberg and [producer] William Goetz [Louis B. Mayer's son-in-law]. . . . Von Sternberg sold all his Impressionists in the 1940s and started all over, collecting the Abstract Expressionists." At the peak of his collecting, von Sternberg owned works by Kandinsky, de Chirico, Grosz, Kokoschka, Brancusi, Archipenko, and many others, all of sufficiently high quality for their sale to keep him comfortable between films.

Stanley Rose's bookshop was next to Musso and Frank's restaurant on Hollywood Boulevard, scene of many frugal and lonely meals in his early days. Professing to loathe books, Rose ran the shop as a pretext to entertain writer friends. Nathanael West wrote part of *The Day of the Locust* in the back room, where, periodically, William Saroyan, James M. Cain, John O'Hara, John Steinbeck, Christopher Isherwood, William Faulkner, and John Fante held forth on literature or played poker. Fletcher Martin called Rose "the least bookish person I've ever seen and I often wondered whether he ever read a book. He ran a shop which was a combination cultural center, speakeasy, and bookie joint. Stanley would get whiskey and/or girls for visiting authors, and Saroyan made him his exclusive agent to the movie studios. The ambience was wonderful, something like your friendly local pool hall. He liked artists and always had a gallery in the back."[5]

This was an ideal environment in which to meet young local artists or those who had just arrived in town, and von Sternberg became a regular. Other habitués included the then-unknown Philip Guston, who supported himself as a movie extra. On *Svengali,* he spent days painting a nude in an atelier scene while John Barrymore emoted in the foreground. In 1935 Rose showed eighty-five pieces by Spanish artist Juan Gris. Von Sternberg bought the only one sold, for $300. He also exhibited work by Peter Ballbusch, a Swiss sculptor and later chief of MGM's montage department, and Richard Kollorsz, a pupil of Otto Dix who was then painting scenery at Paramount. Von Sternberg admired both, employed them as assistants on his films, and in February 1932 sponsored a joint exhibition of their work at the Plaza Art Center in the mainly Hispanic Olvera Street district. Another new friend was Austrian-born architect Richard Neutra. The two would sit up all night discussing art. Their conversations inspired von Sternberg to seek a site in the San Fernando Valley where Neutra could build him a house.

A dilettantish leftism—"swimming pool socialism"—prevailed in the Los Angeles art scene. This was acknowledged in the artists Rose exhibited, many of whom were unapologetically communist, which made them doubly exotic to Hollywood's wealthy collectors. Although von Sternberg never showed much interest in politics, he frequented the John Reed Clubs, a network of Marxist discussion groups supported by the Communist Party. At their shows and auctions, he bought paintings by Diego Rivera and Manuel Orozco. Through Kollorsz he met Ione Robinson, a young painter who had modeled for Rivera and was married to Joseph Freeman, a party ideologue. In 1930 Robinson and Kollorsz persuaded von Sternberg to help Mexican painter and muralist David Alfaro Siqueiros escape from Mexico, where he was under house arrest in Taxco after serving a jail term for his political activities. A local art school was persuaded to offer him a post as a visiting teacher. Von Sternberg's role in this episode isn't clear, although he probably paid duty on the paintings and drawings Siqueiros shipped to Los Angeles.

During his first three months in Los Angeles, Siqueiros directed a team of local students in creating propagandist murals, most of which were effaced by indignant local authorities. Once his visa ran out, he went into hiding with sympathizers such as Dudley Murphy, theater director and friend of Eisenstein. Murphy transformed his house into an art gallery for a three-day show of the artist's work, and in return, Siqueiros executed a mural on the walls of Murphy's patio. The show was a success. Siqueiros sold ten canvases, including two to Charles Laughton and one to von Sternberg. The latter sponsored other exhibitions for the painter, one at Zeitlin's bookshop and another in May at the Stendahl Ambassador Galleries in the Ambassador Hotel. At the Stendahl opening, von Sternberg announced he had commissioned a portrait from Siqueiros. The artist sketched him at work in his office at Paramount and delivered a murky, somewhat sinister oil that von Sternberg chose to unveil as part of an exhibition devoted entirely to likenesses of himself. The show took place on a soundstage at Paramount during the shooting of *Blonde Venus*.

Arthur Millier gleefully parodied the event in the *Los Angeles Times*, particularly the presence of Dietrich in her "Hot Voodoo" costume, including flesh-colored tights, a skirt of red ostrich feathers, and a blonde wig that Millier compared to the hairdo of Harpo Marx. He took the art a little more seriously. It included the Belling bronze, a brass head by David Edstrom, a competent self-portrait by von Sternberg, "a furious silver sculpture" by Ballbusch (the director's favorite), a caricature by "Cugat" (whether Francis Cugat, who executed the cover art for the first edition of *The Great Gatsby*, or his graphically accomplished bandleader brother Xavier isn't clear), and an oil by Boris Deutsch (who worked in the Paramount special effects department). Millier thought Siqueiros's portrait of von Sternberg "ugly, intent, [and] commanding." It captured the obsession and remoteness that made the director such a difficult subject.[6]

Boris Deutsch had the same problem. When he saw the finished likeness, von Sternberg complained that Deutsch had shortened his moustache by an inch on each side and ordered him to correct this. "Go get your moustaches cut!" snapped Deutsch. "I'm a painter, not a barber." Deutsch never signed the painting. Later, he explained why:

[Von Sternberg] was at the height of his career at that time, and he would come over twice a week to pose for a couple of hours. I began to dislike the whole business of painting his portrait be-cause he had a tendency to freeze me. . . . I worked for perhaps four sittings and I was quite disgusted with his attitude: I just couldn't accept those things because I had a certain idea of how to paint it. So I told him I was not going to paint him anymore. By the way, he thought that $250 for the portrait was just about right and of course I didn't agree, but I was only a little mad. But I never signed the portrait! . . . And eight or nine years later . . . he came over to me in my studio asking if perhaps I would be willing to sign the painting. I was working on this painting *What Atomic War Will Do to You*, and he looked at that, and he said, "Why must a person paint things like that? Why don't you paint some flowers or something nice?" . . . And I must say that his poor little painting was left unsigned.

This reflexive aestheticism in the face of Deutsch's leftist propagan-da underlines von Sternberg's political innocence. There's no evidence that his encounter with the John Reed Clubs nor his championing of Siqueiros had any political basis. He failed to anticipate the rise of Nazism and even attempted to set up a production company in Berlin just as Hitler came to power. He is frank in acknowledging that he didn't foresee the annexation of Austria and continued, right up to the last days, to plan a film that relied on Austrian money. Touring the Far East in the late 1930s, he detected no signs of imminent war in Japan or China, even though troops of the first were already occupying large areas of the second. Nor does he deal with politics in his films, except on the most superficial level, such as the Russian riots of *The Last Command* and *The Scarlet Empress* or the radical sentiments of Antonio Galvan in *The Devil Is a Woman*. In a von Sternberg movie, the bedroom is battlefield enough.

Blonde Venus opened on September 23, 1932. Reviews ranged from complacent to hostile, but the box-office returns, though not spectacular, were adequate. Leaving Dietrich and the supporting cast to represent him at the Los Angeles and New York premieres, von Sternberg left with Jules Furthman on October 2 for a month-long trip around the Caribbean. They traveled to Mexico City and Vera Cruz and took a steamer to Havana, where cinematographers Paul Ivano and Lucien Ballard joined them. The party chartered a flying boat from PanAm and continued to Haiti, Jamaica, and Trinidad, ostensibly with the aim of shooting background footage. Ideally, this would have included a real hurricane for a circus story, *The Lady of the Lions,* in which Dietrich was to play a lion tamer. As none of 1932's major storms made landfall near enough to film, von Sternberg contented himself with gathering local color. In Haiti he visited a stockade for the insane, where the afflicted were kept chained to the walls and a woman tried to sell him an invisible apron created with imaginary needle and thread. Such experiences only encouraged his belief that anyone could act and that movie stars were, to a greater or lesser extent, insane. Events to come confirmed this conviction. "Von Sternberg was very strange all through that trip," said Ivano. "He suffered from insomnia, and seemed to be on the verge of a nervous breakdown. He was convinced he was losing Marlene, and he was miserable." He had every reason to be. On December 2, 1932, his contract with Paramount would end. Dietrich had never been more popular, but her discoverer would soon be out of a job.

Russian Dolls

> The evolution of sense is, in a sense, the evolution of
> nonsense.
>
> —Vladimir Nabokov, *Pnin*

VON STERNBERG'S IMPENDING departure left Paramount in a
quandary, since Dietrich's contract ran until February 20, 1933. With
little hope of success, Manny Cohen suggested that while both sides
considered their options, Dietrich might complete another film with
a new director. To his surprise, both she and von Sternberg agreed.
They decided on *Das Hohe Lied* by Herman Sudermann, which had
been turned into a play titled *The Song of Songs* back in 1914 and filmed
twice as a silent. With a minimum of argument, Rouben Mamoulian
was selected to direct, but according to him, he turned down the job
because he thought the novel old-fashioned. In his memory, he agreed
only when von Sternberg and Dietrich visited his office together and
urged him to do it. For his part, von Sternberg announced his intention
to take a long holiday in Europe.

In pushing the production of *The Song of Songs*, von Sternberg and
Dietrich were creating a smoke screen to mask their true intentions—
revealed a few weeks later when Dietrich abruptly refused to appear
in the film. Paramount suspended her in December and took her to
court in January, demanding $182,850.06, the sum supposedly spent
on preparation. The studio also applied for an injunction to keep her

in the United States and sought civil arrest to force her to remain in Hollywood. To demonstrate a risk of flight, von Sternberg's secretary, Eleanor McGeary, testified she had overheard him and Marlene scheming to leave Hollywood for Germany, where they planned to form a company to make their own films. Even as she testified, von Sternberg was in Berlin setting up the production operation, and Dietrich planned to join him. Dietrich didn't deny the charges but attacked her contract, claiming it was so restrictive that it constituted bonded labor. The U.S. courts would eventually accept this principle, but not until 1937. In this case, the court found for the company and issued an order forcing her to remain in the United States. Reluctantly she returned to work, and shooting began on *Song of Songs*.

Dietrich plays Lily, an orphan peasant girl in braids and dirndl (shades of *Dishonored*) who comes to the city to live with her bookseller aunt. Richard, a penniless sculptor (Brian Aherne), asks her to pose for him. Inevitably they become lovers, and he creates a life-size nude statue, as stylized as an automobile hood ornament. Persuaded that she has no future with him, Richard passes her on to a dissolute baron (Lionel Atwill), who marries her. Their wedding night is worthy of von Stroheim, with the old baron dabbing on perfume and ogling a nude sketch of his new wife while the discarded mistress and besotted young estate manager lurk in the garden, staring at silhouettes on the bedroom window. Lily, of course, proves an unsatisfactory consort. Following a scandal, she flees the castle, spends a brief period as a café party girl, and is reunited with a repentant Richard. They consummate their love in a studio littered with fragments of her shattered statue and echoing with quotations from the Bible's Song of Songs.

Superficially, this is a story von Sternberg might have filmed, including the use of Atwill, one of his favorite actors. However, all the parallels in costuming and, occasionally, in Victor Milner's lighting simply throw into relief the differences between his methods and those of the more conventional Mamoulian. Where von Sternberg lingers on scenes, luxuriating in their visual and emotional possibilities, *Song of Songs* overflows with incident—a telling illustration of why von Sternberg preferred anecdotes as a source. Also, although Dietrich has seldom appeared more conventionally beautiful, Milner's flattering lighting lacks the mystery and sadness that only obsession can inculcate. Notwithstanding that Aherne had become her lover in real life as well as on film, Dietrich, it was said, would go to the microphone between takes and whisper, "Jo, where are you?" She explained it somewhat differently. Asked to speak a few words before each shot to establish voice level, she would murmur, "Jo, why hast thou forsaken me?" knowing the executives who watched each day's rushes would hear the rebuke.

The question was rhetorical anyway. As she knew, he was in Berlin. With conspicuously poor timing, he arrived in January 1933, the month Adolf Hitler assumed the chancellorship. On January 30 von Sternberg must have watched the torchlight parade down Unter den Linden that celebrated the event, and on February 27 he would have seen the sky glow red as the Reichstag burned. On March 18 Joseph Goebbels summoned all Berlin's gentile film producers to the Kaiserhof Hotel and laid down the Nazi line on race. The following day, UFA's board met to implement the new policy before the deadline of March 31, designated Jewish Boycott Day. The contracts of all Jewish producers, directors, writers, and performers, including Erich Pommer, Robert Liebmann, Hans Muller, Erich Engel, Werner Heymann, and Ludwig Berger, were dissolved. The board also put on notice Elisabeth Bergner, Conrad Veidt, Fritz Kortner, Friedrich Hollander, and Peter Lorre. The same day Pommer hurriedly left for London, having signed a deal with Fox-Europe.

Some of *The Blue Angel* unit, including Kurt Gerron, remained in Germany and died. Others fled to France, from which most never escaped. Among them was Liebmann, who was deported back to Germany; the date and manner of his death are unknown. Karl Huszar-Puffy, who played the proprietor of the cabaret, was rumored to have died in a Soviet camp in Kazakhstan. John Kahan joined Carl Zuckmayer and Pommer at Alexander Korda's London Films, where Zuckmayer and Kahan remained; Pommer, along with Kortner, Lorre, and many others, moved on to California, where their friends, including von Sternberg, could sometimes help. Actors, even if they had to accept menial roles as waiters and croupiers, fared better than directors and technicians. The Pommers were forced to work in a porcelain factory while waiting for working papers. Hollander and his wife survived by shoplifting food, and his fortunes would not truly recover until Dietrich used him on *Angel* and *Destry Rides Again.*

As a non-Jew, Emil Jannings thrived under the Nazis. So did Leni Riefenstahl, whose first film as director, *The Blue Light,* premiered in Berlin on March 24, in the midst of the Jewish exodus. Von Sternberg saw a preview and apparently complimented her. In later years she inflated his praise into an offer to make her a star in Hollywood. "I've shaped Marlene into this wonderful creation," he supposedly told her, "and I'll do the same for you."[1] Like many of Riefenstahl's statements, this one defies logic. Since von Sternberg planned to set up a European company, he would not have offered her work in Hollywood. As to how Dietrich would have regarded this cuckoo in the nest, one can hardly imagine. Fortuitously for Riefenstahl, *The Blue Light* so impressed Hitler that he invited her to film the 1934 Nazi Party conference in Nuremberg, launching her on an entirely new career.

Von Sternberg returned to the United States on the *Europa* on March 22, 1933, his plan of independent German film production in ruins. The best he had been able to achieve was a meeting with Alfred Hugenberg. But since UFA's owner was shortly to be appointed minister of agriculture and economics in Hitler's first cabinet, he did not receive a sympathetic hearing.

Still a potent figure in Hollywood, and for the moment without studio affiliation, von Sternberg was mentioned in connection with a number of projects, including MGM's notoriously troubled *The Prizefighter and the Lady,* originally intended to be a Clark Gable vehicle. In a letter to Dietrich, he mentions this film, explaining that he had intended to direct it until Gable "got sick (corns or something like that) and I was lucky not to have made [it] since the film wouldn't have been worth it without him, there was nobody else for the part of the prizefighter, the others are just plain pansies."[2] MGM replaced Gable with real-life boxing champion Max Baer, hoping to make him a star as it had other athletes, such as swimmer Johnny Weissmuller. Baer performed respectably, but the film was so punch-drunk with rewrites and reshoots that, although Howard Hawks and W. S. Van Dyke did most of the work, the released version bore no director credit at all.

Other whispers linked von Sternberg to *Red Pawn*, the first screenplay by Ayn Rand. As Alisa Zinovyevna Rosenbaum, Rand had emigrated from Russia in 1926 and lived hand-to-mouth around the film business as a movie extra, script reader, and screenwriter, rising eventually to head RKO's costume department. Universal bought *Red Pawn* for $1,500 and then sold it to Paramount. One can see why people might have thought von Sternberg would direct it, since the story, set in Siberia during the Stalinist purges, deals in the extremes he relished. The heroine bluffs her way into a gulag to rescue her husband, a political prisoner, but falls in love with the commandant. Fleeing, the three are arrested by the secret police, who decide to execute the husband and ask the wife—shades of *Sophie's Choice*—to identify him. She points to the commandant, who meekly sacrifices himself so that the couple can live. Since his next film would have a Russian setting, von Sternberg may have rejected Rand's scenario on that account. It's also possible, albeit unlikely, that *Red Pawn* was the spark that ignited *The Scarlet Empress*. For whatever reason, the moment passed for *Red Pawn*, although it reappeared periodically in gossip about von Sternberg. In 1934 Louella Parsons announced that he would direct it and that Rand was rewriting the script in collaboration, improbably, with French playwright Jacques Deval, best known for the comedy *Tovaritch*. But nothing came of it. In any event, von Sternberg had become fixated on a film about Catherine the Great, with Dietrich as the notorious empress. "I have never started with so much material available," he wrote, "and I have never started with such a wonderful character."[3]

On May 9, 1933, he and Dietrich signed with Paramount for two more films together. Shooting on the first, entitled *Catherine the Great,* was set to begin in October. Dietrich's salary rose to $4,500 a week— $125,000 a picture—making her one of Hollywood's highest-paid stars. Shortly after signing she sailed for Europe, where she remained for the entire summer, mostly in Vienna. There, despite the presence of Rudy and Maria, she plunged into an affair with singer-actor Hans Jaray.

In Hollywood, the Paramount hierarchy fretted with second thoughts. The planned films represented a considerable gamble for the studio: both were costume pictures, which were notoriously expensive and, in the eyes of executives, out of date. Mae West's suggestive *She*

Done Him Wrong and *I'm No Angel* had proved to be the most profitable films of the company's history, all the more so for being cheap and quick to make. Increasingly, such productions would dominate its output.

Von Sternberg didn't intuit any of this, but even if he had, he would not have behaved differently. Far from pulling in his horns following the Berlin debacle, he thrust them out even further. Deciding it was time to have his own home, he bought a "distant meadow in the midst of an empty landscape, barren and forlorn"—a thirteen-acre ranch at Northridge, twenty miles from Hollywood, in the western San Fernando Valley, near where he shot *Shanghai Express*. He commissioned Richard Neutra to build a house to his occasionally eccentric requirements. These included three garages, one with a high ceiling to accommodate his Rolls-Royce, and a 1,000-square-foot living room overlooked by a balcony, where he could display his art collection. Not one for houseguests, he needed only a single bedroom, but with glass walls, the better to enjoy views of the empty valley and the sky. He also dictated that the bathroom doors be without locks. "There is always somebody in the bathroom," he explained to a puzzled Neutra, "threatening to commit suicide and blackmailing you, unless you can get in freely."[4] The requirement may not have been as eccentric as it seemed. In *Sunset Boulevard*, Erich von Stroheim removes all the locks in the home of Gloria Swanson, for the same reason.

When he requested a secluded studio area at the back of the house, plus space for his dogs, Neutra enclosed it within a curved concrete wall rimmed by a narrow lily pond. The press labeled the latter a moat and claimed that both it and the wall were electrified to repel intruders. This was untrue, as was the story of bulletproof window glass. In other respects, however, the house tested the limits of contemporary architectural taste. A raised front patio, suggesting a ship's bow, could seat 200 people. Neutra often incorporated a shallow reflecting pool into his designs, and von Sternberg agreed to such a pool, but on the roof, where it would cool the house in summer. "It worked very well," says author Ruth Beebe Hill, who lived in the house in the 1950s and 1960s. "Richard thought of everything."[5]

Moscow Rules

We're congenitally savage. . . . Sentimental barbarians! . . .
Our souls are still roaming the steppes, wildly—baying
with the wolves at the moon.

—Jacques Deval on the Russian national character in
Tovaritch

IN EVERY CATEGORY, HIS next film took von Sternberg into un-
charted territory. It was set in the eighteenth century—something he
had never attempted. It was also based on a historical character, Catherine II, empress of Russia from 1729 to 1796. It took place in a country
he had never visited. And at a time when the best Hollywood "A" film
cost $400,000, the budget would run to almost $1 million. On paper,
the expense appeared justified. Dietrich would be playing one of the
most sensational figures in European history. Catherine's diaries didn't
list all her lovers, but even if only half the claimants were lying, the
number remained impressive. (According to rumor—false—she died
while attempting sex with a stallion.) Add the monstrous vulgarity of
the Russian court, the lavishness of its ceremonies, and the slaughter of
whole families who threatened Catherine's rule over millions of illiterate, starving, and oppressed serfs, and one had a rich list of ingredients
for a spectacle.

The film is a dizzy balancing act, with von Sternberg walking the
tightrope between his love of décor for its own sake and the dangerously

nihilistic comic invention that almost compromised *Dishonored*. Manuel Komroff, prolific author of historical potboilers, including the popular lives of Marco Polo, Napoleon, and Paganini, extracted a story from Catherine's diaries, and this was further refined by Eleanor McGeary, von Sternberg's production secretary.

Determined to impose his conception of the characters on the cast and eradicate any individual interpretation, von Sternberg ordered the screenplay typed without punctuation marks or capital letters. Actors reading it would know *what* they were required to say, but not the emphasis. Nonplussed, Manny Cohen and Merritt Hurlburd, head of the writing department, called in young writer Joseph L. Mankiewicz, who had a reputation for imaginative solutions to script problems and was well regarded by the director. "All the departments are going crazy," they explained. Mankiewicz asked the director's permission to punctuate at least one copy. "I remonstrated that the property men, wardrobe people, and cutters had to read this," he recalled, "and they were used to reading English." Von Sternberg acquiesced, with the proviso that it not be shown to the cast. "I don't want any actor to come on stage with a preconceived notion of how to read the lines. I want them to learn the words. *I* will tell them how to *say* them." He also encouraged Mankiewicz to improve the speeches if he felt they needed it. This merely indicated how little importance von Sternberg assigned to dialogue, but Mankiewicz took it as flattery and spent considerable time researching Catherine's Russia. He was initially delighted when von Sternberg called to praise his revisions. "I must say that, while they told me you were a talented young man," he began, "I had no idea you were *that* talented." As Mankiewicz preened, he went on. "Your work is so good, I intend to use *several words* of it."[1] Mankiewicz never forgave the slur and thereafter lost no opportunity to mock von Sternberg.

The script presented Catherine as, to quote an intertitle, "the ill-famed Messalina of the North." To von Sternberg, the empress, like Messalina (whom he depicted in *I, Claudius*), was less a scheming courtesan who achieved power by climbing over the bodies of her lovers than a wanton destroyer whose motives for sexual conquest were trivial and perverse. Pique and passion rule Catherine's court. Problems of succession are settled in the bedroom, not the council chamber, and the antics of the courtiers, like their table manners, recall the nursery and the farmyard.

During writing and preparation, long letters to Dietrich in Vienna kept her up to date with his plans, most of which alarmed her. Early versions of the script depicted the future empress's household as "a miniature whorehouse." In these drafts, Alexei, the Russian prince sent to fetch Catherine and with whom she falls in love, is actually the homosexual lover of her future husband. Some versions ended with Catherine beheaded for refusing to renounce Alexei. Dietrich recognized his characteristic folie de grandeur. "Von Sternberg is getting too involved in this film," she supposedly told her daughter. "He sounds like he is planning to make an epic! Why not just shoot a beautiful picture of a tragic Russian empress and leave the big 'to-do' to Eisenstein?"[2] (The reference to Eisenstein is an obvious error: his *Ivan the Terrible* wasn't released until 1944.)

Partly because of her love affair with Jaray, but also because of an unwillingness to cooperate with von Sternberg's fantasies, Dietrich delayed her return to Hollywood, ignoring his increasingly frantic and groveling cables. If anything convinced her it was time to go back, it was a reference in an August 20 cable that Alexander Korda had announced his own film about Catherine, starring Elisabeth Bergner. Dietrich returned to Hollywood in September, ready to immerse herself in von Sternberg's most lavish creation.

Combining the rustic and the luxurious, Von Sternberg created a court at Paramount that was part dacha and part palace, with a hint of a church, suggesting the confused allegiances of Russia's rulers. Rather than construct solid sets for the interiors, Hans Dreier built movable "flats," faced to resemble walls of logs. He interspersed these with vast staircases and doors so huge they required a team of people to heave them open. Richard Kollorsz executed scores of icons and paintings, while Peter Ballbusch created regiments of statues. Smeared together from a mixture of epoxy resin and plaster of Paris, they drooped like figures of softened wax, sagging into poses emblematic of grief and despair.

Von Sternberg trampled over authenticity, originality, and expense. If ideas and even footage from earlier films fit his concept, he plundered them. An overhead tracking shot down the table at Catherine's wedding feast was copied from the Russian drama *The Eagle,* and he hired Louise Dresser, triumphantly vulgar as the dowager empress, to play the same part. Even a scene in which Dresser appeared in a male army uniform to vamp Rudolph Valentino was adapted for Dietrich. He also incensed Lubitsch by extracting a crowd scene from *The Patriot* and slotting it into the film. Von Sternberg simply shrugged off the protests, confident—erroneously, as it turned out—of the rightness of his vision and of the film's inevitable success. When Sam Jaffe, who played the mad Peter, rebelled against his autocratic direction, von Sternberg, citing the popularity of *Shanghai Express,* told him, "Don't you realize, I have five million disciples?" Jaffe reminded him that Christ made do with a dozen.

In this visual torrent, Dietrich is simply swept along, as much a victim of von Sternberg's invention as was Sophia Frederica of the Russian court. Of this film and the later *The Devil Is a Woman,* he wrote, "I completely subjugated my bird of paradise to my peculiar tendency to prove that a film might well be an art medium." Later, he said offhand, "I looked at her back, found a key, wound her up, and off she went." This comment reflects the film's vision of Dietrich/Catherine as a pet or a toy. From the opening scenes, Sophia as a child (played by Maria Sieber, identified in the credits simply as "Maria") is stifled by her Austrian family. "How often do I have to tell you that Sophia Frederica is no longer to play with toys?" her mother snaps to a servant in the film's first line. But Sophia's future consists of little except toys. Automation, ritual, and custom permeate the film, emphasizing the characters' predetermined actions and the mechanical life of the court. An intertitle even refers to the marriage of Sophia/Catherine as "a machine."

The scene in which a doctor calls to cure the child's unnamed spinal complaint reminds us that Sophia is always constrained. "We'll build her a nice harness," he says. Her nurse jokes, "What is he; a horse doctor?" then confides that he's also the public hangman, hurrying from Sophia to one of his "operations." Excited by the capacity to inflict life and death, the little girl, in another reminder of von Sternberg's belief in the implicit sadism of children, asks, "Can I become a hangman some day?" The question triggers a startling montage of the cruelty she is to encounter in Russia: nude women dragged from iron maidens, others tied face-up on torture wheels, still more burned at the stake, four at a time—all dissolving into the vision of a prisoner hanging head-down as the living clapper in a huge bell. This encapsulation of infantile eroticism, sadistic tendencies, and doomed destiny closes with a cynical visual pun—a cut from the dangling prisoner to Sophia laughing on a swing—that carries us smoothly into her young adulthood.

"Suddenly," announces an intertitle, "like a swift storm appeared the messenger of Russia." Sophia is to be whisked across Europe to marry her second cousin, the Grand Duke Peter of Russia, a man she has never met. Her escort is Count Alexei, played with sneering swash by John Lodge, who, in black furs, moustaches, and hussar's uniform, strikes exactly the script's balance of swagger and farce. Lodge, grandson of the right-wing senator Henry Cabot Lodge, was destined to enter Congress and then become governor of Connecticut, but he spent the 1930s as a mediocre movie actor. He was kept from stardom by black eyes that gave him a threatening, even villainous appearance—entirely suited to this part—and by a leaden delivery of his lines.

Eyeing his charge and idly patronizing her provincial family, Alexei rattles off a prepared spiel listing the attractions of her unseen fiancé. "He is the handsomest man in the Russian court; tall, and formed like a Greek god. A model in fashion and deportment which we all strive to follow. His eyes are like the blue sky, his hair the colour of ebony. He is stronger than a team of oxen, and sleepless because of his desire to receive you in his arms. And he can also read and write." Sophia wonders why Alexei has brought a portrait of the dowager empress and not of the prince, but all her doubts are expunged when Alexei seizes the occasion of their first overnight stop to sweep her into an embrace that envelops her in black sables.

"Why did you do that?" she asks as she emerges.

"Because I've fallen in love with you," he replies, "and now you must punish me." He hands her a whip, introducing her to the logic of the Russian court and of von Sternberg's own sexuality—that all pleasure requires an element of punishment. While Sophia ponders this, they are surprised by her mother. "What are you two doing down there?" she demands. Then, noting their guilty manner, says, "Never mind. I don't want to know."

An imperial eagle at the border with Russia reminds us of the director's obsession with birds and the film's fascination with sculpture. To pealing bells, Sophia glides into Moscow by sleigh and is met at the Peterhof by an aging and raucous harridan, the Empress Elizabeth. Receiving Sophia and her mother before another ornate white eagle, and flanked by her powdered dandy of a lover, Shuvolov (Hans von Twardowski), Elizabeth casually changes Sophia's name to Catherine ("more fitting") and directs a doctor to burrow under her clothing to check her fertility, diverting attention with chitchat and by presenting mother and daughter with the Order of Saint Catherine. ("May you both wear it in good health, and be careful it doesn't scratch you.") After the doctor surfaces from his examination, Catherine is whisked off to her first meeting with the man she is to marry.

Grinning maniacally and rolling his eyes, the Grand Duke Peter is a creeping white-haired idiot, trapped in a world of infantile sexuality. The real Peter died at age thirty-four, after reigning less than a year. Though it appears exaggerated, the performance by Sam Jaffe, only ten years older than the original, is close to life. Never without his *équipe* of deformed African servant, black boy with wolfhounds, tutor carrying a sorrowful icon, and the corrupt Princess Elizabeth (Ruthelma Stevens), who is responsible for his "entertainment," Peter is von Sternberg's most cynical combination of cripple and clown, the predecessor of Charles Laughton's Claudius. Peter's fascination with toy soldiers extends to drilling his Hessian mercenaries indoors on wet days. He marches them into Catherine's boudoir with muskets drawn and aimed, before reluctantly calling them off as she disarms him symbolically by impaling her scarf on his sword. Peter's phallic inefficiency, unsubtly suggested in this shot, has its most apt symbol when a discussion between Catherine and the Dowager Empress is interrupted by the spike of an auger weaving out of the eye of a wall painting. "That must be Peter," the empress remarks without surprise, aware that his ability barely extends to spying on his wife, with little hope of consummating the marriage.

Until this production, every von Sternberg film had turned on a love story, but the relationship of Catherine and Alexei hardly deserves the term. It's barely more than a detail, used to add color to scenes of spectacle. At her wedding, Catherine stares hopelessly at her lover through a misting veil while her breath rhythmically excites the chiffon that envelops her. Chants, incense, and candlelight intensify the atmosphere. Authentic Russian choral music would have added to the effect, but von Sternberg preferred a more conventionally European setting of *Kamennoi-ostrow,* a popular piece by mid-nineteenth-century Russian composer Anton Rubinstein.

Two later sequences, almost identical in effect, decisively downgrade the relationship between Catherine and Alexei, making him no more than another toy. In the first, Catherine is attending the old empress, who tells her to blow out the candles and let in her lover, who's waiting at the foot of a secret staircase. To Catherine's horror, it's Alexei. After admitting him, she walks slowly up the stairs, light and shadow playing over her face, signifying mingled love and hate. Her revenge comes after she is crowned empress. Sending for Alexei, she requires him to admit *her* lover, Orloff. A close-up of her awaiting him, cuddled in bed and wreathed in veils, her expression cryptic and hard, recalls the enigma of her earlier walk up the stairs.

With no sentimental story to hold their interest, audiences were left with nothing to enjoy but the spectacle and von Sternberg's sarcastic vision of royalty. Everything in the film is either a joke or an act of chance. Disillusioned with Alexei, Catherine throws his gift of a portrait miniature out her window. In an elegantly contrived shot, the pendant clings to the frozen limbs of a tree, slipping from branch to branch, until it buries itself in the snow. Repenting, she descends to retrieve it and is arrested by a guard who fails to recognize her. He seems determined to consider her a servant girl, and she submits to him and to the game, commenting only, "Well, lieutenant, you are fortunate—very fortunate." A child is born some months later, but congratulations on this "historic event" are turned aside by a courtier's comment: "I'm certain history was far from her mind at the time." When a priest remarks, "I'm afraid you don't know Russia, my child," Catherine replies with some justice, "Father, I'm taking lessons as fast as I can."

Infantile emotions, the motif of toys, the tinkle of a music box that accompanies many scenes, and the use of Mendelssohn's *Midsummer Night's Dream* overture as background music all evoke a playroom rather than a court. Like all his films in which children appear, this one holds up a distorting mirror of the "seven bad years" of von Sternberg's childhood. Even the scale of Dreier's décor suggests this. The enormous doors, with locks above head height, and Ballbusch's larger-than-life statues, contorted and tortured, embody a desire to inflict revenge and retribution on the adult world. In the pantomime climax, Catherine, in the white uniform of hussars, leads a cavalry charge through the palace to Wagner's "Ride of the Valkyries." As her loyal servant strangles Peter behind a looming black cross, her men hoist her on their shoulders and parade her, preceded by one of Ballbusch's twisted, crucified Christs. This spurious image of good rising out of evil is the final joke on the people she leads, who are soon to discover she's as dissolute as her idiot husband.

Shooting was long, difficult, expensive, and punishing on everyone, particularly Dietrich, who noticed an increasing tendency on von Sternberg's part to bully her in front of the cast and crew. The film was still in production when Korda's *Catherine the Great,* directed by Paul Czinner and starring his wife, Elisabeth Bergner, as Catherine and Douglas Fairbanks Jr. as Peter, opened in February 1934 to enthusiastic reviews. At Lubitsch's suggestion, von Sternberg retitled his film *Her Regiment of Lovers* and then *The Scarlet Empress.* Paramount kept it on the shelf for another eight months, hoping to outlast the competition, but when it finally screened in September, the reaction was hostile. Nobody wanted extravagance in a country still obsessed with the Depression. Most critics wrote off the witty visual adventure as self-indulgent nonsense. Advertising played down the period element. Posters showed Dietrich wearing historically neutral gowns that could have come from her own wardrobe, accompanied by texts murmuring vaguely, "Her Whisper Was a Command to Love." Nothing helped, however. Von Sternberg's version of Russian history was no less fantastic and extravagant than that created a few years later by Eisenstein in *Ivan the Terrible.* But Eisenstein was rated an artist, whereas the cultural community belittled von Sternberg. In their eyes, not only had he failed to bite the hand of Mammon; he had kissed it and, worse, become rich on the money it dispensed.

As usual, those outside the film industry were mistaken. Far from being Hollywood's darling, von Sternberg was on the skids. In a series of unusually frank interviews, he even acknowledged *Empress* as a failure. "I got too close to my work," he admitted. "I lost perspective. I turned out a thing of beauty—even my most severe critics granted that—but I permitted it to get out of balance, and in so doing I lost my audience contact." He told another reporter, "I knew it was a bad picture long before the critics ever saw it. I wanted to make it over, but that was financially impractical." Left-wing British critic Paul Rotha conceded that the film "moves with tremendous pace of visuals and a clashing of bells and fanfares of trumpets. . . . If you can stomach the gross over-acting, the monstrous leering background and the superficial direction, you may find moments of interest, even though it requires a mounted Dietrich leading a cavalry charge up the palace staircase to the accompaniment of the Valkyrie Ride to stir you." Even Rotha, however, could not entirely dismiss its bravura and sheer delight in excess. "You cannot help laughing at von Sternberg," he wrote, "for his undisguised show-man's tactics, his fake artistic clap-trap and his succulent debaucheries of photographic slickness. . . . Experience has taught him extravagance. Not one candle but a thousand; not one honest-to-god rape but a skilfully staged scene of perversion. He has reached that delectable state of ecstasy when he can throw away a twenty-five hundred dollar shot on a two-foot wipe and never move a muscle."[3]

It was left to the U.S. press, egged on by the studios, to deliver the coup de grâce—none more deadly than that in *Vanity Fair*. "Sternberg," it charged, "traded his open style for fancy play, chiefly upon the legs in silk and buttocks in lace, of Dietrich, of whom he has made a Paramount slut. By his own token, Sternberg is a man of meditation as well as a man of action, but instead of contemplating the navel of Buddha, his umbilical perseverance is fixed on the navel of Venus."

The End of the Affair

For two full hours now I've been sitting in the Café Bauer,
If you're no longer interested, then tell me to my face!
My cream won't turn sour just because of that.
To hell with you, my sweetheart.
So what! Let's call it quits.
You mustn't think that I'll miss you.

—Erich Kastner, *Der Abschiedbrief* (The Farewell Letter)

ONCE IT WAS FURNISHED to his satisfaction, von Sternberg invited Marlene, Maria, and Rudy Sieber to visit the Neutra house. With the German market now barred to all films with Jewish artists, Paramount closed its Joinville dubbing facility. Sieber moved permanently to the United States—though not, Marlene explained, with any thought of sharing her life, which was too full to accommodate a husband. Rather, he and Tami would live in New York until granted U.S. citizenship. Von Sternberg hoped Dietrich might move into the new house with him, but she derided its isolation and lack of privacy. How could she live there, so far from her friends? And did he really expect her to give up all her lovers and devote herself entirely to him? The idea was really too silly. From that moment, his interest in the house dwindled. Expansion plans were shelved, including a swimming pool designed by sculptor Isamu Noguchi, who was sufficiently proud of the project to exhibit a bronze model in a number of subsequent shows. Indifferent to her mentor's sensibilities, Dietrich later bought land nearby and established Rudy there on his own chicken farm.

The failure of *The Scarlet Empress* was as damaging to von Sternberg's career as had been the shelving of *A Woman of the Sea*. This, combined with his growing estrangement from Dietrich (who realized, after unsubtle hints from the studio, that her future was no longer dependent on his), further eroded his reputation at Paramount. Cohen and Lubitsch, shortly to become the studio's production manager, were poised to oust him the moment his contract expired. Although he and Lubitsch remained superficially friendly and sometimes played chess at the Hollywood Club on Cherokee Avenue, Lubitsch in his role as an executive was a different man. "There was a time," he told the press, "when directors thought that by making silly camera angles and dissolves they were geniuses. They didn't know how to tell a story and they covered up with pseudo-artistry. . . . No man is a genius unless he can deliver honest entertainment."[1]

There remained one last film on von Sternberg's contract and thus one chance to redeem himself. A shrewder operator would have proposed a contemporary sex comedy, with gorgeous gowns for Dietrich and luscious photography—the kind of film that Lubitsch and Frank Borzage would make a few years later when they directed her in *Angel* and *Desire,* respectively. After such a film's inevitable box-office success, Paramount would have pleaded with him to sign a new deal. Instead, von Sternberg perversely began work on a final film with the star that was more ambitious, personal, and prodigal than anything he had previously attempted. Aware that, if given enough rope, he would hang himself, Lubitsch withdrew all executive supervision and ceded complete creative control, a trap into which von Sternberg fatalistically, and perhaps intentionally, fell.

The Spain in which von Sternberg set his last film with Dietrich was a country he had never visited and that no Spaniard would recognize. Pierre Louys, who wrote *La Femme et le Pantin* (The Woman and the Puppet), the 1898 novel that inspired the film, was French; its star was German; and the music was Russian, based on Rimsky-Korsakov's *Capriccio Espagnol,* the film's working title. This is the Spain of operetta and melodrama, reflecting its director's preferred locale and era: Vienna at the end of the nineteenth century.

Of the principal players, only Cesar Romero, born in the United States of Cuban parents, was remotely Spanish, and even his casting was accidental. Lanky Joel McCrea originally took the role of Antonio Galvan, a revolutionary and former member of the *Guardia Civil* who infiltrates Seville under cover of carnival. To assert his domination of McCrea, von Sternberg demanded thirty-five takes of his first shot, in which Galvan sits in a café and orders coffee. After each, the director announced, "That's not the way to ask for coffee. You are not getting it over." The next day he informed McCrea that he had viewed the rushes and couldn't do anything with them. McCrea replied, "That's fortunate, because I don't want to do anything with you," and left the set. Dietrich tried to calm things, telling McCrea, "He speaks to me in German and calls me an old cow. Ignore him." But the actor was adamant.

In urgent need of a tall, slim replacement who could fit into the costumes, Paramount approached Universal about borrowing Romero. Von Sternberg ignored the actor when he arrived on the set, ordering an assistant, "Grab him and put a costume on him." After that, he sat Romero at a table, gave him some lines to read, peered through the camera, and said, "OK. You'll do. Fine."

Since he was gay and, moreover, had started his career as an exhibition dancer, Romero excited only contempt in Dietrich, who dismissed him as "that gigolo dance teacher." He felt more compassion for her, since the director bullied her unmercifully. "He used to bawl her out by the hour in German," Romero recalled. "Marlene would cry. And cry. She had a German maid who used to stand on the sidelines. I used to watch the maid's reactions to what Von Sternberg was saying. He must have been saying terrible things to her because the maid used to start back in horror and clasp her hands to her face. He was rather sadistic. He would make you do things over and over again."[2]

To the satisfaction of cast and crew, these methods sometimes backfired. The public address system was now a feature of every set, and von Sternberg's booming directions reached the furthest corners of the soundstage. After demanding a hundred takes of a scene in which

Romero walked down a staircase and said, simply, "Yes," he announced over his loudspeaker, "I now call upon Mr. Romero to say 'Yes' for the one hundred and first time." Fed up, Romero said, "No," and left the set, accompanied by laughter and applause. He knew that von Sternberg would have to abase himself and lure him back or find yet another actor with the same measurements.

Adaptation of the Louys novel is credited to John Dos Passos. An innovative modernist novelist with intimate knowledge of postrevolutionary Spain, he had never written a screenplay, nor would he again. In fact, it's unlikely that he wrote this one, since preproduction coincided with an attack of his chronic rheumatic fever. As Dos Passos explained in a long, facetious letter to his friend Ernest Hemingway, had he not needed the money, he would have turned down the job, but when Paramount called, he embarked on the zigzag transcontinental flight to California, becoming progressively drunker and vomiting in his hat between refueling stops. On arrival in Los Angeles, he claimed to have staggered off the plane, fallen at the director's feet, and, rising, said, "I declare—Joe Stern of Brooklyn!" If true, this would not have endeared him to the director.

Von Sternberg installed Dos Passos in his hotel and diligently visited him every day to discuss the screenplay, but the writer was mostly too ill to think coherently, and anything he wrote was probably discarded. Certainly nothing in the film calls to mind the author of *Three Soldiers* and *Manhattan Transfer*. Sam Winston had a greater hand in the script, along with the director and two newcomers to screenwriting, David Hertz and Oran Schee. The literary content held little interest for von Sternberg. Of all his films, this one has the flimsiest plot—essentially a shuffling together of Louys's fable and the plot of Mérimée's *Carmen*.

If *The Scarlet Empress* had been a "relentless excursion into style," this was even more so, since von Sternberg used it to introduce, for the first and last time, his most controversial change to studio technique. One awed journalist wrote:

> The sets of *Capriccio Espagnol* reveal a scarcity of color that is startling in its effect. . . . Predominantly gray are all the sets of this feature, with only an occasional splash of color. Von Sternberg

. . . believes that the use of much color on sets gives false values which must be modified through lighting. Hence he is trying to achieve more lifelike and artistic effects through the planned use of tones of gray. At balconied windows hung vines von Sternberg had sprayed with a "half-white" [aluminum] paint, but the occasional plant was left in its natural state. . . . The effect of this set, with its one-way lighting casting only "natural" shadows, and its predominantly gray tones, relieved sparsely by a bright awning, a flower, or Marlene's red and blue costume, is most unusual. The idea is carried out even in the geese, which are white and gray geese. . . . Von Sternberg, who probably spends as much time lighting his sets as he does photographing them, seems to be enjoying himself and his idea. There is often a grin of satisfaction on his face as he rides the crane.[3]

Reasons for the grin are not hard to find. One could debate the artistic value of shooting on monochrome sets, but there was no denying the bonus in publicity. In the corridors of Paramount, nobody was talking about anything else.

After the credits, an intertitle announces, "The action of the story takes place during a carnival week in the south of Spain, at the beginning of the century." The impossibility of maintaining order during carnival is dramatized by the first shots of Seville's crowded streets. Balloons, a motif in the film, float up from the crowd as a picador mocks a man dressed as a bull, men masked as pigs and roosters caper among the streamers, and the disguised Galvan passes calmly through the mob. Intrigued by the crowd around her carriage, he meets and is enchanted by the beautiful Concha Perez. When he follows and tries to enter her house, he is turned aside by, in one of von Sternberg's better visual jokes, a jack-in-the-box containing a note—toy, message, and detumescent phallic symbol all in one.

Waiting at a café for his evening assignation, Galvan meets his old commander Don Pasquale Castellar (Lionel Atwill) and asks if he knows Concha. Pasquale, in a series of flashbacks, reveals that they were once lovers—a relationship that cost him his fortune and his commission. Von Sternberg fills many scenes with images of captivity: cages, a goldfish Concha displays in a tiny glass bowl, and, in a clever extension of the symbol, a cabaret decorated with huge plaster fish and storks— classic victims and predators. Even the familiar nets that drape the café have a new and sinister significance, although the most powerful symbol of imprisonment is the carnival itself, with its shifting reality of costumes and masks that subjugates all of them to its spell.

Costume carries as much of the film's story as dialogue. For the duel in the forest between Antonio and Don Pasquale, Concha appears in black lace, a sheet of rain behind her to accentuate the depths of her veil. After Pasquale allows himself to be wounded, she visits him in the hospital, a figure of mourning like the mutes at a Spanish funeral. White nets around the bed and the bare white walls are a visual accusation, suggesting a change of character that makes her abandon Antonio at the border in favor of her old lover. Does she do so to bleed him of more money? Von Sternberg says no; she returns out of love. But perhaps her love feeds off vanity and the lust to dominate. Joseph Breen, Catholic head of the Hollywood self-censorship office, protested at Concha's going unpunished. He suggested a new ending in which she discovers Pasquale blinded in the hospital and begs forgiveness. He gropes his way to the sound of her voice, only to strangle her, whereupon the guards drag him away. Fortunately, Breen didn't insist.

The Devil Is a Woman raises the question of whether a film can be too beautiful. Much action occurs so far in the background that we barely notice it. Instead, our eye is seduced by palm fronds waving in a mist; flags, sails, and the tips of masts stirring in a mere glimpse of a harbor scene; balloons floating up from a parade in the street. The sense of a framed still life is replaced by that of a window in which the border defines but does not enclose the action. Even when significant detail is isolated in the middle distance, the foreground appears to spread out and disappear, still living, beyond the frame. Aluminum paint sprayed on dresses and backgrounds blends every aspect of his setups into a skillfully graded arrangement of light. It was Dietrich's favorite among her von Sternberg films, and the last word on the director's visual style—perhaps on Hollywood photographic style as a whole—but one achieved at the highest cost to his career. It's also the first film in which he is credited as director of photography (with Lucien Ballard). To do so, he had to be accorded membership in the prestigious American Society of Cinematographers—an honor not begrudged by any cameraman who had worked with him.

As noted, the incidental music (and the film's original title) is Rimsky-Korsakov's *Capriccio Espagnol*, although before making this choice, Dietrich had approached Kurt Weill, composer of *The Three-penny Opera*, to produce an original score. She had met him in Paris in 1933, during one of her excursions with Hans Jaray, and asked him to set Erich Kastner's poem *Der Abschiedbrief* (The Farewell Letter) to music for her. Shortly after, she wired him, "Would it interest you to come here and work with von Sternberg and me on a musical film length about six months stop Please let me know if you want and can stop Paramount will take care of the rest Fondly yours Marlene."[4] Weill welcomed the offer, since, with the banning of U.S. films from German cinemas, his ten-year contract with Universal had just lapsed. However, the project came to nothing. The only music heard in the film is by Rimsky-Korsakov, with an additional song by Ralph Rainger and Leo Robin.

The mayor of Seville, Don Paquito, was played by Edward Everett Horton with his usual harassed verve. He queried whether someone like him—self-evidently homosexual and not even remotely Hispanic—would be the mayor of a Spanish city, and von Sternberg assured him that parts of Spain had been settled by people from northern Europe, so his presence was entirely authentic. Visitors to the set included Charles Laughton, who donned a mask and participated in one of the carnival scenes. He was just about to conclude a Hollywood stint on the high point of *Mutiny on the Bounty* before returning to Britain, where he was under contract to Alexander Korda. That Laughton, Korda, and von Sternberg would be working together in only a few years' time, with Dietrich intimately involved, never occurred to any of them. Nor would they have imagined that such a collaboration would end in disaster.

Taking a gloomy satisfaction at having engineered his own downfall, von Sternberg wrote of *The Devil Is a Woman*, "I paid a final tribute to the lady I had seen lean against the wings of a Berlin stage." He saw the film as encapsulating their relationship. The fragmented nature of the Concha-Pasquale affair, the references to money, and Pasquale's attempts to retain her love by guaranteeing her material comfort also relate to von Sternberg's involvement in Dietrich's career. Most of all, the sense of frustration, self-criticism, and resigned melancholy are comments on a collaboration that inspired him, at the cost of his independence. Atwill is not merely physically similar to von Sternberg (as Warner Oland, Stuart Holmes, and Adolphe Menjou had been); he is an exact replica down to the moustache, the impeccable clothing, and even the style of speech. Her daughter's memoir claims that Dietrich denied any resemblance, but even at the time, journalists noted it. Wood Soames, writing in *Screen and Radio Weekly*, remarked, "Von Sternberg, I might explain, looks not unlike the character portrayed by Lionel Atwill in the film, and those who hunt for symbols regard it as somewhat autobiographical."

This, von Sternberg's most beautiful film, is also the most vicious, an act of revenge on the woman who dominated his life. Its characters are at physical and emotional war. Flying objects fill the air. Dietrich's first close-up is engineered when Antonio, sniping at balloons with his slingshot, pops those around her coach window, but his next missile is diverted with a thrown kiss. When Concha and Pasquale meet for the second time, a worker in the cigarette factory flicks a ball of paper into the supervisor's eye. After her song in the cabaret, Concha is bombarded with hats, one of which strikes Pasquale, and her kisses are neutralized by the cigar smoke another watcher puffs in his face. This combative theme culminates in the duel that Pasquale feels he must fight with Antonio.

Throughout the film, Dietrich is swathed in white lace, with vast white hats or mantillas covering her face, dresses whose geometric contrasts of black and white decorate her body, as a curious scroll of hornlike curls ornaments her forehead. As a result, one doesn't immediately realize the deficiencies in Dietrich's performance. Most beautiful in repose, her face is allowed to become a stage across which a succession of grimaces, frowns, and moues pursue one another, apparently at random. However, as in *Shanghai Express,* von Sternberg appears unconcerned with the failure of her behavior to even approximate that of real life. For his subject to be beautiful is, as always, more than enough.

As part of the promotion of *The Devil Is a Woman,* von Sternberg helped assemble and took directorial credit for a ten-minute short, *The Fashion Side of Hollywood,* which edited together a series of lighting and costume tests featuring Dietrich, Joan Bennett, Carole Lombard, Claudette Colbert, Mae West, and George Raft. Expressionless, Dietrich parades before the camera in Concha's costumes or slouches in a chair while a narration by Kathleen Howard—character actress, magazine editor, and former opera singer—heaps praise on costumer Travis Banton in a reverberant mezzo.

The Devil Is a Woman hammered the last nails in the coffin of von Sternberg's Hollywood reputation. On February 6, 1935, Lubitsch took over as production manager. He interfered little, except to change the title to *The Devil Is a Woman.* (*Capriccio Espagnol* would puzzle U.S. audiences, he said; they wouldn't even know how to pronounce it.) In March 1935 the film previewed in Los Angeles. Shortly after, Paramount issued a dismissive press statement, which was paraphrased in a newspaper report: "Following the preview the other evening of *The Devil Is a Woman,* the studio indicated that no attempt would be made to hold Mr. von Sternberg and that, in spite of certain financial loss, the film would be released in its present form, without retakes. The temper of the new production regime was described as favouring the immediate departure of the director, with the whole thing charged off to experience."[5] Von Sternberg's contract was not renewed. He was told unequivocally that his Paramount days were ended. In his words, he was "liquidated by Lubitsch."

Put into general release in May, the film won unexpectedly good reviews in the major papers. "This column regards *The Devil Is a Woman* as the best product of the Dietrich/von Sternberg alliance since *The Blue Angel,*" commented Andre Sennwald in the *New York Times.* "It is not hard to understand why Hollywood expressed such violent distaste for Josef von Sternberg's new film. For the talented director-photographer . . . makes a cruel and mocking assault upon the romantic sex motif which Hollywood has been gravely celebrating all these years. His success is also his failure. Having composed one of the most sophisticated films ever produced in America, he makes it inevitable that it will be misunderstood and disliked by nine-tenths of the normal motion picture public."[6] As Sennwald foretold, the film pleased only the carriage trade. Dan Thomas, whose column was syndicated to hundreds of regional papers, confirmed its failure in "the nabes," as neighborhood theaters were known. "Frankly, I think the title should be changed to 'The Devil is von Sternberg,'" he wrote. "During the production of this film, von Sternberg was so intent upon keeping the spotlight focused upon Marlene and himself that he forgot his audiences entirely."

Distribution outside the United States began after the summer holidays, the doldrums in terms of moviegoing, and almost immediately elicited a protest from the Spanish government. In October, Madrid complained officially that the film parodied Spain and "insulted the Spanish armed forces." The Spanish embassy informed a puzzled Paramount that "the film was refused admission to Spain when it was learned at a preview that it contained a scene of a civil guard drinking in a public café,"[7] presumably a reference to the conversation between Antonio and Don Pasquale. The following day, Spain's Foreign Ministry warned that if *The Devil Is a Woman* were not withdrawn, it would bar all Paramount films from Spain. Anxious to safeguard a trade agreement under negotiation throughout 1935, the U.S. State Department petitioned Paramount for a token of contrition. Adolph Zukor feebly agreed to suppress the film if the objections were "on sound grounds," adding, without conscious irony, "we do not make pictures with any idea of depicting real life."[8] In November he promised it would be withdrawn "after contracts with its distributors were satisfied"—which meant, effectively, when the maximum profit had been extracted. This didn't satisfy the Spanish, so a formal auto-da-fé was arranged in Washington, and a so-called master print was burned in the presence of the Spanish ambassador. Significantly, that week the trade bill was reported to be under discussion by the Spanish cabinet.

Ironies abound in the subsequent history of *The Devil Is a Woman*. Despite the scorn of Paramount, the 1935 Venice Film Festival awarded the film first prize for cinematography and acknowledged von Sternberg's role in lighting by presenting it jointly to him and lighting cameraman Lucien Ballard.

Civil war broke out in Spain early in 1936, so no trade agreement was ever negotiated. Responding to the headlines, Paramount immediately began production of films about the war, such as James Hogan's *Last Train from Madrid,* which used von Sternberg's leftover sets. And although it was regarded for many years as a total loss, the film was restored to circulation when Dietrich revealed that she had held back a private print, since she regarded it as the film that showed her at her most beautiful.

Paramount, though anxious to be rid of von Sternberg, was equally keen to retain Dietrich, to whom it offered a new contract. But before the release of *The Devil Is a Woman,* von Sternberg announced their split. "Miss Dietrich and I have progressed as far as possible together," he announced. "My being with her will not help her or me. If we continued, we would get into a pattern that would be harmful to both of us." Dietrich corroborated this. "I didn't leave von Sternberg," she said. "He left me. That's very important. He decided not to work with me any more, and I was not very happy about that."[9] Maria Riva agrees that the announcement came as a complete shock to her mother—but what other decision was possible? A notorious 1937 advertisement, inserted in the trade papers by rebellious exhibitors, would brand Dietrich, along with Katharine Hepburn, Fred Astaire, Mae West, and Greta Garbo, as box-office poison, but von Sternberg was even more toxic to her career. Any future collaborations could take place only if she forced him on the studio—which, given their joint unpopularity, would be professional suicide. Von Sternberg remembered how Mauritz Stiller, Garbo's mentor, had hung around too long, an impediment to her love life and an embarrassment to the industry. Stiller had been unceremoniously deported to Sweden, where he met an early death. Von Sternberg decided it was better to jump before he was pushed.

Cardboard Continental

To go wrong in one's own way is better than to go right in someone else's.

—Fyodor Dostoyevsky, *Crime and Punishment*

WITH TIME ON HIS hands, von Sternberg took refuge in art, organizing an exhibition of his collection at the Los Angeles County Museum. Urged by Preston Harrison, a prominent collector and donor, the museum devoted most of its wall space in June and July to forty-three oils, fifty-five watercolors and drawings, and thirty-five sculptures. Along with works by Modigliani, Picasso, Pascin, Kandinsky, Nolde, Vlaminck, Dix, Grosz, Archipenko, and Kokoschka, the show included most of the self-portraits first displayed on the set during the making of *Blonde Venus,* plus work by von Sternberg protégés Peter Ballbusch and Peter Kollorsz and a painting of his own so fresh that it was initially too wet to hang. The *Los Angeles Times* reviewed the show respectfully, remarking that von Sternberg's choice of art, like his films, could "aggravate some people" but that both showed "the same flair for bold adventuring in the realm of plastic form, color and movement."[1]

Meanwhile, Ben Schulberg once again threw him a lifeline. Ousted from Paramount, Schulberg had signed a production deal in April 1935 with Columbia, the tightfisted but energetic organization of Harry Cohn. At the height of the furor over *The Devil Is a Woman,* Schulberg offered von Sternberg a two-picture contract. He accepted eagerly, though not without a sense of having come down in the world.

As soon as he arrived at Columbia, von Sternberg's fortunes became linked to those of another European émigré, Peter Lorre, whom Cohn had also signed to a two-film deal. The Hungarian-born actor bore a reputation from his theater work in Germany with Bertolt Brecht and Kurt Weill and his starring role as the pedophile in Fritz Lang's *M.* He had just appeared in Alfred Hitchcock's *The Man Who Knew Too Much* in London and was anxious to establish himself in Hollywood. The ideal role, he decided, would be the young killer Raskolnikov in Dostoyevsky's *Crime and Punishment.* It is the story of a brilliant student who, inspired by Napoleon and driven by the conviction that a superior will transcends morality, murders an old pawnbroker and her sister. Although he gets away with it, his own remorse, his love for the saintly prostitute Sonya, and the cunning of Porfiry, a policeman investigating the crime, lead him to confess. He is sentenced to seven years' imprisonment in Siberia. Sonya accompanies him, holding out some hope for redemption.

Cohn had never heard of the book, so Lorre prepared a simplified summary for his benefit. After reading it, Cohn's first question was, inevitably, "Can we get the rights?" He was delighted to hear that Dostoyevsky's work was in the public domain. Shrewdly, Cohn offered Lorre both carrot and stick. At MGM, Karl Freund was remaking the horror story *The Hands of Orlac.* Lorre had been proposed, probably by Freund, to play the doctor who, catastrophically, replaces the severed hands of a pianist with those of a murderer. If Lorre agreed to be lent to MGM for the Orlac film, now called *Mad Love,* Cohn promised to produce *Crime and Punishment,* with von Sternberg directing. It must have seemed as good a deal to Lorre as it did to Cohn. The actor would be launched in the U.S. cinema in a classic text directed by a major name, and Cohn, by loaning Lorre to the wealthy MGM at a multiple of his salary, would profit substantially.

Lorre was ill throughout the production with the chronic respiratory diseases that would lead to his addiction to heroin. A former student of Sigmund Freud, he strove to create a psychologically accurate portrait of Raskolnikov to rival his role as the child murderer in Lang's

M. Von Sternberg, however, recognized the novel's deficiencies as material for a commercial film. "At best it can be no more than a film about a detective and a criminal," he said, "no more related to the true text of the novel than the corner of Sunset Boulevard and Gower is related to the Russian environment." The only possible approach was to shoot it as a detective story, but one in which the murderer is known from the moment of the crime. A connoisseur of ironies would have noted that while von Sternberg knuckled down to a B-budget murder movie at Columbia, back at Paramount, Dietrich was also playing a criminal—in her case, a seductive jewel thief—opposite Gary Cooper and directed by Frank Borzage in the film initially called *The Pearl Necklace* but now renamed *Desire*.

Sam Lauren, who had worked on *Blonde Venus,* rewrote Joseph Anthony's screenplay when it was decided that the film would be cheaper to shoot if it were updated. The action no longer takes place in nineteenth-century St. Petersburg but, as a prologue warns us, in "any time [and] anyplace where human hearts respond to love and hate, pity and terror." A cast was assembled, consistent with the film's starvation budget. Columbia contract players joined inexpensive freelancers—including, von Sternberg claims, "some who have made the jump to the screen from the trampoline of a mattress." Edward Arnold played Porfiry. Jovial, but with an edge of menace, he specialized in ruthless tycoons who mellow in the last reel, a role he would hone in Frank Capra films such as *You Can't Take It with You* and *Meet John Doe*. Marian Marsh was Sonya. A pretty blonde, she had been Trilby in the Barrymore *Svengali*. As Harry Cohn habitually bedded the blondes in his employ, she was presumably the target of von Sternberg's "mattress" gibe, although the Garboesque Tala Birell was also a candidate.

In a piece of notably eccentric casting, Mrs. Patrick Campbell played the pawnbroker. The darling of London's Edwardian stage, Stella Campbell was deeply admired by George Bernard Shaw, who wrote the role of Eliza Doolittle in *Pygmalion* for her. At the end of her career she supported herself by selling off Shaw's love letters and making the occasional regal appearance on Broadway and in movies, always with her Pekingese Moonbeam. She inspired George S. Kaufman and Edna Ferber to create aging stage star Carlotta Vance in *Dinner at Eight,* played memorably in the film version by Marie Dressler. Baffled by her presence in *Crime and Punishment,* Campbell had read neither script nor novel, but she busked her role with aplomb, bantering with von Sternberg in between takes, to his confusion. Used to being either feared or loathed, he couldn't deal with amused indifference.

Despite the efforts of cinematographer Lucien Ballard and Stephen Goosson (credited as set decorator rather than designer, since the budget didn't allow for new décor), we never forget that, after Lorre and Marsh depart, these staircases and alleyways will echo to the yells and thumps of the studio's biggest moneymakers—the Three Stooges. Statues, icons, and paintings help, and von Sternberg manages some coups, such as Lorre slumping forward to reveal a portrait of his hero Napoleon, which he strikingly resembles. Edward Arnold fails to get the measure of Porfiry. Aside from narrowing his eyes to indicate suspicion, he captures none of the character's sly intelligence, although he and Lorre play effectively against each other in a scene in which the detective interrogates a suspect in Raskolnikov's presence, pressing the real killer for his opinion as to whether the trembling innocent could have committed the murder. Marian Marsh benefits from von Sternberg's lighting skill and later wrote that he had told her he planned to make her "another Dietrich," but it would take more than the shadow of a beret slanting across her face to evoke virtue shining through despair.

As if to show contrition for his excesses on *The Scarlet Empress* and *The Devil Is a Woman,* von Sternberg involved himself in every aspect of the production. To the surprise of his shopworn cast, he held two days of script readings and rehearsals, and once shooting began, he didn't flinch from the most menial tasks, moving equipment and touching up sets with a paintbrush. In the time saved, he put the bewildered actors through numerous takes, though without noticeable improvement, a fact that began to erode his temper. One of the busiest members of the cast, Arnold was so tired on his first day that he yawned in the director's face. A troubled Lorre asked him, "Did you tell him you were sorry?"

"No, why should I?" Arnold demanded. "It was nothing personal. I'm dead tired. I worked all night on retakes at Universal."

"Well, if you don't do something about it," said Lorre, "he'll take it out on the rest of us."

Their relationship didn't improve. In his memoirs, Arnold called von Sternberg "a raper of egos . . . who crushes the individuality of those he directs in pictures."[2]

Crime and Punishment ended shooting in October, five days under the thirty allocated, but the surprise is that it took that long. A B-movie sense of one-size-fits-all pervades not only the sets but also the costumes and even the cast, down to the incongruously well-fed urchins to whom Raskolnikov gives money. Lorre mugs willingly, screwing up his mouth or reeling back in horror, but it would take a far greater actor to convey a rational will struggling to overcome an inborn sense of guilt. Only a few moments come to life, among them the opening sequence of Raskolnikov being singled out from the college graduating class. Ballard and von Sternberg light the faculty and students half-shadowed against side-lit white walls, with Lorre, in a favorite effect, stepping from among the silhouettes into the light of approbation. Lorre and Marsh also manage an atmospheric scene on a rickety wooden staircase above the river. As they desultorily discuss their predicament, the water lies below them, still and black, an invitation to death. The staircase, draped with nets, and the 1930s clothing worn by both characters give an erotic languor that one associates with film noir. Nevertheless, the scene, like the film, has little to do with Dostoyevsky, and in retrospect, the decision to treat the story as a psychological detective story seems the only honorable way out of an impossible situation.

Andre Sennwald of the *New York Times,* normally a von Sternberg supporter, couldn't say much for the film or its star. "Although Peter Lorre is occasionally able to give the film a frightening pathological significance," he wrote, "this is scarcely Dostoievsky's drama of a tortured brain drifting into madness with a terrible secret. It is Dostoievsky eviscerated and converted into nickel-plate detective melodrama." As a vehicle to launch Lorre's new career, the film also misfired. *Mad Love,* though shot later, was released first. After glimpsing those goggle eyes and hearing Lorre's corrupting *mittel-European* purr, audiences wanted more of him as a figure of menace, a category from which he rarely escaped for the rest of his working life. Graham Greene, who admired Lorre in *Mad Love,* had no time for *Crime and Punishment,* calling it "vulgar as only the great New World can be vulgar, with the vulgarity of the completely unreligious, of sentimental idealism, of pitch-pine ethics, with the hollow optimism about human nature of a salesman who has never failed to sell his canned beans."[3] The film's most distinguished critic, Jorge Luis Borges, then a weekly movie reviewer, was even more scathing. "For this time," wrote the great magic realist, "von Sternberg has renounced his customary *marottes* [fads]. Unfortunately, he has not replaced them with anything. . . . Formerly, he seemed mad, which at least is something; now, merely simple-minded."

Von Sternberg's second film for Columbia, and also his break with the company, resulted from an attempt to reproduce the lushness and scope of his Paramount period romances on a reduced budget. Cohn signed soprano Grace Moore after the success of Victor Schertzinger's *One Night of Love* and cast her in a film of Fritz Kreisler's *Cissy*, a piece of strudel about the courtship of Princess Elizabeth of Bavaria (aka "Cissy") and her cousin, the young Emperor Franz Josef (Franchot Tone). Considering his Austrian background and skill with female stars, von Sternberg seemed the obvious choice to direct and was assigned Sidney Buchman's script, now retitled *The King Steps Out.*

To Moore's embarrassment, word had spread that her acclaimed singing in *One Night of Love* had been achieved by editing together a number of performances. Cohn's promise that there would be no such tinkering on *The King Steps Out* made her nervous, which von Sternberg's reputation only increased. "I was terrified of meeting the self-convinced genius," she wrote.

Harry Cohn brought me over to the set and locked von Sternberg and me in his room. . . . Von Sternberg began by modestly declaring he was the greatest director in Hollywood. As to personalities, he said, if I hated him at first, I would certainly end up by loving him; everyone did. . . .

"I know," declaimed the Great One, "exactly what to do with the music. I saw the *première* in Vienna. I know what to do with you. I am just the one to bring you and the music together."

But in spite of the back-room oratory, von Sternberg apparently didn't know what to do with the music or me. I found myself standing by a big piano most of the time, like a lump of a log, singing. The great action scene came when I had to milk a cow, singing at the same time.[4]

In fact, the scene in which she sings while milking a cow comes early in the story. Although included in the trailer, it was cut from the film, where we see Moore handing a bucket of milk to her mother and telling her, "Compliments of Bessie." As for the claim that she was trapped at a piano, almost without exception she sings in the open air, often in crowds, and sometimes while dancing, with not a piano in sight. Given the requirement that all music be recorded on the set, von Sternberg handled the sequences with efficiency and style.

The King Steps Out is von Sternberg's first and only attempt at comedy, and not a very successful one, although he appears to enjoy ringing changes on the plot of *The Scarlet Empress*. Cissy's bucolic father Duke Maximilian (Walter Connolly) schemes with his daughter against his wife and the dowager empress, who are determined to marry off Cissy's sister, sight unseen, to Franz Josef, heir to the Austrian throne. As in *The Scarlet Empress,* an early scene shows Cissy and her father setting out for the court, this time in a donkey cart, a journey as uncomfortable as the one Sophia's mother complains of in the earlier film. Social-climbing mother (Elizabeth Risdon) and beer-swilling father both fit the pattern of Sophia's family, and when Cissy's sister (Nana Bryant) is presented to Franz Josef, her unseen fiancé, she comments, "I'm overcome. His Majesty is so unlike his portrait," a reminder of the meeting between Sophia and Peter. After a good deal of confusion, with Cissy pretending to be a seamstress to beguile the duke, as Sophia impersonates a maid when accosted by the "fortunate" lieutenant, the sister is married to her lover (Victor Jory), and Cissy and Franz Josef are united at the fade.

The film often looks sculpted in sugar and decorated with whipped cream. Its artificial forests sparkle with aluminum paint. Every sign bears a decorative spatter of shadows, and the interiors of the palace, a succession of blindingly white apartments, are crammed with lavish furniture. The inn where Cissy and her father lodge is a riot of gingerbread carving, trophy animal heads, and tables covered with foaming beer steins. The visit paid by Cissy and the incognito Franz Josef to a carnival is another reminiscence of the Prater of von Sternberg's childhood. As a pantomime dragon weaves through the crowd, the lovers evade the bumbling imperial Secret Service to compete at a shooting gallery, and Cissy flirts with a contingent of hussars.

The director's feud with Moore became as notorious as that between Mae Murray and von Stroheim on *The Merry Widow.* "I got so tired of seeing [von Sternberg] in his velvet coat and velvet beret," wrote Moore, "sliding his personal microphone around, carrying on, declaiming, stamping his foot, shooting off constant sparks of what he perhaps wishfully assumed was genius."[5] Character actors such as E. E. Clive had their roles truncated when scenes were recut around some outburst, but that still left plenty of opportunities for Walter Connolly, Raymond Walburn, and, in particular, Herman Bing as an innkeeper, a role that aroused him to paroxysms of broken English. As Graham Greene wrote, his "rolling eyeballs, his enormous splutter, his huge lack of understanding have never been given such generous room. He bears the whole film on his wildly expressive shoulders." If anyone gives an unconvincing performance, it is Moore. She speaks as she sings, with a shrill animation that suits the songs but grates in dialogue. Greene dismissed her acting as "the exaggerated vivacity of a games-mistress letting herself noisily go on the last night of term."[6]

Periodically, Harry Cohn summoned von Sternberg and Schulberg to his office for "script conferences" about their projects and those of other directors. Frank Capra felt that Cohn convened these meetings merely to illustrate his dominance, in particular over Schulberg and von Sternberg. Capra, like the rest of Hollywood, perceived the two of them as sad figures, once great but now slipping inexorably down the ladder. Capra had submitted a screenplay that cast Gary Cooper as a hick who inherits millions and comes to the big city, where he's parodied for his odd habits, such as playing the tuba and feeding donuts to horses. Von Sternberg urged Capra not to make it. "A hero must be noble, not imbecile," he said.[7] Fortunately, his advice was ignored. *Mr. Deeds Goes to Town* became a classic and was nominated for three Oscars, of which Capra won one for best director.

Far Cathay

Bai wen bu ru yi jian. (Seeing it once is better than being told a hundred times.)

—Zhou Chongguo, Han Dynasty

VON STERNBERG REPUDIATED *The King Steps Out.* It became the only film he specifically requested be omitted from any retrospective. The Columbia experience, with its contrasts to the prodigality of Paramount, shook him. In an effort to regain his confidence, he developed some projects to be produced independently. Perhaps inspired by Lorre's use of a classic novel in the public domain, he wrote a treatment of Émile Zola's *Germinal,* the story of a coal miners' strike in northern France that ends in violence. One can hardly imagine a project less likely to attract a Hollywood studio, but he tried anyway, with a conspicuous lack of success. In a last-ditch attempt, he took the script to the talent agency of B-movie producer Edward Small, only to find that its representation of writers was in the hands of an old adversary, Riza Royce's friend Frederica Sagor. "I could not say which of us was more uncomfortable when Eddie Small left us alone," recalled Sagor, who relished von Sternberg's humiliation. "Adversity had had a salutary effect on his personality. I found him chastened, affable. Gone was that air of superiority he affected to diminish others, that air which, in the end, helped topple him. He was almost humble now, eager to please." Any such humility did nothing to ingratiate him with the Hollywood establishment. "When I sampled the hostility everywhere at the mere mention of his name," said Sagor, "I did not push him or his story."[1]

Once again, Dietrich tried to throw him a lifeline, in the form of *Hotel Imperial*. Lajos Biro's story, already filmed in 1927 with Pola Negri, looked ripe for a remake. Between the lines of some Ruritanian war, the hotel of the title is successively occupied by officers from both sides as the advantage shifts. After a girl jilted by an officer is driven to suicide, her sister takes a job as a maid in the hotel to unmask the guilty man. She doesn't know his name or even which side he fights for. She knows only the number of his room—and naturally, she falls in love with its current occupant.

Henry Hathaway proposed a new version titled *I Loved a Soldier*, with him as director. Lubitsch concurred, on the condition that he use Charles Boyer and persuade Dietrich to star. She was interested, until Hathaway explained how he intended to film her—plain and unglamorous while she masqueraded as a maid, but becoming progressively prettier once she fell in love. Dietrich balked; no star chooses to look ugly. Hathaway persuaded Lubitsch to let him cast Margaret Sullavan, only to be frustrated again when Sullavan broke her arm. At this point, Dietrich, to the studio's surprise, expressed renewed interest—on the condition that von Sternberg replace Hathaway as director. Lubitsch refused, and the film was canceled. Had von Sternberg made a romantic comedy like *I Loved a Soldier* instead of *The Devil Is a Woman*, his career at Paramount might have been saved, but it was too late. The film would eventually be made in 1939 by Robert Florey, with Isa Miranda and Ray Milland.

To add to von Sternberg's troubles, his brother Fred, in declining health since his gassing at Belleau Wood, was hospitalized with stomach cancer. Conferring with two surgeons in the corridor of the hospital, a distracted von Sternberg forgot his superstition and lit cigarettes for all three from the same match, an action regarded as unlucky (and employed as such in *Dishonored*). At that moment, Fred died.

The King Steps Out opened on May 12, 1936, to good reviews, at least from the better papers. It was even invited to the Venice Film Festival. But the experience had soured von Sternberg on Hollywood. Shortly after, he sailed on the Japanese liner *Chichibu Maru*, which plied regularly between San Francisco and Yokohama. He intended the voyage as the first leg of a lone westward cruise to Asia and the Far East that would also take him to Britain.

He claims that, somewhere in the China Sea, the *Chichibu Maru* accidentally ran down a Chinese junk. Passengers heard the screams of those on board, but after circling the wreckage twice, the ship sailed on, on the pretext that because it was carrying mail, it could not be delayed. Such events were a common consequence of the heightened tension in the Pacific as Japan, China, and the European powers maneuvered for position in the struggle for territory and resources that developed into World War II. With their usual skill, the Japanese hid political realities behind an inscrutable amiability. This, and the beauty of the Orient, misled von Sternberg, who socialized almost entirely with Europeans, both on the boat and during stopovers.

In Japan he even found a German director at work. Arnold Fanck, former geologist and convinced Nazi, whose "mountain films" such as *The White Hell of Piz Palu* had launched Leni Riefenstahl, was making a contribution to the Berlin-Tokyo axis by codirecting *Die Tochter des Samurai* (A Daughter of the Samurai) with Japanese director Mansaku Itami. Von Sternberg knew the film's producers, Princeton-educated Yoshio Osawa and Nagamasa Kawakita, who had studied at Heidelberg. Kawakita spoke fluent German and admired German culture to such an extent that after World War II he was exiled from Japan as a class B war criminal and barred from the film industry for five years. In the film, a Japanese man returns home with a German wife, and his former fiancée tries to kill herself in the traditional Japanese manner, by jumping into a volcano—a mountaineering element that explains Fanck's involvement. It was an unhappy set. Itami so detested the attempts to introduce Nazi ideology that he insisted on making his own alternative version, with Fanck shooting by day and Itami at night.

Intending to continue to Shanghai, von Sternberg learned that, in another sign of deteriorating relations with China, Japanese cruise ships no longer called there. Tourists were relegated to what one passenger called "a dirty little tub of a mail steamer" (von Sternberg added "rat-infested"), which left not from Tokyo but from Shimonoseki, on the western tip of Honshu. Alighting from the train there, he was surprised to find a young fan waiting to welcome him, provide him with food, and take him on a tour. As he admired the picturesque coastline, his new friend said, "It is as beautiful as if you had directed it."

After a rough crossing, von Sternberg spent a few hectic days in Shanghai, where he concentrated on the more decadent sights, such as an opium den, and the *Da Shi Jie* (Great World), an entertainment complex on picturesquely named Yangjingbang West Street in the former French concession. As many as 20,000 people flooded through each day, dazzled, like him, by its "gambling tables, singsong girls, magicians, pickpockets, slot machines, fireworks, bird cages, fans, stick incense, acrobats . . . actors, jugglers, pimps, midwives, barbers, and earwax extractors." His descriptions of China on the eve of World War II are suffused with the same delight in spectacle and sensuality that he relished in the Vienna of his childhood. Political realities did not intrude. In July 1937 the Japanese would seize the whole of eastern China, but although he traveled by train through Korea and Japanese-occupied Manchuria, von Sternberg claimed to see no militarism, beyond a pleasant Japanese officer with whom he shared a compartment and, in Mukden, Manchuria, a theater where soldiers with fixed bayonets lined the front of the stalls, facing the potentially restive audience. The many pages of *Fun in a Chinese Laundry* devoted to von Sternberg's travels in Asia conflate two cruises, the first in 1936 and the second in 1947. They shuffle together images of Oriental strangeness; brothels, temples, gambling dens; a vast, unknowable reality that reminds us of the ersatz Asia invented for his films. In his telling, *Shanghai Express,* *The Shanghai Gesture,* and *The Saga of Anatahan* appear more original for being nothing like the real thing.

In October 1936 he embarked on the next leg of his cruise. In Bali he visited sculptor Dora Gordine, who had resettled in Singapore. While in Java he fell ill with what he called an "abdominal infection"— probably appendicitis. Flying to London, he was admitted to the London Clinic and operated on for bowel inflammation and peritonitis, suggesting that his appendix had ruptured. Recuperating, he must have felt that, at forty-two, his career was at an end. But he had been in that situation before and retrieved his fortunes with *The Blue Angel.* Maybe he was due for another visit from the gods of good fortune.

The Claudius Trap

> For God's sake, let us sit upon the ground
> And tell sad stories of the death of kings.
> —William Shakespeare, *King Richard II*

PLENTY OF OLD FRIENDS from Berlin had taken refuge from Hitler in London, and they brought grapes to von Sternberg's bedside and commiserated. Even Marlene Dietrich was there, juggling lovers while playing a fugitive Russian grand duchess in *Knight Without Armour* for Alexander Korda. Since von Sternberg had seen Korda off at Union Station in Los Angeles five years before, the devious Hungarian, thanks to substantial funding from Prudential Insurance Company, had become a movie magnate, transforming a mansion at rural Denham into the studios of his London Films. It seethed with cronies and relatives, including his brothers Zoltan and Vincent. There was also a regiment of refugees, among them old associates of von Sternberg's such as Erich Pommer, Carl Zuckmayer, and Lajos Biro, who was head of its script department. (Jokers suggested that the three flags that flew above the mansion signified the number of its British-born employees.) Although Korda enjoyed a few hits, in particular *The Private Life of Henry VIII* and *Rembrandt,* he was never more than one step ahead of disaster. "The art of filmmaking," he wrote, "is to come to the brink of bankruptcy, and stare it in the face." When von Sternberg arrived, Korda was doing so again, having gambled on importing Dietrich to star with

Robert Donat in *Knight Without Armour.* Not only did it incur a huge loss; he still owed Dietrich $100,000 of her $350,000 fee.

Korda's most valuable asset was Charles Laughton. An instinctive actor, he relied on an almost mystical mental equilibrium to create a performance. "Laughton needs a midwife, not a director," moaned Korda. *The Private Life of Henry VIII* made £1 million, but clashes during *Rembrandt* led Korda to keep Laughton on contract at £700 a week for the next two years without making a single film. Now, with that contract ending in April 1937, he risked having to write off every penny.

Laughton's friendship with von Sternberg suggested a solution. Korda arrived at the director's bedside preceded by a fruit basket from London's leading emporium, Fortnum and Mason. With it were copies of Robert Graves's novels *I, Claudius* and *Claudius, the God,* about the life of Emperor Tiberius Claudius Drusus, as well as a screen adaptation by Biro and Zuckmayer in which Korda had planned to direct Laughton. After the dramas of *Rembrandt,* however, he had assigned it to William Cameron Menzies, the gifted production designer who made *Things to Come.* Now Korda invited von Sternberg to take over. In return, he offered either a partnership in London Films or a reputed (and much exaggerated) fee of £25,000—equal to about £1.25 million today, or US$2 million—at a time when the biggest stars received about $100,000 per film (at the peak of his Hollywood career, von Sternberg earned only $20,000 a week). Whatever sum Korda proposed, von Sternberg, suspecting (rightly) that London Films was teetering, took the cash.

The story and character of Claudius immediately appealed. An aging cripple who became emperor by outwitting his contemptuous family and subjects was a character of Shakespearean stature, and his near destruction by his nymphomaniac child-wife Messalina gave the story added spice. But von Sternberg had a larger vision. "My plan," he wrote, "was not only to bring to life an old empire, but to hold it up as a mirror to our own tottering values, and to investigate the diseased roots of excessive ambition." Elsa Lanchester, Laughton's wife, claims the two men wanted "to show the world the fall of the Roman Empire and point up the comparison with the current unsettled times."[1] Von Sternberg may have been thinking of his own "excessive ambition." Had recent failures made him introspective? Did the capricious Caligula, with his mad changes of mood, mirror Hitler? Or was his gibe aimed at the Hollywood executives who had undermined him? In the latter case, the film offered rich material for von Sternberg's favorite pastime—getting his own back.

A contemporary summary of the plot hints at the film's scope:

> The story deals with the life of Claudius, Emperor of Rome, born 10 B.C. When the film opens, Tiberius is emperor, and Claudius, whose nervousness causes him to stutter, is an object of ridicule to the court and amusement to the public. He is more happy on his Capua farm than amongst the intrigues and vice of the Roman Court. Caligula murders Tiberius, proclaims himself emperor, dragging the unwilling Claudius from his obscurity and forcing him to marry the beautiful Messalina. When the army revolt and kill Caligula, the generals choose the apparently harmless and easily controlled Claudius to succeed him. But Claudius's studies prove useful, and sharing his enormous power with his wife Messalina, whom he has come to love and trust, he proceeds to set right the evils of Caligula's reign, to bring prosperity to the Roman empire and to lead his victorious armies in the subjugation of Britain. He is proclaimed a god during his lifetime, for the first time in history. Heartbroken at Messalina's infidelity during his campaign in Britain, he leads the army against Rome, punishes his enemies for their treachery and in a terrific final scene signs her death warrant. Then the great Claudius, god and emperor, rules alone.[2]

Korda set a budget of £120,000, later increased to £150,000— between $7 million and $10 million in today's terms, and vastly more expensive than other films of the time. As well as Laughton, the cast would include, as Messalina, the beautiful Eurasian Merle Oberon, Korda's mistress and later wife; Flora Robson as the Dowager Empress Livia; and Raymond Massey, John Clements, F. Forbes Robertson, and Robert Newton in supporting roles. Vincent Korda had designed extravagant sets, Georges Périnal was to shoot it, and Agnes de Mille would create the choreography. Although those who knew von Sternberg's inexperience with action might have wondered how he hoped to handle the film's battles and parades, it appeared that with such a crew, it would be difficult to fail.

As a further encouragement, Korda presented him with what he called an important large bronze of a female nude by Aristide Maillol, declaring seductively that, when it came to directing women, von Sternberg had no peer. The magnolia-skinned Merle, he wheedled, could not be in better hands. But Oberon was anything but happy about the casting. She feared that von Sternberg would see through the lie on which her fame rested. Far from being, as her publicity claimed, the child of pure Anglo-Saxon parents from Tasmania, remotest corner of the white British Commonwealth, she had actually been born in Colombo, Sri Lanka, the illegitimate daughter of a mixed-race girl of fourteen and her white lover. Revealing this would condemn her to roles as domestics and Asian temptresses. Korda convinced Oberon that she had nothing to fear and promised the role would make her as famous as Dietrich. Such was her vanity that she swallowed this story, despite clear evidence that Laughton would dominate *I, Claudius,* and Messalina would be as peripheral as the Anne Boleyn she had played in *The Private Life of Henry VIII.*

To direct *I, Claudius,* Laughton much preferred von Sternberg to Korda, but he remained uncertain in the face of two other alternatives. Erich Pommer had proposed that they form their own production company, and Laughton had also been offered the role of Louis XVI in the forthcoming *Marie Antoinette,* opposite Irving Thalberg's wife, Norma Shearer. He was depending on an informal agreement under which, when his contract with Korda ended in April 1937, he would return to MGM, which had made him famous with *Mutiny on the Bounty* and *The Barretts of Wimpole Street.* He had just arrived back from Rome after a research trip with Vincent Korda in September 1936 when he heard of Thalberg's sudden death. It was a professional and personal blow. Fearing he would be forced to make films he disliked with producers he despised, he agreed to the formation of a Pommer-Laughton company, Mayflower Films.

In addition to the Laughton contract deadline, Korda had another incentive that he didn't reveal. Dietrich, taking pity on her former lover (and assuming Korda would find some way to avoid paying her anyway), offered to waive the $100,000 owed for *Knight Without Armour* if Korda hired von Sternberg for *I, Claudius.* Douglas Fairbanks Jr., her lover at the time, was in awe of her generosity. "In many ways," he said, "Marlene was superior to Von Sternberg, and had this 'thing' of gratitude towards him. She went to such exaggerated lengths of defense and promotion, helping him and talking people into helping him—getting *jobs* for him. She would never hear the slightest criticism, even when he was terrible to her. He was always bitching about her, and she took it. She'd just smile sort of ironically, and the money would flow out. She was certainly his most loyal friend."

Von Sternberg was indeed "terrible" to his former partner. For decades he depicted her as someone he had created and who had repaid his largesse with ingratitude. In a particularly magniloquent interview for *Cahiers du Cinema* in 1963, he turned history on its head: "On finishing *The Blue Angel*, I had finished with Marlene," he told the journalist. "I did not want to make any more films with her. But she followed me back home, as do most women." Here he laughed before he continued:

And I had to direct her in *Morocco.* After finishing *Morocco,* I had finished with her for the second time. But the company called me and said, "You have saved the company from bankruptcy. . . . Please keep going." About a year later, I made *Shanghai Express,* also with Marlene. And again, I wanted to be finished with her after finishing the film. But she came to see me and told me [she] could not work for another director, that she would readily state publicly that I was a good film-maker and she was a bad actress, and added that I had no right to do this to her. I realized that Marlene was right, and we decided to continue working together until she could stand on her own feet.

During their collaboration, Dietrich, in his version, was little more than his maid-of-all-work. "She has the energy of a thousand oxen," he told *Cahiers.* "She was my best assistant. If I needed a chair, she was the first to bring it to me; if I didn't like the eggs at lunch, she would go out and get me others, and if she couldn't find any she was capable of laying them herself [laughs]. In any case, she was the ideal tool for me."[3]

Dietrich had troubles of her own. In the summer of 1936 she had sailed to Europe with Rudy and Maria, planning to visit her family in Berlin. When she arrived at the German embassy in Paris to renew her passport, the ambassador, Count von Welczeck, handed her a personal letter from Joachim von Ribbentrop, Hitler's former roving representative who was about to become ambassador to Great Britain. Aware of her plans to leave Hollywood and make films in Europe, the German government urged her to return and become "the reigning queen of the German film industry." (As a Jew, von Sternberg was not included in the invitation.) Although its Jewish associations barred *Der Blaue Engel* from public screening, and officially, all prints had been destroyed, Hitler owned a private copy that he would show at the slightest excuse. French diplomats complained of being forced to sit through four hours of Dietrich, including *Der Blaue Engel*, during which they were forbidden to speak or even smoke.

The letter shook Dietrich, as she later explained to the FBI. Her reaction was described by an interviewing officer in a report to director J. Edgar Hoover: "Dietrich said that after von Ribbentrop's messenger left her, she debated with herself for two hours whether she should call Hitler directly, telling him that she would go to Germany to visit him, and then, when she arrived there, make some plan to kill him. She described Hitler as being 'not a normal human being mentally,' and described his evident feeling for her as 'he has a tick for me.'"[4] (This may be a mistranslation of *Der hat ja einen Tick*, meaning, "He's really off his rocker.")

Though the homicidal impulse passed, the warning made her prudent. Sailing for the United States on the liner *France* on September 20, she declined, in the words of one report, "to comment on her reported refusal to return to Germany and to confine her motion picture work to its studios." The report continued, "It is regarded as significant . . . that Miss Dietrich was returning on a French ship, after having come to Europe on a German liner, and that she did not ever cross the frontier into Germany during her three months' vacation abroad."[5] Once back in California, she applied for U.S. citizenship.

And what if she had followed her instinct, made the phone call, and been welcomed into the presence of the Führer? Could she have gone through with her plan to murder him, knowing it would lead to certain death? How ironic that World War II might have been averted because of von Sternberg's eagerness to show off Dietrich's legs.

News of *I, Claudius* appeared in the trade press just after Christmas 1936. But that December, nobody spoke of anything but Edward VIII's threat to abdicate unless he could marry American divorcée Wallis Simpson. Not even von Sternberg knew that Dietrich had volunteered her expertise in averting this constitutional crisis. "Send me!" she supposedly said to her friend Prince George, Duke of Kent. "I can do *it* better than Wallis Simpson—and with me, you can be *sure* I won't try to be the Queen of England!" The bisexual, morphine- and cocaine-using prince was perfectly capable of engineering such an exploit. Unfortunately for this lurid legend, the king remained sequestered at Fort Belvedere, on the grounds of Windsor Castle many miles from London, and saw only his intimates. Even if Dietrich did somehow find her way into his bed, she failed to change his mind, since he abdicated on December 11.

On January 13, 1937, the press noted, "Josef von Sternberg has taken over his Denham offices and is busy with preparations for *I Claudius*. . . . He personally supervises all suggestions from set designers, costume experts and property departments as well as working on final touches to the script." These meetings shook the tranquil Denham regime. Paul Tabori wrote, "von Sternberg arrived, summoned all the technical staff and then had the doors locked so that no one could get in or out. He went through the script line by line, explaining every scene and passage, demanding opinions, conducting long arguments with each technician involved. The meeting started in the morning and was still going in the late afternoon. Finally the staff, hungry and exhausted, were rescued by Korda."[6]

Shooting began in mid-February. Cast and crew smirked at von Sternberg's choice of working clothes: riding breeches, laced boots, a bulky jacket, and a Javanese bandanna wound around his head. He was more colorfully dressed than the cast, among whom he immediately had to adjudicate. Actors who had tested for and been promised parts found themselves replaced, and Raymond Massey withdrew to protest having to work with Laughton, who was fitfully brilliant but puzzled by the character. He forgot his lines and misjudged the physical tricks that required him to limp, twitch, and stutter. Pommer's assistant John Kahan, who was on the set for some of the shooting, agreed that "artistic arguments" were common. "Korda was weak," he says. "He couldn't stand up to Laughton, but von Sternberg did."[7] Others suggested a different interpretation—that von Sternberg left his friendship for Laughton at the door and tyrannized him, both to extract a better performance and to assert his superiority. Their relationship deteriorated until, according to actor David Tree, "von Sternberg was not on speaking terms with Laughton. When he walked in, the other walked off."[8]

On March 11 Laughton told the press he would be leaving London Films and *I, Claudius* on April 21. Korda, meanwhile, fretted about costs. After five weeks' shooting, von Sternberg had completed mainly dialogue sequences, not the elaborate and expensive spectacles. In addition, he had ordered Vincent Korda to construct all the main sets and keep them ready for use at any time, in case Laughton decided to depart from the schedule. When Kahan, at Korda's request, diplomatically asked how long the film would take, the director, in his words, "blew up. 'You, an old friend, ask me such a question!' he said. 'I am just warming up. How should I know when I finish? It could be Christmas, it could be next spring.'"[9] He then returned to one of his most elaborate sequences, a procession with Laughton at the head of his army, marching out of Rome to defeat the Britons. After a day of lighting tests and rehearsals, the scene was still unshot. With more than two-thirds of the budget spent and the film not half finished, Korda began to despair.

His phenomenal luck saved him. On March 16, Merle Oberon was involved in a collision in her chauffeured Rolls-Royce. Thrown to the floor, she hit her face on the metal footrest of the folding passenger seat, sustaining cuts to her left eye and ear and a possible concussion. The seriousness of these injuries has been much debated, but at the time, newspaper reports suggested she would recover in a few weeks. Korda cautiously suspended *I, Claudius.* Phoning California, he asked if Claudette Colbert could take over Oberon's role, but she was busy. Calculating von Sternberg's slow pace and the soaring costs, Laughton's threats, the indifferent quality of many scenes with the star, and the fuss from Oberon if she was replaced, he decided to get out while he could. Three days later, on March 19, he announced the cancellation of *I, Claudius.* It was the prudent move. He had everything to gain from shutting down the production and little to lose, since insurance covered the costs. He could also write off Dietrich's $100,000. Recouping his costs from Prudential, he gave Laughton his freedom in a violent leave-taking with recriminations on both sides, and put aside the material that had already been shot.

In 1965 the BBC discovered the remnants of *I, Claudius,* fifty-eight cans of negative, sound negative, and print, stored in Denham's derelict editing rooms, formerly its stables. Interviews with von Sternberg, Oberon, Emlyn Williams, Flora Robson, and other survivors were combined with extracts from the preserved footage to create the documentary *The Epic That Never Was,* narrated by Dirk Bogarde. From luxury exile in Mexico, Oberon insisted that the film had been "built around" her and that von Sternberg's autocratic handling of Laughton had caused its collapse. Williams and Bogarde pushed the same theory. Laughton needed "warmth" from his director but received only "cold, cold, cold."

The material held by Britain's National Film Archive doesn't support this interpretation. The total footage, including discarded takes, mute offcuts, and "scrap," runs almost two hours, but only five reels represent edited sequences, rough-cut, with synchronized sound. Von Sternberg had completed six major sequences, but they made up only about a quarter of the film.

The first sequence is also one of the most ambitious—an extended piece of scene-setting in which the principals arrive at the temple and are greeted by crowds around the ornately decorated columns and wide staircase. Inside the temple, as Caligula and Claudius lounge on the steps beside the empress's throne, Livia warns them of each other, presaging at the same time her own death, foretold by her soothsayer. Caligula accepts her low estimate of him with indifference, while Claudius, watching him depart, stammers only, "An unpleasant youth." Emlyn Williams's Caligula builds on his performance as the serial murderer in his own play *Night Must Fall,* but adds a layer of waspish camp. This is reinforced by his interviews in *The Epic That Never Was,* where he mocks the whole enterprise, particularly his costumes—"two hostess gowns, and a couple of cocktail numbers."

The scenes that follow, of worshippers filing into the temple with its towering statue and of veiled virgins, each with a palm and candle, are all that remain of the film's epic element, but they show the entente von Sternberg established with Georges Périnal, who acknowledged how much he learned from the director. Costume designer John Armstrong, less enamored, complained that von Sternberg flouted historical accuracy. Strictly speaking, the temple housed only six virgins, but he demanded sixty—all of them naked, though draped in additional veils (again historically inaccurate) to enhance the effect of backlighting.

Caligula brings Claudius to Rome, probably to have him killed. As Claudius waits disconsolately to be admitted to the imperial presence, Messalina passes, surrounded by giggling friends. A long tracking shot follows her along the colonnade, her face losing and gaining highlights in the shadows. Claudius is obviously smitten, but as the girl looks back, she flashes a malicious smile at her grotesque admirer. Once face-to-face with Caligula, Claudius resourcefully flatters him, inspiring the mad young man to order his uncle and Messalina to marry. "I have decided you will die an exquisite death; an old man, married to a beautiful young girl." He turns to Musa, his doctor. "That would be of medical interest too, doctor. Consider it; a remote descendant of Julius Caesar married to a remote descendant of Augustus. What do you think would be the result?"

"A pair of crutches," Musa replies glumly in a double entendre that almost certainly would not have escaped the censors.

Two sequences shot in the large Senate set with more than 200 extras complete the existing material. In the first, Caligula takes command of the governing body, appointing his racehorse Incitatus as senator. There is a furor, but the Senate is too cowardly to protest. Standing behind a bronze Roman eagle, a senior senator formally welcomes the animal. In the second, the army, after murdering Caligula, nominates Claudius to replace him. Laughton's speech to the Senate, the film's most effective piece of acting, wasn't easily achieved. Twenty takes survive, in whole or in part. He starts with a tentative statement that he will rule only if the Senate supports him. As he sticks on a word, someone crows derisively, but Claudius, given courage by this response, observes, "I did not know that your talents extended to imitating a chicken. I thought you confined yourself to neighing like a horse." A chastened Senate listens as he dictates his terms. "I, Claudius," he concludes, "will break everything rotten in this Senate like an old dry twig." He demands to confront the murderers of Caligula and, after condemning the brutality of their act, notwithstanding its justification, asks them to name the appropriate penalty for their betrayal of trust. They answer, "Death," and Claudius, softening, says, "For that reply, I will take your family under my care."

Visually, *I, Claudius* shows von Sternberg in a restrained mood. Nets and veils are less in evidence, statuary is used sparingly, and shadow patterns are kept to a minimum. Light is almost always soft and diffused, so that the characters glow against the gloomy hang of curtains and the intricacy of friezes and mosaics. There are few elaborately lit close-ups. Oberon is consistently shot in dim light, her eyes shadowed. As for her claim that the film was built around her, and Korda's insistence that her injuries made it necessary to shut down production, the surviving footage suggests that her replacement would have been not only possible but desirable.

Watching the edited footage of *I, Claudius* leaves no doubt that Laughton was responsible for the film's cancellation. Von Sternberg printed only usable takes. When he was doubtful, he retained a selection, as with Edna Purviance on *A Woman of the Sea*. In the case of Flora Robson's performance and, to a lesser extent, Emlyn Williams's, he kept only one or two takes. But for Laughton's scenes there seemed to be no limit, as if he regarded all as equally unsatisfactory. More than ten takes survive of his arrival at the temple, as well as numerous fragments of the Senate speech, long passages mixed with whole or partial retakes. In most of them, Laughton, having missed a word or wrongly emphasized a sentence, stops and corrects himself, in one case bitterly criticizing his pronunciation as bad East End Cockney. Even after five weeks of shooting, the correct voice for Claudius continued to elude him and, with it, the essence of his character. One morning he surprised von Sternberg by playing a disc of Edward's abdication speech, insisting that it provided the elusive key. Von Sternberg wasn't convinced; nor, apparently, was Laughton, since no hint of that prissy, sulky tone is detectable in his performance.

In *Fun in a Chinese Laundry,* von Sternberg also blames Laughton's homosexuality and masochism. Multiple takes were necessary to shoot the scene in which Claudius is thrown into a room with Messalina and says, simply, "This is not how I would have wished to appear before you." Laughton suggested that, for greater realism, someone should kick him into the shot. An assistant was assigned to do so, but he fluffed his line on take after take, necessitating a multitude of kicks. Shooting wrapped for the day with the scene still not completed but Laughton's backside thoroughly bruised. That night, Oberon experienced her fortuitous accident. No part of this sequence survives, so von Sternberg's claim, like his charge that Purviance's drinking aborted *A Woman of the Sea,* just adds another mystery to the many that surround what he called "the *Claudius* trap."

There is little doubt that Korda played von Sternberg, luring him into a project that, when it collapsed, would divert all blame from himself and Laughton. It was a skill of which he was a past master. *I, Claudius* left its director vilified and discredited, but Korda, far from being condemned for his recklessness, was knighted in 1942. Typically, von Sternberg dismissed the debacle as "a warning to waste no longer the little I had to contribute, and . . . fortified my resolution not again to be harnessed by others." Privately, however, he never forgave Laughton. According to his widow, "he had no grudges against anybody, except Charles Laughton. Him, he wished he'd never met."[10]

On April 14, 1937, less than a month later, von Sternberg stepped off the *Queen Mary* in New York. With no prospect of finding work in the studio system, he directed his efforts toward setting up an independent production in Europe. After a concert (von Sternberg says in London, but she never sang there), he approached Czech opera singer Jarmila Novotna with the suggestion that she star in a film, but she wasn't interested. Although she had made films with Max Ophuls and others, her ambition was to become a diva in the United States, which she achieved in 1940. For a time he considered filming a 1933 book by

Franz Werfel, *The Forty Days of Musa Dagh,* about the Armenians who resisted Turkish genocide following the First World War. He discarded the idea, however, when he found Austrian interest in his screenplay for *Germinal.* As Hitler hungrily eyed his German-speaking neighbor, Austrians wished to assert themselves and to remind the world they had a culture.

In September he was back in Europe, staying at the Palazzo Vendramin in Venice, which Vollmoeller had again rented for the summer. Dietrich was there too, with German fashion model Karin Stilke and novelist Erich Maria Remarque. The author of *All Quiet on the Western Front* soon became one of her most durable lovers. In Vienna in the autumn, von Sternberg began to assemble *Germinal.* The heterogeneous production would be shot mainly in London, in both German and English. French actor Jean-Louis Barrault was cast as Etienne, the labor leader who foments the strike, with Croatian newcomer Hilde Krahl as his partner Catherine. Von Sternberg became even more optimistic when the Austrian government approached him to undertake another project. In his words, "I was to be guardian of the arts, its vast arts, its poets, its dancers, its music, and its talented men and women—mine to guide and to inspire." One wonders what the government was thinking, since his qualifications as an administrator hardly inspired confidence, and his race and reputation would have been no recommendation. In the event, nothing came of it, since Hitler had other ideas.

Protected by his American citizenship, von Sternberg visited Berlin, where he celebrated the arrival of 1938 at the Palast Hotel with Leni Riefenstahl and a party of her friends, including Prince Ernst Ruediger von Starhemberg and his new wife, the Austrian actress Nora Gregor. According to Riefenstahl, he praised *Triumph of the Will.* "*Maedchen,*" he supposedly told her, "this film will make movie history. It is revolutionary."[11] According to Riefenstahl, he also reaffirmed that once he was finished with *Germinal,* he intended to mold her into a star as he had molded Dietrich. She claims that she told him she was anxious to escape from documentary films and would be delighted to cooperate.

Most histories blame the collapse of *Germinal* on the *Anschluss* of March 1938, but events overtook it months before. In January, von Sternberg returned to Britain to make final preparations for filming.

In a London hotel room, his overstrained constitution, weakened by surgery and the experience of *I, Claudius,* "snapped like an elastic that has been stretched too far." He was admitted to the psychiatric ward of the Charing Cross Hospital with acute exhaustion. At the end of February, without having returned to Austria, he sailed on the *Queen Mary,* docking in New York on March 4. It wasn't until eight days later, on March 12, 1938, that Hitler annexed Austria, and *Germinal* "joined the long list of other projects that went up in smoke."

Von Sternberg made his last prewar journey to Europe in the summer of 1939, primarily to help friends and relatives escape Germany and Austria for the United States. He personally smoothed the way for at least twenty people, including the publisher of *Daughters of Vienna* and his wife. After leaving Berlin, he joined Dietrich on the Côte d'Azur. Also holidaying nearby, at the Hotel du Cap, were Joseph Kennedy, U.S. ambassador to Britain since 1938, and his family, including twenty-one-year-old son John. The Kennedys and Dietrich had been there the previous year as well, and forty-nine-year-old Joe couldn't resist showing his interest. Since she seldom refused anyone personable who asked for sex, Marlene and the elder Kennedy enjoyed a number of erotic encounters in the secluded cabanas lining the Mediterranean. Her sexual involvement with the Kennedys didn't end there. At a ball thrown by indefatigable hostess Elsa Maxwell, she ensured that young Jack would always remember their dance to "Begin the Beguine" by slipping her hand into his trousers. Years later, when Jack was president, he seized the opportunity to enjoy a quickie with Dietrich during her visit to the White House. Afterward, he inquired conversationally if she had ever slept with his father. Dietrich, fearing some Oedipal conflict, said, "He tried, but I refused," at which JFK said with satisfaction, "I always knew the son of a bitch was lying."[12]

Relishing his access to the circles of diplomacy, von Sternberg chose to ignore Kennedy Senior's anti-Semitism, arrogance, and pro-Nazi sentiments, and passed on some gossip picked up in Berlin (supposedly at the Spanish embassy) about an impending nonaggression pact between Hitler and Stalin. The same person may have warned of the imminence of war, since a rumor soon swept the holidaying Americans. On June 21, von Sternberg and Dietrich were in Paris, attending the races at Auteuil. On August 18 they stepped ashore from the *Normandie* in New York. As Hitler and Stalin signed their pact on August 23, Nazi troops poured into Poland. Von Sternberg would not leave the United States for the next eight years.

Family Ties

The Father a Cop . . . The Son a Killer.
—Publicity line for *Sergeant Madden*

EVEN THOUGH *THE DEVIL Is a Woman* effectively terminated von Sternberg's career as a filmmaker of the first rank, it inaugurated the growth of his legend. Of the personalities with whom he was most often compared during the 1920s and 1930s, Murnau had died in a 1931 car accident. Pabst refused to risk his reputation on the international scene and made a succession of negligible if exotic program films for the Continental market. Reinhardt would die in a New York hotel room in 1943, having achieved nothing of note in exile. Although Eisenstein survived until 1948, his last works, *Bezhin Meadow* and *Ivan the Terrible II: The Boyars' Plot,* were suppressed by Stalin and never released in his lifetime. Meanwhile, von Stroheim spiraled down into character acting, feeding on the legend of his mutilated directorial masterpieces. Von Sternberg alone commanded the moral high ground. Refusing to concede his role as the great artist, he accepted occasional journeyman work, but only on his own terms, abandoning a project when it fell below his standards—which it invariably did. If each new encounter added to the list of his enemies and reduced even further the chances of serious work, he regarded that as no more than the price one had to pay.

In 1938 MGM imported French director Julien Duvivier to make *The*

Great Waltz, vaguely based on the life of "waltz king" Johann Strauss the younger. He started shooting in May with a cast that included Luise Rainer, Fernand Gravey, and Estonian soprano Miliza Korjus (pronounced "gorgeous," as MGM's publicists helpfully pointed out). At the end of June, Duvivier returned to France, unaware that, almost immediately, MGM assigned Victor Fleming to reshoot many sequences. The film was too dark, the studio executives said, both visually and in its political references, and Korjus was deemed "brittle." Fleming called in von Sternberg to direct the complicated conclusion, described by Michael Sragow as "a montage of Strauss's melodies winning the hearts of waltzers across the Continent and beyond as his sheet music pours off the presses." According to Gravey and Dorothy Barrett, who plays a dancer from Spain in these scenes, von Sternberg did "all the montage shots . . . all the little intricate shots and trick shots."[1]

He finished work on *The Great Waltz* in September, and in October MGM offered him another job. Following a pattern that had become tediously familiar, he was hired specifically for his expertise in photographing actresses, in this case, fellow Austrian Hedy Lamarr. She had been under contract to MGM for some time, but no project had satisfied Louis B. Mayer, who had taken a personal interest in her Hollywood debut. By chance, another producer became responsible for Lamarr's first onscreen role in the United States. Charles Boyer met Lamarr at a party and persuaded Walter Wanger, to whom he was under contract, to borrow her to star her opposite him in *Algiers,* a remake of the French crime melodrama *Pepe Le Moko.* Wanger and Mayer negotiated a deal under which Lamarr would appear in *Algiers* and Boyer agreed to play Napoleon in MGM's lackluster *Conquest,* with Greta Garbo as his Polish lover Marie Walewska.

Lamarr was electric in *Algiers* as the thrill-seeking Parisian beauty who proves to be the downfall of gangster Boyer, and MGM producers pressed Mayer to cast her immediately as a femme fatale in a thriller set in some atmospheric and exotic locale. Mayer hired von Sternberg as director, with orders to make Lamarr over, using Dietrich as the model. However, Mayer chose the unrepentantly domestic *New York Cinderella* as the vehicle and, as her screen lover, the all-American Everyman Spencer Tracy. The story originated with Charles MacArthur, with some help from Ben Hecht. Tracy plays a public-spirited New York doctor who, returning by liner from the Yucatan, prevents jilted fashion model Lamarr from jumping overboard. Back in New York, they marry, and she joins him in his slum clinic, until memories of the married man who dumped her tempt her back to the high life.

Mayer interfered constantly, even correcting the way Tracy read his lines. He receives no screen credit, but this may be the only film personally produced by the studio head. For her part, Lamarr still had problems with English. According to her biographer, Ruth Barton, Lamarr was "distressed by not receiving her lines until the night before shooting and not being allowed to work with her regular voice coach, Phyllis Laughton, but instead having to make do with Laughton's assistant." After eight days, von Sternberg resigned. "Each detail of this film, on which I worked not more than a week, was pre-determined by a dozen others," he complained. "Other directors were better fitted to participate in this kind of nonsense, though this may well be beyond the ability of anyone." According to Barton, Mayer "scrapped everything except a few good shots of Hedy, then hired Frank Borzage. What Borzage didn't realize was that Mayer regarded this as his project and they fought for weeks. Then Spencer Tracy was sent for by 20th Century-Fox to work on *Stanley and Livingstone*. Once again production was halted, once again the director left (or was fired if you believe Mayer's version), and once again, most of the footage was scrapped."[2]

Already $800,000 in the red, *New York Cinderella* sat on the shelf until January 1939. In the interim, Lamarr acquired a husband, screenwriter Gene Markey, and a child. Frustrated with the mediocre roles being offered, she announced her intention to appear on Broadway in a production of *Salome*. MGM took her to court, demanding a re-straining order. Lamarr argued that the studio had voided her contract by failing to utilize her talents, having made only one film with her, the lackluster *Lady of the Tropics*. Hurriedly, *New York Cinderella* was dusted off. James Kevin McGuinness rewrote the script, which W. S. Van Dyke shot with Tracy and Lamarr but an entirely different support-ing cast. Walter Pidgeon, Lana Turner, and Fanny Brice disappeared, to be replaced by Kent Taylor, Laraine Day, and Verree Teasdale, herself a replacement for Ina Claire. The film emerged in February 1940 as *I Take This Woman*—more aptly titled, someone suggested, *I Retake This Woman*—and, predictably, flopped.

Early in 1939 MGM, apparently sympathetic to von Sternberg's special problems on the Lamarr film, invited him to discharge his contract by making a crime story with Wallace Beery, *Sergeant Madden*. "I did the best I could," he wrote, "though this could never be good enough. It is not possible for a director, no matter how skilled, to carry out someone else's orders on how and what to direct. However, everyone was pleased; everyone but me, and I left." His main complaint was against the bearlike Beery, a Metro institution for decades and, in the actor's view, above direction. After an early difference of opinion, Beery went over the director's head and protested to the front office that von Sternberg was demanding rehearsals and in general disturbing the even tenor of Beery's well-paid career. Von Sternberg was summoned and, in his words, "ordered not to waste any time in teaching someone who knew more than I did."

Despite this, Beery's performance in *Sergeant Madden* is among his least maudlin, an indication of his eventual acceptance of the director's vision of the story as not simply another sentimental tale of New York's finest but a throwback to European fables of parental duty. "Wallace Beery changed his mind," von Sternberg commented, "when he noted that my instructions were carefully heeded by the others." As soft-hearted New York cop Shaun Madden, whom von Sternberg uses as a symbol of the inflexible and sinister beneficence of fatherhood, Beery, though still prey to coy grins and cries of "Aw, shucks," is unusually subdued and believable.

Wells Root's screenplay gave von Sternberg a chance to review his own troubled relationship with his father. Shaun, like Moses Sternberg, is big and slow. The first third of the film chronicles his painful rise from beat cop to sergeant, via a series of brow-wrinkling examinations. His brogue, banter, and habit of adopting street kids make him a metaphor for parental tyranny. He stifles those around him, not viciously, like von Seyffertitz in *The Case of Lena Smith*, but with a refusal to accept any point of view except his own, even when it leads to the death of those he claims to love.

His son Dennis (Alan Curtis), dissuaded from becoming a boxer, is cajoled into entering the police academy and marrying one of the sergeant's wards, Eileen (Laraine Day). Another adopted stray, Al (Tom Brown), also becomes a cop, but with more enthusiasm than Dennis. When Dennis is forced, under pressure from this parental ideal and Al's threatening competition, to shoot a young criminal (David Gorcey) in the hope of attaining a quick promotion, gangster "Piggy" Ceders (Marc Lawrence) frames him for murder. Madden, disinclined to believe in his boy's innocence, resigns from the force in shame. On the train to imprisonment in Sing Sing, Dennis escapes and takes to crime, until Madden, shrewdly callous, sets a trap at the hospital where Eileen is having Dennis's baby. Despairing, Dennis lets himself be killed in the trap his father has laid, and the family gratefully returns to respectability. Al graduates from the police academy and takes Dennis's place as husband and father, after which the cage of social necessity settles once again over its complacent victims.

The resonance with German cinema gives *Sergeant Madden* more than usual interest. The theme of the adopted child mastering and replacing the natural son appears frequently in German theater and film. Even its minor characters might have passed unnoticed in UFA films of two decades before. "Piggy" is a ratty spiv out of Fritz Lang, and Ma Madden (Fay Holden) is the classic hausfrau, content with *kirche, kuche und kinder*. As for Eileen, no young wife could be more dutiful. At her most tranquil when she bears the "bad" son's child in a delivery conspicuously free of pain, she cheerfully gives herself to the "good" son, conscious only of the necessities of the system they serve.

A chase through a warehouse shows some film noir flair, but von Sternberg employed mostly slow traveling shots, detached framings, wet streets, and softening filters to re-create some of the morose grayness of Murnau. Veteran John Seitz became the preferred cinematographer of Billy Wilder, for whom he shot *Double Indemnity* and *Sunset Boulevard,* both of which share some of the same character.

Ironically, *Sergeant Madden* was the last film von Sternberg made while his father was still alive. On February 2, 1940, Morris died at his home in Lynbrook, Long Island. The brief *New York Times* obituary described him as "beloved husband of Abigail, and father of Josef von

Sternberg of Hollywood, Calif.; Hermine Tobias of Valley Stream, L.I., Mollie Sternberg of Brooklyn, NY, Henry Sternberg of East Rockaway, L.I., and the late Fred Sternberg of Hollywood, Calif." The number of fraternal associations listed in his obituary attest to his sociability. One of von Sternberg's few mementos of his father was his Masonic ring, which he kept for the rest of his life.

The War at Home

Remember, remember always that all of us, and you and I
especially, are descended from immigrants and revolutionists.
—Franklin Delano Roosevelt

WITH WAR NOW DECLARED, an estimated 25,000 Europeans
flooded into American show business, but they found closed doors everywhere. "Not yet at the alarming stage," noted the *New York Times,*
"Hollywood's refugee problem is nevertheless giving some concern to
certain people here." Newcomers could expect invitations to parties but
few offers of work. The *New York Times* reported in March 1941 that
"forty or fifty well-known film workers have been more or less recently
employed by the studios . . . and there are twice or three times that
number waiting around on the off-chance that a job will be found for
them. Technical jobs are pretty well protected by guilds and unions. . . .
A scattering of secretaries, research workers, readers, messengers and
the like have been brought in."

Any person of foreign extraction in Hollywood, even someone
like von Sternberg, who had lived there for years, needed to be careful
about his or her friends. When he and Dietrich dined with newly arrived
French director René Clair, each was under individual FBI surveillance.
Austrians and Germans were routinely suspect, and Clair attracted attention because the American authorities distrusted all those who didn't
declare themselves antifascist—something many exiles hesitated to do,

particularly if family or friends remained in Nazi territory. In particular, Dietrich's lover of the time, Jean Gabin, came under suspicion for his refusal to condemn Vichy.

The FBI received numerous anonymous letters, most barely literate, accusing Dietrich of Nazi sympathies and of spying during her USO visits to military bases. One informer claimed that meetings of the banned German-American Bund took place at her home and that she climaxed such events by singing "The Horst Wessel Song." Despite the flimsiness of the charges, the FBI used them as a pretext to open her letters and monitor both her bank accounts and her sex life. During 1941–1942 it noted affairs with Gabin, Erich Maria Remarque, John Wayne, and actress Kay Francis. Her relationship with Rudy puzzled the Bureau, which collected many pages of anodyne information about Sieber's life in a New York hotel with Tami Matul (who passed as his "ward") and the $200 Dietrich sent him each month.

Von Sternberg attracted the attention of the FBI by protesting the construction of a military airport near his Chatsworth home, but he satisfied the Bureau that his objections were based entirely on the noise potential. Of more gravity was his friendship with Karl Vollmoeller, who was interned as an enemy alien in December 1941. Fearing guilt by association, von Sternberg volunteered to give information about the writer and was interviewed by the FBI on June 16, 1942. According to an internal report, he described how "in the summer of 1939, Vollmoeller . . . tried to get Marlene Dietrich to meet representatives of the German movie companies in Paris to discuss possible contracts for the making of pictures in German. But Dietrich, von Sternberg stated, was furious at such overtures and would have nothing more to do with him because she wanted to have no connection with anything German."[1] Vollmoeller, who was never particularly political, may have been guilty of simply pursuing his activities as a go-between. Though eventually released, he never recovered from his imprisonment and died in 1948.

Shortly after Max Reinhardt arrived in Hollywood in 1937, he took over direction of an acting school that had been financed by a consortium of studios to find new talent. The Max Reinhardt Actors Workshop for Stage, Screen, and Radio graduated a number of later stars, including

Jane Russell, Robert Ryan, and Robert Stack. Von Sternberg, encouraged by the presence on the faculty of composer Erich Wolfgang Korngold and writers such as Gert von Gotard, resurrected a plan to restage Reinhardt's 1924 Berlin production of Luigi Pirandello's *Six Characters in Search of an Author* and to film it, with Reinhardt both producing and playing the stage manager.

In 1930 Jesse Lasky had optioned some of Pirandello's works and brought the author to Hollywood on a generous retainer to discuss how they might be filmed. Almost immediately, they ran into censorship problems, particularly with his best-known work, the aforementioned *Six Characters*. In Pirandello's story, while a play is in rehearsal, six members of a family mysteriously appear in the theater and insist on acting out their personal tragedies, in competition with the invented action. These include suicide and an incident of near incest when a father unwittingly encounters his own daughter in a brothel. Pirandello's stage directions gave producers wide latitude. In 1924 Reinhardt audaciously used ultraviolet light to have the family materialize from the dark— "like departed souls in Hades," wrote one awed critic, "yearning for life-giving blood. [The purple light created] an unearthly glow, accentuating their nature as splits of imagination, and heightening the element of guilt."[2] Such possibilities for creative lighting, combined with the chance to work with Reinhardt, made the project almost irresistible to von Sternberg.

Unable to solve the censorship problems, Paramount gave up on the plays, ceding the rights of the most accessible, *As You Desire Me,* to MGM as a vehicle for Garbo and von Stroheim. Pirandello won the Nobel Prize in 1934 and died in 1936. Management of the estate passed to his secretary, Saul Colin, who placed a high value on the late author's work. When Reinhardt inquired about filming *Six Characters,* Colin demanded $80,000 for the rights. After much haggling, a contract of sorts was negotiated, under which Reinhardt would stage the play with student actors, working for little or no money. He and von Sternberg would produce and direct a film of the production but would receive no payment until the film was sold. Even then, all rights would revert to the estate after only one year. On November 25, 1940, they wrote a joint letter to Colin, confirming the agreement but complaining that it still hadn't been ratified by the Pirandello family. It never would be. With the U.S. declaration of war against Germany and Italy, Reinhardt dropped the project, closed the acting school, and moved to New York, where he died in 1943.

From the rarefied reaches of Pirandello, von Sternberg descended to the depths of Oriental depravity. Producer Arnold Pressburger, despite a long career in Berlin and Vienna, was having difficulty gaining a foothold in Hollywood. He owned the rights to John Colton's 1926 play *The Shanghai Gesture,* which ran for more than 200 performances on Broadway but had always proved too hot for Hollywood. For the next two decades, a series of writers and producers tried and failed to adapt it for sound. Pressburger approached von Sternberg, attracted, he said, by the director's reputation as difficult, presumably in the hope he would stand up to the censors.

Von Sternberg hadn't read *The Shanghai Gesture* and was startled by its frankness. "You would be amazed at the garishness of the original stage play," he told the *Los Angeles Times,* "both in its setting and its plot. We found it quite hopeless." Colton, the son of an American diplomat, had been raised in Japan, lived there for many years, and knew Oriental vice intimately. He owed his reputation to a stage version of Somerset Maugham's short story "Rain," about a missionary who tries to drive a slut from a Pacific island, only to succumb to lust and cut his throat in remorse.

The Shanghai Gesture deals no less enthusiastically with the decay of Western morality under the influence of the Orient. It's set in 1920s Shanghai, filled with refugees from the Russian Revolution, many of whom prostituted themselves to survive. Opium, forced on the Chinese by the British in return for tea, the nation's most valuable export, was commonplace. In her brothel, "Mother Goddam," a Manchu princess turned madam, caters to wealthy expatriates and sensation-seeking tourists who goggle at the whores dangling naked in bamboo cages. The set piece is a banquet to celebrate Chinese New Year, thrown by Mother Goddam for Sir Guy Charteris, whose China Trading Company is buying up properties like hers for redevelopment. During dinner, the madam reveals that she was once a whore herself, enslaved when her

Western husband-to-be stole her dowry and disappeared. Shuttled with other girls from port to port, she was prevented from fleeing by having the soles of her feet slit and small stones sewn inside, making it agonizing to walk. Her former lover, of course, is Charteris, and Mother Goddam has planned an intricate revenge. At the climax of the party, she produces Charteris's daughter, Victoria, who has become an opium addict and, as "Poppy," one of the brothel's most popular attractions. Charteris then turns the tables, revealing that Victoria is also Mother Goddam's daughter, whom he took at birth and raised. In the gory denouement, Poppy turns on her mother, who murders her.

Paramount optioned the play in 1926, United Artists and Universal in 1929, Columbia and Tiffany in 1930, and RKO, Mascot, and Warner Brothers in 1932. Universal persisted the longest, with studio head Carl Laemmle Jr. pleading with Will H. Hays and Colonel Jason S. Joy of the MPPDA that his company needed a "red-hot smash" to stave off collapse. Hays counseled Laemmle, "The play deals with a bawdy house which at times is unusually attractive and at other times wretchedly sordid. Into this background is woven miscegenation, illegitimacy, white slavery, murder, and an opportunity to incur the ill-will of other countries. If the story were re-written so as to avoid all of these difficulties, as it would have to be, it is my honest opinion that it would be so emasculated as to thwart the purpose you have in mind."

Laemmle persisted. Through a succession of draft screenplays, and over Colton's objections, the brothel was downgraded to a casino. "Mother Goddam" became "Mother Satan," then "Mother Gin Sling." Victoria Charteris remained "Poppy," but her opium habit was diminished to indiscriminate gambling and drinking. Hays and his successors continued to read new scripts and reject them, until the total stood at thirty-two. Meanwhile, Universal, having clawed its way out of recession with horror films such as *Frankenstein*, dropped the project. In 1933 United Artists announced a production, eliciting a testy telegram to the MPPDA from Harry Warner, who had been ready to buy the rights until warned off by the association. Hays reassured him that *The Shanghai Gesture* remained as unfilmable as ever, and interest lapsed again until Pressburger, with von Sternberg's help, convinced United Artists he could "lick" the story.

Attaining respectability for *The Shanghai Gesture* involved radical revision. In the new version, Victoria Charteris (Gene Tierney), traveling incognito as "Poppy Smith" and looking for excitement in Shanghai with her escort (John Abbott), enters the gambling house of "Mother Gin Sling" (Ona Munson). Learning that Poppy is the daughter of Sir Guy Charteris (Walter Huston), Mother sees a way to save her business. She orders one of the casino's hangers-on, Dr. Omar (Victor Mature), to seduce Poppy and encourage her to run up huge debts at roulette. The rest follows, more or less, Colton's original.

Von Sternberg took credit for the screenplay, "with the collaboration of Geza Herczeg and Jules Furthman." Vollmoeller also worked on the adaptation, but Pressburger prudently removed his name. Although Paul Ivano is listed as cinematographer, von Sternberg pointedly inserted "Directed by Josef von Sternberg, ASC" to emphasize his membership in the exclusive American Society of Cinematographers and assert responsibility for the lighting. Boris Leven designed the film, but as always, von Sternberg contributed, both with original ideas and by employing artists he had met in the course of his collecting. One of these was actor Keye Luke, who executed the murals in Mother Gin Sling's dining room. Before becoming familiar as Charlie Chan's "Number One Son" in the series starring Warner Oland, Luke was a commercial artist who not only decorated the walls and ceiling of Grauman's Chinese Theatre on Hollywood Boulevard but also drew the press-book artwork for *King Kong*.

In the cleanup, Mother Goddam's brothel takes on some of the coziness of Rick's Café in *Casablanca*. Whores no longer hang in cages. In fact, there are no whores at all, although as part of the New Year celebrations, some girls, fully clothed, dangle over the street in what's described as an ancient ritual but looks like an auction. The worst vice practiced on the premises is roulette, which takes place in a cockpit-like *salle* reminiscent of both the set built for the operating room of *Vanity's Price* and the atrium of the Great World in Shanghai. Players and spectators peer down from concentric terraces, and a basket is periodically lowered to collect the house's winnings from the sour-faced appraiser and cashier.

Like Rick's Café, the casino attracts a floating clientele of European and Eurasian riffraff—in one case, the same riffraff, since Marcel Dalio plays the croupier in both films. Otherwise, most actors are cast against type, sometimes startlingly so. Mike Mazurki, usually seen as a thug in a double-breasted suit and snap-brimmed fedora, is the "Coolie," an Asian rickshaw man. German émigré Albert Basserman is the police commissioner, and perennial English butler Eric Blore plays Caesar Hawkins, the casino's handicapped accountant, limping on crutches. Phyllis Brooks is Dixie Pomeroy, another addition to Colton's original; she's one of those itinerant wisecracking floozies who turn up in many 1940s crime stories as victims or convenient plot devices, in this case, to supply some background on Walter Huston's Charteris. More puzzling is the presence of Maria Ouspenskaya, who, as the Amah, appears in only one scene and never says a word. Von Sternberg took particular relish in casting the role of the appraiser, who lurks in a booth behind the roulette table, peering through a loupe at the trinkets players offer for credit. The performance of Russian actor Mikhail Rasumny is modeled on Mr. Kamenetzky, who once employed von Sternberg to sell costume jewelry.

Bette Davis was rumored to covet the role of Mother Gin Sling—not such eccentric casting if one recalls her merciless Regina Giddens in *The Little Foxes* that same year. A better candidate existed in Gloria Swanson. After seven years offscreen, she had just launched a tentative comeback with the romantic comedy *Father Takes a Wife,* with Adolphe Menjou. While it awaited release, she was optimistic about her chances for a new career, and the *Los Angeles Times* described her as "the strong candidate" to play Mother Gin Sling, adding that "the signs of the zodiac look propitious." Pressburger probably anticipated Swanson's casting and had the costumes cut to fit her petite five-foot-one-inch figure. Once negative reviews of *Father Takes a Wife* sent her recoiling into obscurity for another seven years, von Sternberg was faced with a situation similar to that in *The Devil Is a Woman,* when the departure of Joel McCrea forced the casting of Cesar Romero on the basis of his shirt size.

In this case, the search led to five-foot-two-inch Ona Munson. In one sense, she was an obvious choice, having played brothel-keeper Belle Watling in *Gone with the Wind.* Although she probably got the part exclusively because of her height, von Sternberg courteously attributed

Munson's casting to her "mentality" and understanding of the role—not entirely implausible, since she could well manage its chill asexuality and misanthropy. Bisexual, and another of Mercedes de Acosta's many lovers, along with Dietrich and Garbo, she was also a former mistress of Ernst Lubitsch and would commit suicide in 1955 after a career plagued by bouts of depression.

As easy as it is to mock its pretensions, *The Shanghai Gesture* was closer to the essence of von Sternberg than any film since *Shanghai Express*. Without Dietrich, he was free to indulge himself with a hand-picked ensemble. Tense, mask-faced, dressed in exotic mixtures of Eastern and Western styles, they move like marionettes across his white-walled stage, manipulated like the wax figures Mother Gin Sling caresses as she plans her dinner. This film has no von Sternberg surrogate, no languishing, cane-carrying discarded lover. Instead, it's the omnipotent, manipulative Mother in whom he is reflected. The terraced pit, with the roulette wheel at its core, is her domain, as the cinema is his, and the gamblers—desperate, elated, indifferent—who peer down at it belong to both. Attended by her acolytes, she confers and denies, chiding a loser who tries to kill himself, accepting his kiss on her hand as she extends further credit. Poppy dimly sees the true corruption of this empire. "It has a ghastly familiarity," she says the first time she walks in, "like a half-forgotten dream. Anything could happen here." But the real speaker is surely von Sternberg, and his target the cinema.

Since Poppy, in this emasculated text, does not succumb to opium, the writers invented a nemesis in Dr. Omar. A Eurasian voluptuary in fez, cape, and tuxedo, he looks the "thoroughbred mongrel" he claims to be. Asked of what he's a doctor, he says, "Doctor of Nothing" but "a poet of Shanghai and Gomorrah." As such, he's in the right place, since these people don't have a belief among them. It's for his loose-lipped indolence Poppy falls, lubricated by emollient quotes from Edward FitzGerald. British critic C. A. Lejeune, in a review titled "Rude Gesture," dismissed him as someone whose "idea of a Levantine mystic is to quote the more hackneyed stanzas of 'Omar Khayyam' ('A loafer bread, a jugger wine, and Thou')." Omar's affair with Poppy, conducted in the shadow of the censor, is of necessity played out in glances and unspoken invitations. Only when she declares her love does any feeling show through those luminous eyes. The scene in which she visits his apartment and, as he lies casually among cushions, surrenders herself to his indifference, encourages us to mingle lust with dismay. Not for the first time, we see what von Sternberg looked for in a love object—a kind of emotional slavery.

The worst fault of *The Shanghai Gesture*, both in design and in casting, is overcrowding, signaled by the opening scene of a congested, smoky Shanghai intersection re-created on the set, with traffic being directed, improbably, by a heavily bearded and turbaned Sikh. With only $1 million to spend, Pressburger hired the old Hal Roach studios in Culver City, dismissed by von Sternberg as "a concrete warehouse." The gambling pit hogged most of the space, along with the dining room, which was lined with floor-to-ceiling mirrors decorated with Keye Luke's life-size Chinese figures in oils and gold leaf. Because of these large sets, others were skimpy. The bar from which Michael Dalmatoff dispenses his misanthropic wisecracks is barely more than a corner; Omar's apartment and Mother Gin Sling's office likewise.

With so many characters, few get more than a couple of scenes, and these are seldom developed. Too often, von Sternberg seems to be lost for ideas, cutting away to a sneering Eric Blore propped on his crutch like Long John Silver or to Ona Munson posed in her voodoo hairdo, curls varnished hard as toffee. (She hated the costumes of *Shanghai Gesture* and particularly the makeup, which induced headaches.) Gene Tierney has the lioness's share of screen time, enthroned at the bar while her admirers fawn, attracted and chilled by the languid emptiness of her beauty. If only she could act. Her career had been underwritten by her wealthy family, and Tierney was slow to develop credible dramatic technique. The *New York Times* spoke for many when it acknowledged that she is "fabulously svelte" in gowns designed by her husband, couturier Oleg Cassini, but as an actress "gives a fair imitation of a second lead in a boarding-school play." Lejeune suggested that she "plays Poppy with the abandon of a child who can't have her second helping of chocolate cake."[3]

The Shanghai Gesture severely taxed von Sternberg's health. He experienced a recurrence of the anxiety that had caused his nervous breakdown and also the first symptoms of the heart disease that would kill him. A young nurse, Jeanne McBride, was hired to care for him during shooting and his convalescence. He directed part of the film while lying on a cot. However, he was sufficiently mobile to give a few press interviews, designed to correct his reputation as a curmudgeon. One reporter, the Associated Press's Sigrid Arne, was accorded a rare visit to the set. She evoked his reputation for working "like a miniature artist. Taking, re-taking, changing, shading, until actors turn white with fatigue. Or purple with rage." But the man she watched directing Victor Mature at the piano was a pussycat. After the actor ended his scene and strode past her off the stage "like a race horse," Arne got her moment with this new von Sternberg, "a middle-sized man, paunchy, with thick gray hair. He had a pleased-with-von-Sternberg smile. He shook hands, saying, 'How would you like to meet the old heavy?'" During the interview he took pains to show a sunny side, hitherto unsuspected. "Oh, you should have known me ten years ago," he told her, "when I had no friends. Now I am growing old and kind."[4] In most Hollywood circles, this statement would have elicited a hollow laugh.

Anticipating objections to the film from the remnants of Chiang Kai-shek's Kuomintang administration, which, though barricaded on Taiwan, remained the "legal" Chinese government in U.S. diplomatic eyes, Pressburger retained Tom Gubbins, an expert on Chinese culture, as technical adviser. In addition, a wordy preface to the film reminds the audience that this Shanghai is a fantasy city—"a distorted mirror, . . . a refuge for people who wished to live between the lines of laws and customs, . . . a modern Tower of Babel, neither Chinese, European, British nor American." Nonetheless, T. K. Chang, of the government in exile's Los Angeles consulate, protested the scenes of women suspended in cages, insisting that there was no such practice in China. He also complained about the murder of Poppy, which was hardly conceivable in terms of good morals, whether in Shanghai or in Hollywood. Chang visited the set and met von Sternberg and Pressburger, but his many complaints about the characters and the story were ignored. Pressburger, echoing Adolph Zukor's defense of *The Devil Is a Woman* to the Spanish government, insisted that "*Shanghai Gesture* is not meant to portray reality, but to display a world of fantasy. This imaginary world has no connection with the realistic aspects of today."

And what is the meaning of the title? Since "to shanghai" means to kidnap (as in seizing a drunken seaman and forcing him aboard a ship about to leave for Asia), it could refer to the enforced prostitution of Mother Gin Sling or that of the caged girls. Alternatively, it may hint at the sexual technique called the "Shanghai squeeze" or "Casanova clip." Otherwise known as *fang chung-shu*, this skill, one of the Taoist arts of the inner chamber, permits a woman to tighten her vaginal muscles during sex, constricting blood within the penis and, as one description put it, making "a matchstick feel like a Havana cigar." Persistent rumor claimed that Wallis Simpson, who had spent a year in Shanghai after separating from her first husband, a U.S. Navy pilot, frequented a brothel like that of Mother Gin Sling and learned such expertise, which she later used to beguile the future Edward VIII.

Shot between August and October 1941, *The Shanghai Gesture* had a brief New York screening starting on Christmas Day, three weeks after Pearl Harbor, to qualify it as a 1941 release for the following year's Academy Awards, but it didn't open nationally until January 15, 1942. In light of the new war against Japan, this eccentric take on Asia left reviewers bemused. *New York Times* reviewer Bosley Crowther, a mouthpiece for the major studios and no friend of von Sternberg, predictably dismissed it as "so utterly and lavishly pretentious, so persistently opaque, and so very badly acted in every leading role but one [Walter Huston's Charteris] that [it] finally becomes laughable. . . . The director was apparently so interested in shooting magnificent scenes that he overlooked the necessity of fitting together a lucid film."[5] All the same, Leven's set design would be nominated for an Academy Award, as would Richard Hageman's music score.

Americana

'Tis the gift to be simple.
—"Simple Gifts," an old Shaker hymn

ON JULY 29, 1943, von Sternberg married Jeanne Annette McBride, his twenty-one-year-old secretary/nurse. It's difficult to imagine who he might have married if not her. No man was less inclined to date, and throughout his life he maintained a distance from women that was at best courtly, at worst icily polite. The ceremony took place at the North Hollywood home of Dr. Hans Schiff, a noted German photographer. The groom cheated his age a little for the press, giving it as forty-five instead of nearer fifty. The union was sufficiently newsworthy to rate a listing in *Time* magazine, which described him, inaccurately, as the "magniloquent discoverer and first director of Marlene Dietrich."

The couple settled in North Hollywood, at 1919 Outpost Drive. He had abandoned the Neutra house, which was up for sale. He could not get gas for the Rolls, his Japanese servants had been interned, and Royal Canadian Air Force pilots from the nearby air base (constructed despite his vehement protests) flew practice bombing runs on the isolated building. "He was getting dive-bombed every night," said his widow. "It was driving him crazy."[1]

With time on his hands, he agreed to another show of his art collection at the Los Angeles Museum. In many senses, it was a valedictory exhibition, since he was already culling some works and contemplating the sale of his entire holdings, both for living expenses and for possible investment in his own company. Interviewed about his activities, he mentioned his own production plans and a government job, the nature of which he could not discuss. The company never eventuated, but his government project did. Having volunteered his services after Pearl Harbor, he was at last asked by Philip Dunne, then managing propaganda production for the Office of War Information, to direct the fourth in a series of one-reel documentaries, a more relaxed version of the "Why We Fight" model called "The American Scene."

The Town is a picture of Madison, Indiana, during a few days of summer 1943. It is a typical community, but one whose roots, the film stresses, spring from the foreign culture American forces were then defending overseas. Intended as an antidote to isolationism in small-town thinking, it's persuasive in its thesis that American life, both in outlook and in culture, owes much to Europe and Europeans. Von Sternberg later dismissed it, complaining he had been "told what to say and what to do," but the film does have charm and occasional flashes of imagination, although these are often stifled by a spoken commentary that is hectoring or unctuous by turns.

The opening, with its art history slant and mildly flippant approach, is characteristic of the film. As the camera glances at an Italian campanile, a Palladian portico, and a Renaissance fountain, the commentary asks rhetorically in what town such a mixture of features could be found. Then the film reverses to show that the fountain belongs to the local swimming pool and the portico to the courthouse; the campanile is the Madison Fire Brigade bell tower. Sun-filled and clean, the images establish an interesting tension between these adopted elements and the landscape in which they are set. The calm chiaroscuro of the library, a school seen across a forest of bicycles, the teacher in class framed by a desk and a dominating globe, cattle jammed into a stockyard gate—these pieces in the mosaic give us the feel and flavor of the community. *The Town* is the work of a man reacting without bitterness to a project considerably beneath his abilities.

The marriage to Jeanne McBride didn't survive the war. They parted in 1945. In 1944 a jeweler named Lou Bach had bought the Neutra house at a bargain price—less, Jo lamented, than it cost to put in the tennis court. Bach sold it to Ayn Rand and her husband, actor Frank O'Connor, for a mere $24,000. Rand wrote her best-seller *Atlas Shrugged* there. In 1963 she resold it for $175,000. A property developer demolished it in 1972.

David O. Selznick retained a respect for von Sternberg's visual flair, if not for his reliability as a director, and periodically offered him small jobs, most of which he declined. One came in mid-1944 when Alfred Hitchcock, after wrangling for months with Selznick over a surrealist dream sequence for *Spellbound,* designed by Salvador Dali, was unable to finish shooting it before leaving for Europe. Von Sternberg declined to take over, intuiting that if Selznick was difficult to deal with, Dali would be worse, and the two together impossible. William Cameron Menzies completed the sequence but declined credit.

A year later Selznick proposed another contract, which von Sternberg accepted. Just as von Sternberg never entirely severed his connection to Marlene Dietrich, Selznick lived in the shadow of *Gone with the Wind.* With each new film, most of them starring his wife Jennifer Jones, he strove for a similar epic grandeur, inflating the material far beyond its limits. *Duel in the Sun,* a simple western, bulged with Homeric detail: a murderous conflict between brothers played by Joseph Cotten and Gregory Peck; a war against the encroaching railroad generaled by their crippled cattle-boss father, Lionel Barrymore; and a love affair that ends with Peck and Jones dueling to the death in the desert, earning the film the label "Lust in the Dust."

Not content with action and spectacle, Selznick strove for glamour too. Director King Vidor recalled, "Selznick thought highly of the contributions that von Sternberg had made with his films, and in his handling and photographing of Marlene Dietrich. . . . He thought that von Sternberg could do the same for his wife." Von Sternberg joined Otto Brower, William Cameron Menzies, and Chester Franklin as one of the second-unit directors. "His work was more or less in line of assistant to the director," said Vidor. "I suppose it's possible that he made some of the isolated atmospheric scenes without members of the principal cast."[2]

There's no evidence that von Sternberg lit any shots of Jones that appear in the film. He had never worked with color and was further challenged by the fact that Jones, playing a mixed-blood Mexican, wore dark makeup throughout. Rather, according to Vidor:

He directed, and I suppose lighted, some of the make-up tests and costume tests of Jennifer. During some of the scenes in Arizona where we wanted Miss Jones to look terribly wet with perspiration from the intense heat, Von Sternberg would take on the job of throwing a bucket of cold water over Miss Jones after the cameras were going and just before she entered the scene. . . . He would rehearse dialogue or whatever was necessary to do. He had an eye for colour and costumes and very often would make suggestions about how to improve the dress or appearance of any one of the many characters in the picture.[3]

Only once was he given leeway to do more than assist Vidor, and the result was unfortunate. Vidor recalls:

I left the set one afternoon at five o'clock (we usually kept going until seven) and asked Von Sternberg to take over a scene which I had rehearsed of a sheriff and his deputies searching through the patio of the house for Greg Peck. A few days later, Selznick called me in. . . . Von Sternberg kept going until nine or ten o'clock that night and had shot 4,500 feet of film [about fifty minutes]. It was a very simple scene of men walking along a terrace and opening doors, but Von Sternberg, in his usual way, kept going hoping to make something big out of it.[4]

The Seven Bad Years

Demoniac frenzy, moping melancholy,
And moon-struck madness.

—John Milton

TO BE A FLUNKY, even for a director of Vidor's stature, must have crushed what remained of von Sternberg's old spirit. With no work in sight, he began writing an original screenplay called "The Seven Bad Years." Based on his own childhood, it dealt, in his words, "with man's fixation on an infantile level, and its purpose was to demonstrate the adult insistence to follow the pattern inflicted on a child in its first seven helpless years, from which a man could extricate himself were he to realise that an irresponsible child was leading him into trouble." His outline suggests a work of self-analysis that would have confronted for the first time the issues introduced elliptically into his earlier films, but no producer offered more than polite interest, followed by a refusal "on commercial grounds." One suggested that it might help if he called it "And a Little Child Shall Lead Them," but since von Sternberg was no writer, it's hard to see how any script of his would have found favor.

Dispirited, he took another cruise to China. In Shanghai he once again had an expatriate friend to show him around. Hungerford Howard had been one of his numerous poorly paid assistants before entering the U.S. Foreign Service and being posted as vice-consul to Chungking and Shanghai. On his return to the United States, von Sternberg put some

241

of his paintings up for sale, including a Gauguin. In 1947 freelance art appraiser Meri Wilner (née Otis) visited him with art dealer Gus Gilbert, for whom she worked and who had done business with von Sternberg in the past. "Hallmark Cards was looking for some paintings to buy," Meri remembered. "At that time, any big business who wanted to decorate with precious paintings could write off the expense, believe it or not."[1] Wilner was a war widow with a young daughter, Catherine, born on May 5, 1944. In October 1948 Meri and von Sternberg married.

Von Sternberg's next job came from an unexpected quarter. After writing the controversial western *The Outlaw,* Jules Furthman was promoted to producer on the staff of Howard Hughes, aircraft manufacturer, sometime filmmaker, and, at the time, owner of the RKO studios. Hughes involved himself exhaustively in the technical aspects of filmmaking, which, to him, transcended content. He would tinker with a film for years, "correcting" details such as hairdos and accents, unconcerned that, with each delay, turning a profit became less likely. Believing in ideas of proven worth, he decided to produce an ambitious flying epic, the *Hell's Angels* of the jet age, to equal if not better the film he had made in 1930.

Shooting on *Jet Pilot* commenced with another director, whom Hughes fired. Furthman, asked to suggest replacements, came up with five candidates, including von Sternberg, whose photographic experience, he argued, might be ideal for the beautiful young Janet Leigh. Hughes agreed, with the proviso that all five candidates film a test sequence. Von Sternberg was philosophical. "My job is to transfer the script to the screen," he told Ezra Goodman. "I have no freedom whatsoever beyond that. I don't see why I should have. At this point they want to see if I can make an actor walk across the set."[2] The "actor" in his case was Italian actress Gina Lollobrigida, one of Hughes's conquests, with whom von Sternberg filmed a screen test. Hughes had flown her to Hollywood to continue their affair, but once the relationship petered out, so did the promise of a U.S. career. "La Lollo" returned to Italy and didn't make her English-language debut until *Beat the Devil* in 1953.

In November 1949 von Sternberg signed a contract for two films, the first of which was *Jet Pilot,* starring John Wayne. Furthman and

Hughes told him unequivocally that they did not want an elaborate excursion into eroticism but a strict reading of the script, with prominence given to the glamorous Leigh, the many flying sequences, and the anticommunist message, endorsed by both Hughes and Wayne. Soviet pilot Anna Marladovna (Leigh) lands at an Alaskan U.S. Air Force base and requests political asylum. The commanding general (Jay C. Flippen) rightly doubts her motives and assigns Shannon (Wayne) as her guide in the hope that she will divulge some useful information. Through a series of midair dialogues, the couple progresses from respect for each other's flying ability to affection and love. Holidaying in Palm Springs, where the American way of life is spectacularly on show, Shannon hears that Anna has been refused asylum and will have to return to Russia and, he believes, a firing squad. Smitten, he marries her. The twist comes with a Secret Service revelation that Anna is actually an agent, charged to lure someone like Shannon back to Moscow. He acquiesces, offering bogus information. Meanwhile, primitive Soviet amenities—doorknobs come off in her hand, lights don't work—remind Anna of the West's superior lifestyle, and when her stolidly comic superiors threaten to brainwash Shannon, she engineers their escape. Predictably, they celebrate with huge steaks, symbols of the American way.

Though Hughes encouraged von Sternberg to shoot Leigh in costumes that emphasized her ample figure, the film is almost coy. In contrast to the priapism of the military men in *Morocco, Dishonored,* and other 1930s films, their 1950s counterparts shun sex as inconsistent with their responsibilities. Any wooing in *Jet Pilot* is left to Wayne's adjutant, an aging and miscast Paul Fix, who is merely embarrassing when expressing lustful thoughts about the fresh-faced Leigh. Wayne is hardly better, behaving like a high school boy when he's forced to search her on arrival and examine her clothes as she discards them.

The filming of dialogue scenes didn't commence until December 8, 1950. Hughes was more concerned with the flying sequences, for which the U.S. Air Force offered him Chuck Yeager, test pilot on the Bell X-1 rocket-powered plane. The air force also allowed access to the first X-1, *Glamorous Glennis.* Because the X-1 had to be carried to launching height on a Boeing B-29 Superfortress, it was recast for the film as a Soviet "parasite fighter." In the meantime, the RKO publicity office did its best to relaunch von Sternberg as a mature and amiable artist. The press was not easily convinced. One report called him "synonymous with the Hollywood that used to be—the Hollywood of white bearskin rugs, limousines with gold-plated fenders, and temperamental exotic stars." Von Sternberg denied such charges, as well as accusations of intransigence. "Difficult? Rubbish!" he said. "When I returned to Hollywood, my desk was piled with telegrams from people wishing me luck. Does that indicate I'm 'difficult'?" As for closing his sets to visitors, he blamed that on Dietrich. "She was nervous," he insisted.[3]

This "new" von Sternberg didn't survive for long. "He was a very difficult man," said Janet Leigh. "I am an easy-going person, but he had the most quietly infuriating way of saying something. He had marvellous effects, and he did things that were provocative without being openly displayed, which to me is always more interesting. Von Sternberg was really better than I wanted to admit, because I didn't particularly like him."[4] Wayne would only remark, philosophically, that the director scared him stiff, although the fact that both had shared Dietrich's bed should have induced a spirit of comradeship.

Shooting finished in May 1951, and in August von Sternberg started work on his second film for RKO, a romantic adventure called *Macao*, produced by Sid Rogell, with a budget of $1.4 million. In what must be a record for a Hughes production, *Macao* emerged little more than eighteen months later, but with so much reshooting and revision that nobody is entirely sure who was responsible for it. Stanley Rubin and Bernard C. Schoenfeld receive screenplay credit from a story by Robert Creighton Williams, but George Bricker, Edward Chodorov, Norman Katkov, Frank L. Moss, and Walter Newman all contributed to the script. Rubin and Chodorov wrote early drafts that were never used. The scenario on which von Sternberg began shooting was by Schoenfeld, but Katkov, a prolific writer for TV, received $3,000 for rewrites and was assisted by Newman, whose $500 stipend suggests their relative contributions. Two producers, four directors, and eventually seven writers worked on *Macao*, justifying von Sternberg's terse summary that "instead of fingers in that pie, half a dozen clowns immersed parts of their anatomy in it."

Despite an opening intertitle's evocation of the ex–Portuguese colony as "a fabulous speck on the earth's surface," *Macao* could be taking place anywhere. The theme, of expatriates trapped by legal constraints in a remote corner of the world, mostly echoes *Casablanca*. Vincent Halloran (Brad Dexter), unscrupulous owner of Macao's biggest gambling den, the Quick Reward, is wanted by the American police, who send their man Trumble (the serviceable William Bendix) to lure him beyond the three-mile limit, where he can be arrested. Nick Cochran (Robert Mitchum) and Trumble arrive on the same boat from Hong Kong, along with Julie Benson (Jane Russell), a nightclub singer who dabbles in petty larceny. Halloran, who has a thriving sideline converting hot jewels into cash, hires Benson, to the resentment of his croupier girlfriend Marge, played by Gloria Grahame, a late replacement for Hughes's recently discarded companion Jane Greer (so memorable opposite Mitchum in Jacques Tourneur's *Out of the Past*). Chases, attempted murders, fistfights, and misunderstandings follow. The most memorable sequence, however, is quite new and deserves inclusion in any anthology of von Sternberg's best work. Cochran is pursued by Halloran's Japanese knifeman (Philip Ahn) among the bobbing junks and fishing nets, light sliding over their faces as they leap from boat to boat, a cat's eyes glinting in a darkened window as the men run by, until Trumble, mistaken for Cochran, is stabbed on the dock through a screen of hanging nets.

Attempting to rule his set with the autocracy of his Paramount days, von Sternberg quickly discovered that the technique no longer worked. Power lay with the front office, which in turn deferred to the stars. Robert Mitchum, who ate directors for breakfast, looked on him almost with pity. "He was very short," he said. "He wore suede trousers, and scarves. He used to stand on a box. And our cameraman, Harry Wild, when he lost patience, would throw down his hat and kick it. Once he kicked the apple box and Von Sternberg fell off backwards. I think Von Sternberg sort of lost heart at that point."[5]

On the principle of divide and rule, he tried to turn the stars against one another. "He would try to butter me up and talk about Mitchum," Russell recalled, "and then he would go to Mitchum and butter him up, and talk about me." To Mitchum, he confided, "We both know this is a piece of shit and we're saddled with Jane Russell.

You and I know she has as much talent as this cigarette case." But this simply excited Mitchum's scorn. When von Sternberg, as usual, banned eating and drinking on the set, the actor brought bags of hamburgers and sodas and distributed them among the cast and crew, ostentatiously leaving greasy scraps on the lectern where von Sternberg kept his copy of the screenplay. Others in the crew indulged in practical jokes, such as smearing pungent cheese on the engine block of von Sternberg's prized Jaguar and toppling a tent while he was inside changing his clothes.

Hughes was anxious that the underwire push-up bra, which he had designed for Jane Russell in *The Outlaw,* was seen to similar advantage on *Macao.* After viewing rushes of Russell in a clinging gown, he sent a memo to the costume department: "The fit of the dress around her breasts is not good, and gives the impression, God forbid, that her breasts are padded or artificial. They just don't appear to be in natural contour. . . . It would be extremely valuable if the dress incorporated some kind of a point at the nipple. . . . I want the rest of her wardrobe, wherever possible, to be low-necked . . . so that customers can get a look at the part of Russell which they pay to see."[6] Grahame, feeling ignored, wired Hughes after two weeks and complained of a lack of consistency in her role, which "varied in interpretation from Eurasian to White Russian to 'Marge' in a mere fifteen minutes of laborious discussion." Hughes ignored her. His interest in the film began and ended at Jane Russell's nipples.

Producer Sid Rogell left at the end of primary shooting and was replaced by Samuel Bischoff (*Two Yanks in Trinidad, The Corpse Came C.O.D.*), who, when he saw von Sternberg's cut on October 19, ordered many of its distinctive visual details removed on the grounds that they slowed down the action. Von Sternberg had no further contact with *Macao,* which passed through a succession of hands, beginning in February 1951 with Robert Stevenson (*Son of Flubber, Mary Poppins*), who shot new footage with Mitchum, Russell, and Ahn. On April 4 a Pasadena preview audience approved of the chase across the junks and a few other scenes but didn't think much of either Mitchum or Russell; they wanted to see more of Grahame. Hughes decreed further retakes but delegated nobody to write them. "Jane and I looked at one another," recalled Mitchum, "and finally Jane handed me a pencil and a piece of paper.

I wrote one line and ad-libbed it from there. . . . We worked about three weeks [on the retakes]."[7] Grahame, meanwhile, left RKO and signed with Paramount. On July 18 she was recalled and found actor Mel Ferrer, who had performed similar chores for Hughes on *Vendetta* and *The Racket,* ready to direct her in new material written by Katkov and Newman. Still later, she was summoned by yet another replacement producer, Jerry Wald, to be directed in additional scenes, this time by her soon-to-be-ex-husband Nicholas Ray. "If you can cut me out of the picture entirely," she told him, "I won't ask for any alimony."[8]

Once he finished *Macao,* and with no more directing work in prospect, von Sternberg taught a one-year course at the University of Southern California. After that, he moved his family to New York. Meri von Sternberg recalled, "Jo had taken me to Crown Heights, Brooklyn, and a few other places, to see if I would like to live there. Finally we went across the Hudson to Weehawken, New Jersey. When I saw the Palisades, I was stunned. We took up residence in a house overlooking the Hudson on Kingswood Road in Weehawken."[9] The two-story house was a new one, built to von Sternberg's specifications. To pay for it, he sold his art collection. A total of 107 items went under the hammer at Parke-Bernet, New York, on November 22, 1949, raising more than $100,000. His first and only child, Nicholas, was born in January 1951, while the house was still under construction. Von Sternberg had an ulterior motive in relocating. He hoped to switch from directing films to directing Broadway plays. One vehicle of this change was to have been a stage musical based on *The Blue Angel.* Dietrich, then having an affair with Harold Arlen, persuaded the songwriter to see the film with E. Y. "Yip" Harburg and Burton Lane, who wrote *Finian's Rainbow.* However, according to Leo Lerman, the three "made funny jokes, such as 'I've got an angle on the *Angel,*' German pronunciation (*Engel*) making it funnier. This infuriated her, for they were not taking it all seriously."[10]

After this project fell though, von Sternberg lived on the proceeds of playing the stock market, for which he showed a considerable facility. When Hughes asked Nicholas Ray to reshoot portions of *Macao,* Ray advised the Directors Guild of the request and also called von Sternberg to alert him. If he objected, Ray said, he wouldn't touch it, but von

Sternberg allegedly told him, "Oh no, Nick. I'm here in New Jersey with my rose garden. I'm close to Wall Street and my art gallery. Go ahead."[11] Some years later he was less forgiving. "Nicholas Ray is an idiot," he told Kevin Brownlow. "He did terrible things to *Macao*. He cut it and ruined it. His name did not appear, but mine did. It was a great injustice."[12]

Ray added a new opening montage that establishes the geographic location of Macao, but with the exception of the curtain-raiser chase and murder of the New York cop and a fistfight that's obviously Ray's, many of the scenes that follow could hardly belong to anyone but von Sternberg, since they use elements from his earlier films. From *The Docks of New York* are the stokers shoveling coal in the boiler room of the ferry from Hong Kong, and their pause to admire chalk drawings and clippings of nude women on the stokehold walls. Also from *Docks*, Mitchum dives overboard to save a life. Russell plays another member of "the foreign legion of women," sister to Dietrich in *Morocco* and Phyllis Brooks in *Shanghai Gesture*, faking it around the Far East cabaret circuit and trusting that something will turn up. More visual signatures, recycled mostly from *Shanghai Gesture*, include a Sikh traffic policeman; a rickshaw man; an Arab along the lines of Dr. Omar; the limping accompanist "Gimpy," recalling Eric Blore's handicapped accountant; and, most notably, the Quick Reward, a scaled-down version of Mother Gin Sling's casino, with croupiers shuttling baskets full of money to the office above.

Beyond these sequences, von Sternberg is recognizable in those shots where overhead lattices and bead curtains cast shadow patterns on Russell's lamé gowns and Mitchum's white suit. In a succession of shimmering metallic evening dresses, combining sexuality with a reminder of wealth, Russell, tight-wrapped and toothsome as a liqueur chocolate, rebuffs Mitchum's mooning, impractical romantic suggestions with the contempt they deserve. Persistence brings few rewards and some outlandish rejections, such as the pass she fends off with an electric fan. As he defends himself with a pillow, the room fills with von Sternbergian feathers. Occasionally, however, the wisecracks wear thin, exposing their vulnerability. "I was lonely in Times Square on

Christmas Eve," Mitchum confesses, and Russell, atypically melting, agrees that she's "tired of running." Not only the decorative elements but also the Viennese *weltschmerz* echo von Sternberg's observation in the commentary for his last film, *The Saga of Anatahan:* "the only real enemy most of us ever have is lonesomeness."

Because I Am a Poet

Delight, then sorrow,
aboard the cormorant
fishing boat.

—Matsuo Basho

ON JUNE 13, 1944, bombers sank three small Japanese cargo ships moored near the tiny Pacific island of Anatahan in the Marianas, 100 kilometers north of Saipan. Thirty-three of the crew swam ashore. In February 1945 a U.S. Navy party sent to retrieve the bodies from a crashed B-29 discovered what remained of the group. It included an Okinawan woman, Kazuko Higa, who had been on the island when the castaways arrived, living with the former overseer of a now-derelict plantation.

No one was ready to surrender. In particular, one noncommissioned officer, Nakagawa Ichiro, remained fanatically loyal to the emperor and threatened to kill any backsliders. For five years they lived off coconuts, taro, wild sugarcane, fish, and lizards. They made huts and clothes from palm fronds. Dried papaya leaves provided a kind of tobacco, and they brewed coconut wine, called *tuba*. The wreck of the B-29 yielded useful plunder, ranging from parachute fabric for clothes to aluminum for cooking pots. They also retrieved two guns. One of the less combative survivors, Michiro Maruyama, used wire to make a samisen. He also kept a diary, from which he later compiled a book about their life there.

Pamphlets air-dropped by the United States, explaining that the war was over, were taken to be a trap and ignored. Periodic attempts by the navy to coax the group out of the jungle failed until, in June 1950, Kazuko Higa signaled to a boat moored off the island, indicating that she wished to be removed. Once she identified the remaining castaways, the Japanese government dropped letters from their relatives, begging them to return. On June 30, 1951, the nineteen survivors left Anatahan. Even when they arrived back in Tokyo, their "commander," Nakagawa, continued to dominate them. "All attempts at conversation were brushed aside," wrote one reporter. "They muttered something incomprehensible, pointed to one member of the group, and seemed waiting for orders."

Also in 1951, von Sternberg was visited in New York by Nagamasa Kawakita, producer of Arnold Fanck's *Daughter of the Samurai*, which he had watched being filmed in 1937. Kawakita had become Japan's largest distributor of non-Japanese films. "We talked about a co-production between Japan and the US," said Kawakita, "which would in a way make up for the stupidity of the war. Von Sternberg proposed the story of *Anatahan*. He showed me the book."[1] As Maruyama's book didn't appear in European languages until 1954, it's more likely that Kawakita saw the July 16, 1951, issue of *Life* magazine, which included an article on the survivors, with photographs.

The world press took some time to ferret out the full story of what took place on Anatahan, but when it did, the reports were sensational. The *Los Angeles Times* headline read: "Only Woman on Island with 31 Tells of Romance. 'Queen Bee' Insists Only Two Men (Not Six) Died for Her Love—One Shot, Other Stabbed." Calling Kazuko a "source of passion, love, intrigue, hatred and murder," the *Times* continued: "The 4-foot-8-inch 32-year-old woman indignantly charged that lurid newspaper and magazine stories that six men were killed because of her were misleading. 'Actually,' she said, 'only two died because of me. One was shot and the other stabbed to death.'" The report concluded, "She plans to go on the stage of one of Tokyo's largest theatres to tell the audience her story—daily for four weeks."[2] Though skimpy, these pieces contained all the essentials of the film von Sternberg and Kawakita would make. As for the idea that filming the story would "make up for the stupidity of the war," that aim disappeared in favor of turning a profit.

Hoping for a speedy production that could be released while the story was still news, Kawakita approached the Toho company, where his old partner Yoshio Osawa was president. It had produced a number of Akira Kurosawa's films and also owned a chain of cinemas in the United States. But Toho was switching almost exclusively to monster movies and had no interest in drama, no matter how topical. Momentum faltered until Osawa resigned from Toho and he and Kawakita formed a new company, Daiwa, solely to make *Anatahan*. Even then, progress remained slow. Rather than leave his wife and baby son in New York, von Sternberg decided to take them along. "[He] arrived in Japan with his family," recalled a somewhat aggrieved Kawakita. "It took quite some time before [they] settled down comfortably. Then, he started writing a scenario which he had promised to complete before his arrival. We had great admiration for his genius, so we gave him a complete free hand."[3]

As usual, von Sternberg adapted the original story to reflect his preoccupation with the destructive power of a woman. Reducing the survivors to a more manageable dozen, he reinvented the homely Kazuko Higa as Keiko, a glamorous and sensual temptress. Assuming that they will soon be rescued, his castaways fish, brew *tuba*, harmonize on old songs, but mostly eye Keiko, who is soon sneaking away for assignations with the younger and more handsome of them. The Nakagawa character loses his authority in a fistfight, and the discovery of two handguns in the crashed B-29 redistributes the balance of power. Keiko, far from suppressing the violence, mirrors Concha in *The Devil Is a Woman*, relishing her status as "Queen Bee." As the corpses pile up, she watches impassively until one day, for no obvious reason, she wades naked into the ocean and swims away. The survivors never see her again, but when they arrive back in Japan, she watches impassively as they leave the airplane, followed in her imagination by the ghosts of those who died for her.

An intertitle in the English-language version proudly states that *Anatahan* was "filmed in a studio specially constructed for the purpose in Kyoto, the ancient capital of Japan." Actually, it was an wartime aircraft hangar, converted to an exhibition hall, in Kyoto's Okazaki Park.

Speaking no Japanese, von Sternberg needed expert local help, which was provided by Shuji "Shu" Taguchi, a newsreel cameraman and the former New York bureau chief of Nihon News. The few special effects were the work of Eiji Tsuburaya, whose first job in movies had been on *Daughter of the Samurai*. Tsuburaya's credit on *Anatahan* sits oddly in a career devoted mainly to creating the bestiality of Japanese movie monsters—Varan, Mothra, Furankenshutain, and even Gojira, aka Godzilla.

Von Sternberg recruited actors from Kabuki companies and a dancing school. Most had never appeared in a film, nor would they again. In Akemi Negishi, however, he discovered a true star. Nineteen years old and a dancer in the chorus at Tokyo's Nichigeki Music Hall, she exuded sexuality with her broad, sullen face and lips set in a sensual pout. Inspired to showcase her sulky sex appeal, von Sternberg filmed her dancing on a table for the diversion of the castaways. In a flagrant piece of soft-core erotica, he showed her slipping out of her kimono during a rainstorm and, in full view of the men, bathing naked in a tin bath, coquettishly raising her leg in a classic pinup pose. Once he revealed her photogenic qualities, Negishi had a long career, particularly in films by Kurosawa.

Familiar motifs appear from the first sequence of lazily swinging ropes and a boat moving heavily in its lashings. On the island, Keiko is given Dietrich lighting for her sulky and impassive face. Shells decorate her home and body, shadows sliding and flaring over their metallic surfaces; these, like a shot of two castaways with fish and an octopus slung over naked shoulders, recall the sea that pounds the rocks, emphasizing their isolation. To create an artificial jungle, von Sternberg uses dredged-up swamp trees, inverting them so that the branching roots create a canopy of vegetation. He sprays trunks and leaves with aluminum paint or wraps them in cellophane for moonlight scenes set under a lattice of shadows in a forest of dead, silvered trunks. With his characteristic long tracks and soft wipes, he lingers on visual detail as an illustration of character. When Keiko, on a night consecrated to the remembrance of dead ancestors, creeps into the jungle to meet a lover, the cold moonlight is an apt simile of her heartlessness.

As in every von Sternberg film, characters are driven by lust or duty to act against their best interests and finer inclinations. *Anatahan* creates neither heroes nor villains, just victims. With a similar lack of editorializing, he reassesses two of his favorite characters: the Rath-like Nakagawa, an authority figure humiliated in his fight to keep control, and the passive, emasculated "husband" Kusakabe, who, with von Sternberg's beard and eyes, could have been another doomed Chang or Don Pasquale. Yet we're encouraged to feel indifference for the former, who adjusts too complacently to the loss of the traditions that gave his life meaning, and contempt for the latter, whose glowering and snarling make him a less sympathetic figure than La Bessière or Ned Faraday.

In *Fun in a Chinese Laundry,* he mocks the Japanese for their rituals, their obsessive politeness, their literalism. It amused him to note that if he pointed, the crew peered not at the object of his interest but at his finger. Conversely, he responded to their fatalism, their reverence for tradition and form. He understood, as they did, that emotional, cultural, and psychological necessities override intellect. Travels in Asia had altered his European sensibility. From an admiration for clear white planes, smooth curves, and the architectural clarity of glass and steel, his tastes turned to the religiously charged tribal art of the Third World, of which he accumulated a large collection during the 1960s.

Since there was never much hope of telling the Anatahan story in a form equally comprehensible to Japanese and Western audiences, Kawakita decided on a dramatized reconstruction rather than a drama. Characterization and dialogue were kept to a minimum, and the story was told in a commentary from Maruyama's book. Japanese audiences were comfortable with this narrative technique, which recalled the *benshi,* an actor who sits at the edge of the stage in traditional Japanese theater and explains or amplifies the plot. As an institution, *benshi* adapted to cinema and survived to the end of the silent era, elucidating the often baffling relationships and motivations of Western movies.

Anatahan opened in Japan in June 1953 and, despite right-wing nationalist objections, succeeded modestly. Some critics resented a foreigner dealing with an event that, whether viewed from a militarist or a pacifist perspective, reflected badly on Japan. In particular, they objected to the inclusion of newsreel footage showing defeated Japanese servicemen returning home. "It is most probably an error," von Sternberg conceded, "to assume that human beings will pay admission to inspect their own mistakes rather than the mistakes of others."

Making the film accessible to Western audiences proved a taller order. New credits were shot—of fish swimming under rippling water—and the film was retitled *The Saga of Anatahan,* with the subtitle *A Postscript to the Pacific Conflict.* In place of the Japanese commentary, von Sternberg wrote his own and narrated it himself in a voice-over. This may have been his version of the Joycean "inner monologue" Eisenstein proposed for *An American Tragedy,* but more likely he was influenced by Chaplin, who re-released his silent *The Gold Rush* in 1942 with a similar spoken summary. Superficially, von Sternberg acts as *benshi* for *Anatahan,* explaining the story, interpolating philosophical observations, and translating portions of the dialogue, but he exceeds that role by assuming the characters of the castaways, explaining what "we" did or thought and even anticipating the action. Audiences for the English-language version were puzzled and chilled by his detached, almost uninflected voice and his refusal to find anything either alien or reprehensible in the events on the island. There is no moralizing, no propaganda. The effect is one of an entomologist peering into a nest of insects. Reflecting his detachment, he credits performers and technicians only by surname and segregates the cast according to the insect metaphor, listing Keiko as the "Queen Bee" and her hapless lover-victims as the "Drones."

The solipsistic tone of his narration resonated as well with von Sternberg's assertion that everyone in his films, even the female stars, represents an aspect of himself. Asked by a British journalist about his resemblance to a number of his characters, he answered, "Everyone in my films is like me."

"Physically? Morally?" the questioner pressed.

"Spiritually," he replied.[4]

Kawakita screened a subtitled English-language print at the West Berlin Film Festival in 1953, but it aroused little interest. In 1954 *The Saga of Anatahan* opened at two Los Angeles cinemas. The general reaction was summarized by Philip Scheuer in the *Los Angeles Times.* Identifying von Sternberg as "an Occidental director not unknown in Coast circles," he called the film a curiosity among motion pictures that may have some esoteric interest but that to this itinerant filmgoer is largely a bore. . . . At his former best a camera painter of no mean distinction, Mr. von Sternberg has always favoured a slow, introspective tempo—and he still clings to this habit. More, here he is dealing with a bunch of men (and one woman) who have no place to go and consequently begin to get on each other's nerves—an affliction to which the fellow in the audience is hardly immune. A third deterrent to any rousing enthusiasm is Mr. von Sternberg's spoken narrative, in both its tone and content. The tone is Brooklynese by way of Vienna (or vice versa) and the content, while given to occasionally pungent observations, has an unfortunate way of editorializing about what is yet to come and thus killing off such small suspense as may be germinating in the beholder.

In 1957 the film's title was changed yet again to *The Last Woman on Earth*. It won a French release as *Fievre sur Anatahan* (Fever on Anatahan). In the English-language market, however, it dropped out of circulation until the only intact copies were those in the hands of von Sternberg himself. Even *Fievre sur Anatahan* disappeared, replaced by the U.S. version with subtitles. By all objective standards, von Sternberg's final film was an ignominious flop—the consummation his enemies had long and devoutly wished. It was not so to him, however. At last he had made a film over which he exercised complete creative control. Compared to that triumph, its commercial success or failure was irrelevant. As critic David Thomson observed, "it needed the ridiculous impossibility of *Anatahan* to end his filmmaking career."

The Lion Is Loose

Play off everyone against each other so that you have more
avenues of action open to you.

—Howard Hughes

ALTHOUGH EDITING ON *Jet Pilot* concluded on February 8, 1950,
the film sat on the shelf until 1955, when General Teleradio bought
RKO, primarily for its film library. The same year, CinemaScope arrived
and permanently altered the form of the epic film, and Anthony Mann's
Strategic Air Command unveiled wide-screen flying scenes almost identical to those in *Jet Pilot*. Stung, Hughes paid Teleradio $12 million to
buy back *Jet Pilot* and another John Wayne epic, *The Conqueror*. A new
team prepared the former for belated release. Up-to-date air footage was
added, and the film was reformatted for the wide screen. Supervising
editor Jim Wilkinson and three assistants recut some dialogue scenes,
and performers were recalled for yet more retakes—those who were still
alive. Some, such as Jack Overman and Richard Rober, had died.

Hughes also ordered the opening reels spiced up, emphasizing Janet
Leigh's impromptu striptease. Even thermal underwear can be provocative on a body like hers, and its removal, layer by layer, is achieved with
erotic expertise—crudely undermined, however, by a sound track of
simulated wolf whistles disguised as the noise of jets whizzing overhead.
This sequence also incorporates some static close-ups of Leigh's face in
partial shadow. Since these don't fit the style of the remaining footage,

they may have been salvaged from camera tests. Their irrelevance to the story makes Leigh's status as a sexual object even more flagrant. French critic Luc Moullet was in no doubt that *"Jet Pilot* is a film on and for Janet Leigh."[1] More thoughtfully, François Truffaut observed, "It isn't a likable film and it isn't inspired by any ideology. . . . Still, amazingly enough, it is a successful, even a beautiful film." It opened on September 25, 1957, in Los Angeles, followed by a Manhattan premiere at the Palace Theatre on October 4. Making a virtue of necessity, the distributor (Universal) tried to turn the film's belated emergence into a selling point: "So BIG It Took Years to Make!" After moderate commercial success, it was again withdrawn by Hughes, at an estimated overall loss of $4 million.

In 1957 von Sternberg gave up on Broadway and moved back to Los Angeles, driving alone cross-country in his Jaguar while Meri and the children traveled by train. The new owner of the Weehawken house was the Baroness Pannonica Rothschild de Koenigswarter, famous for befriending jazz musicians such as Charlie Mingus, Thelonious Monk, and, in particular, Charlie Parker, who died in her suite at the Stanhope Hotel in 1955. She continued to shelter ailing musicians in Weehawken, and Monk died there some years later. Jazz insiders knew it as "The Cathouse"—not only for their hostess's liberal sexuality but also for the jazz cats who fetched up there and the felines to whom the baroness also gave a home.

At a time when other directors of his age enjoyed active careers, von Sternberg's languished. Few younger producers knew his work, and those who did were cautious of his reputation as a troublemaker. Hopeful of succeeding as an independent, he optioned a 1951 novel by Shelby Foote called *Follow Me Down*, which he planned to film as *The Temptation of Luther Eustis*. Eustis, a respectable, pious Mississippi farmer, retreats to a deserted island with a young girl and, after a three-week idyll, murders her. Foote, better known as a Civil War historian, based his book on a 1941 trial in Greenville, South Carolina. In describing events from the perspective of eight participants, the novel recalled Akira Kurosawa's 1950 *Rashomon,* which may have been von Sternberg's motive for acquiring the option. However, he had no luck finding a backer.[2]

In 1959 Twentieth Century–Fox planned a remake of *The Blue Angel* as a vehicle for Marilyn Monroe and Spencer Tracy. Both turned it down, so, after briefly considering Fredric March as Rath, the roles fell to the undistinguished Curt Jurgens and Swedish newcomer May Britt. Edward Dmytryk directed a screenplay by British novelist Nigel Balchin, who ignored Mann's novel and simply adapted the 1929 script, moving the setting inland, to Landsburg, and making Rath a teacher of biology, the better to trade on the irony of his belated discovery of the birds and bees. More galling to admirers of the original was a newly imposed happy ending, in which Rath's old friend, the school principal, restores him to his former job.

Dietrich persuaded Leo Lerman to accompany her to the Paramount theater in New York's Times Square to see the new version, insisting on sitting at the back of the balcony so as not to be recognized. They left before the film ended. "It was agony for Marlene," wrote Lerman.[3] He took her to Café Geiger on East Eighty-eighth Street, the nearest thing New York had to a Berlin *kondoterei*, and fed her coffee and pastries *mit schlag* while the string quartet played "Falling in Love Again," "Jonny," and other tunes from her past to cheer her up. Although Carl Zuckmayer, Karl Vollmoeller, Robert Liebmann, and Heinrich Mann received screen credit on the remake, von Sternberg wasn't mentioned. Incensed, he sued Fox for $1 million, for plagiarizing his adaptation and for creating a film "so inferior that it decreased the value of the original." Dietrich gave a deposition on his behalf, and although the case had dubious legal merit, Fox thought it more politic to settle out of court.

Between 1959 and 1963 von Sternberg taught eccentrically personal courses in cinema aesthetics at the University of California in Los Angeles, using his own films as examples. He made no secret of his bitterness that contemporary Hollywood would not employ him. Many felt the classes represented von Sternberg "review[ing] his life." His students included Jim Morrison and Ray Manzarek, who went on to form The Doors. Both found von Sternberg mesmerizing. "It changed my life," wrote Manzarek:

He opened my mind to the possibility of making movies that were deeply passionate, mysterious, and psychological. Perhaps even slightly kinky, who knows? I know he had a profound effect on The Doors' music. . . . Von Sternberg took us into bungalow 3K7, the screening room where all the films were shown, and said, 'Boys and girls. Students. . . . Watch and learn. In particular, watch the lighting. If anything with my films, I'm most pleased with the lighting. I'll show you how I lit Dietrich when we go to the sound stage. I call it the butterfly light. High up, straight overhead. It casts the shadow of a butterfly under the nose. Of course the cheek-bones must be perfect. . . . ' And of course von Sternberg's mise en scène was discussed endlessly. We talked about his lighting, his sets, his filling of the negative space in front of the camera, his stories of men as fools for a blonde goddess, his Orientalism, his exoticism, his languid pace fraught with psychological tension. . . . Von Sternberg's vision of sophistication and the darker side of the human condition was perhaps the single greatest influence on the music of The Doors.[4]

Others in the class included Curtis Harrington and Gregory Markopoulos, both later directors of experimental films. Harrington subsequently entered the mainstream (*Games, Whoever Slew Auntie Roo?*) but remained a von Sternberg acolyte, compiling the first critical study of his films. Such scholarship had become difficult. Most studios destroyed prints of their silent films to retrieve the silver in the emulsion or let them deteriorate through neglect. While television's hunger for cheap programming kept sound films in circulation, prints were often scratched or incomplete. Many films owed their survival to collectors who squirreled away discarded or bootlegged copies, hiding them from an industry that was seemingly determined to stamp out any sense of a U.S. film heritage. Among these collectors was Los Angeles cineaste David Bradley. A failed filmmaker, Bradley, like Henri Langlois, founder of the Cinematheque Francaise, was a relentless and largely nonjudgmental accumulator. Thanks to a personal fortune and an elastic attitude toward legality, he built an impressive collection. Fortunately, he admired von Sternberg and lent him pristine prints of his own films. Festivals and archives were soon able to offer retrospectives of von Sternberg's work, which he frequently attended as a guest.

In 1960 he was feted at the festival in Wiesbaden, Germany, which was also attended by Dietrich. In August 1961 he was honored by the Venice Film Festival, which screened *The Devil Is a Woman*. William Bast, sometime close friend, roommate, and biographer of James Dean, was also there. "Stopping at the Excelsior [Hotel] bar for a drink my first night," Bast wrote,

I was introduced to a sturdy little man with a handsome crop of gray hair, who turned out to be . . . Josef von Sternberg. . . . Given my credentials, von Sternberg immediately wanted to know all about James Dean. Relieved that he was only interested in Jimmy's acting, we talked until the bar closed. Before parting, he asked me to join him the next evening for the festival's tribute to him. . . .

Throughout the screening, von Sternberg, who turned out to be as garrulous as he was opinionated, reminisced continuously about the making of the film, so much so that I found the movie itself difficult to follow at times. Confiding to me in a running commentary of whispered asides, he pointed out all his personal touches. Faulting the limitations of the art director, for instance, he indicated that the surreal sets he'd had to re-design using makeshift things like cutout tree trunks and wisps of toile for foliage. The lighting director didn't know his job, he complained, so of course he'd had to come up with special lighting effects. The cameraman was also a dead loss, I was informed, so of course he'd had to invent his own ingenious camera angles. I began to wonder who, if not von Sternberg, had selected his team for the film in the first place, though I lacked the courage to ask. I also wondered how two such perfectionists as Dietrich and von Sternberg managed to survive each other for as long as they did.

While browsing the shops off the Piazza San Marco with von Sternberg the following days, I kept my eye open for a gift to take Pat Cavendish, whose guest at La Fiorentina I was to be in a few days. Some small token, I thought, classy but not ostentatious. Ahah! Von Sternberg found the "perfect" gift, a singularly unremarkable scarf from a rather tacky tourist shop. Rather than offend him, without objection I bought the thing, thinking Pat at least might enjoy the idea that it had been handpicked by "the man who created Dietrich," Josef von Sternberg himself. Later, prudently, I sneaked off to pick up a bottle of Balmain's *Vent Vert* as a backup.[5]

Other festivals, such as Locarno in Switzerland, followed. After a 1996 tribute, the Mannheim Festival instituted a prize in his name.

His family accompanied him on some of these trips, during which he spent time in Vienna, visiting the scenes of his childhood. This encouraged him to begin work on an autobiography. When *Fun in a Chinese Laundry* was published in 1965, critics who had hoped for a concise summary of his relationship with Dietrich, the truth about his adventures with Chaplin, detailed descriptions of the circumstances underlying his Paramount films, and some new anecdotes about Hollywood personalities were chagrined to read instead a rambling, provocative meditation on motion pictures as they relate to the graphic arts. References to his own films are so cryptic that only the dedicated student can unravel them. Paradoxically, his intransigence in refusing to follow the fashion in Hollywood autobiographies guaranteed his book a place in the literature of cinema long after less oblique works had been remaindered.

"Why Have I Not Been Given a Woman?"

> Those who are weak don't fight.
> Those who are stronger might fight for an hour.
> Those who are stronger still might fight for many years.
> The strongest fight their whole life.
> They are the indispensable ones.
>
> —Bertolt Brecht

INCREASINGLY ILL WITH THE heart complaint that would kill him, von Sternberg made an exhausting trip to Australia in 1967 as a guest of the Sydney Film Festival. Of all the exotic corners of the world he had visited, few were more alien. Preoccupied with sport, Australians regarded more sophisticated cultures with suspicion, even while, paradoxically, acutely desiring their respect.

Since 1954, the Sydney Film Festival had done its best to represent world cinema, despite being subjected to ferocious censorship and physically confined to the campus of the city's oldest university. Changes began with the appointment in 1966 of a British director, David Stratton. On his first visit to Los Angeles later that year, he met David Bradley, who screened some films from his collection, including Rouben Mamoulian's 1931 version of *Dr. Jekyll and Mr. Hyde*. Because Mamoulian was still alive and enjoying a revival of interest in his work, Stratton contemplated inviting him as a guest of the festival. Bradley argued instead for von Sternberg, who eventually agreed to attend.

Stratton flew on to Sweden, where he met Finnish-born director, filmmaker, critic, politician, and businessman Jorn Donner. Able to seduce any woman and drink any man under the table, Donner charmed everyone, and Stratton was delighted when he offered not only to enter his latest film in the festival but also to accompany it to Sydney. The stage was set for a confrontation of styles and some moments of high comedy.

Donner, robust and Nordic, contrasted startlingly with frail, gray-haired von Sternberg, though the extent of the difference wasn't immediately apparent. The festival's opening reception might have been designed to showcase the latter's European politesse. Women responded instinctively to a man who obviously enjoyed their company—and none more than voluptuous Javanese-German actress Laya Raki. Attending the party with her husband, Australian actor Ron Randell, Raki wore the kind of gown that prompted columnist Earl Wilson to comment, "she looks as if she only wears the zipper and has forgotten the material."

"If I had known you would be here," she purred on being introduced, "I would have worn something more discreet; more . . . Sternbergian."

Von Sternberg contemplated the canyon of her décolletage. Shifting his cane to his left hand, he took a scarf dangling from her shoulder strap and draped it across her breasts.

"Not at all," he said. "I have seen naked women on many occasions."

In other respects, however, he proved a difficult guest. Two journalists with whom he was to have dinner were late arriving at the restaurant, so he was left alone at the table. When Stratton (also late) got there, the atmosphere was frosty. Intuiting von Sternberg's essential masochism, Stratton, hitherto formally polite, slapped him on the shoulder and said heartily, "Well, Jo, I'm sure it's not the first time you've been kept waiting in your life." Von Sternberg immediately relaxed, and each day he turned up at the festival office and asked politely, "What do you require of me today?"

His patience was tried more than once in the weeks that followed. Dissatisfied by unimaginative studio lighting for his TV interviews, he ordered the lights reset. He often encountered technical shortcomings in the various decrepit theaters around the city that had been rented by the festival. At a presentation of *The Saga of Anatahan,* the public address system broke down, so he had to speak to the audience without amplification. The official opening ceremony was staged twice, with the guests whisked across town from one cinema to another. At the second ceremony, too few seats were provided on stage, so the dignitaries, blinded by the ancient footlights, stumbled about, playing musical chairs. As von Sternberg rose to speak, he left his cane on his chair; another man, groping for the vacant seat, sat down on it, to the amusement of the audience. In his speech, the festival president, pursuing an elaborate metaphor, characterized the event as being like a young woman who, having attained her eighteenth year, was bringing home boyfriends. He indicated von Sternberg and Donner, who glared back in unison.

Worse was to come. Both guests had been given a guide and helper —in Donner's case, an attractive young woman from whom he soon became inseparable. This didn't go unnoticed by von Sternberg, who, a few days into the event, summoned the festival committee to air his grievances: cars had not turned up on time; his films were being shown in the wrong ratio; and a board erected in the lobby of the main cinema invited people to rate the titles on a scale of 1 to 10, and dismissive 1s and 0s for *The Saga of Anatahan* were not appreciated. However, he had a much more pressing matter to discuss.

"Why have I not been given a woman?" he demanded.

The committee members gaped. Society matrons, businessmen, and academics, they were like butterfly hunters confronted by a tiger.

"A . . . woman?"

"Mr. Donner has a woman. Why have I not been given one?"

"But . . . she's his *helper,*" someone stammered.

Von Sternberg snorted.

Fortunately, with a little urging from the more sophisticated members of the committee, two female students agreed to attach themselves to him. Thereafter, he insisted on having them seated on either side of him at every public event. Two women trumped Donner's one.

The festival scheduled von Sternberg to spend a day at the government documentary film studio—a risky decision, since its director, Stanley

Hawes, had begun his career as office boy to one of von Sternberg's early *bêtes noirs*, John Grierson. I worked there at the time and presented my copy of *Fun in a Chinese Laundry* for the author to sign. Emboldened, I also proffered Andrew Sarris's appreciative but sometimes revisionist *The Films of Josef von Sternberg*. He regarded it with venom. "You have my signature," he said, and I was dismissed. Perhaps he took exception to Sarris's brisk summation of his work as "the cinema of illusion and delusion, of men deluded by women, of men and women deluded by surface appearances."[1]

That afternoon he addressed the staff on the studio's soundstage. His text, summarizing his theories of filmmaking and the primacy of image over text, probably also served as his introductory lecture at UCLA. It restated his belief that "the best source for a film is an anecdote" and reformulated the cliché as "every picture *transliterates* a thousand words," making the point that text is implicit in the picture it replaces, which should be as clearly readable as a printed page. Although future directors Peter Weir and Donald Crombie were on the staff, as well as cinematographer Donald McAlpine, I don't remember seeing them in the audience. To most Australians, von Sternberg appeared to be a figure from the antediluvian past, outdated and irrelevant.

But a few of us found his visit mesmerizing. In the presence of this stooped, graying man, the six degrees of separation that normally distanced us from the great days of American cinema became one. With the help of a complaisant projectionist, we sneaked away the prints of his films each night and screened them in my apartment, sometimes running them twice. We knew the films only from television, where they had been interrupted by commercials, sometimes truncated to fit the time slot, and invariably scratched and worn. These prints were pristine, protected by meters of creamy leader. Opening each of Bradley's custom-made carrying cases was an occasion for reverence. We felt blessed. This was the Grail.

I didn't know at the time that a scandal was brewing over at least one of these films. Stratton had been unable to locate a copy of *The Docks of New York* and was startled when von Sternberg produced a 16mm print from his luggage, having carried it through customs without declaring it—a serious breach of import and censorship laws. Even worse, he had "borrowed" it from David Bradley's collection without permission.

Von Sternberg left Australia as he had arrived, in a flurry of confusion. Refusing to be separated from his new haul of tribal art, he demanded that it be shipped on the same plane. He declined, however, to take the print of *Docks of New York* and asked Stratton to ship it back to Bradley. Already angry at the unauthorized loan, for which he held Stratton partly responsible, Bradley became apoplectic when, upon the film's return, he detected a scratch on the leader. Claiming that the shock affected his health, Bradley demanded that the festival pay his medical expenses. When Stratton refused, Bradley warned that if he ever showed his face in Los Angeles again, he risked horsewhipping.

Von Sternberg lived his last years in a town house in the Los Angeles suburb of Westwood, close to the campus of UCLA. Age did not diminish his capacity for the grand gesture. Critic Charles Higham, there for an interview, found him "at 4 PM, sitting in a chair under a skylight through which the late afternoon sun conveniently bathed him in a single beam of light. He was leafing through a book of poems of [Hafiz-e Shirazi] in ancient Persian, pretending to read a language with which he was not familiar. He led me downstairs to a study, where I was surrounded by primitive carvings obtained from his travels."[2]

David Stratton also visited him there and was warmly welcomed:

On 4 December [1969] Jo arrived at my small hotel in his elderly Jaguar and drove me back to his house, stopping on the way to buy fruit at Farmers Market. . . . In the evening, he took us out to a Japanese restaurant, where he insisted on showing me how to use chopsticks, an art I hadn't at the time mastered. He left the table at one point to go to the men's room and Meri told me, rather anxiously, that he hadn't been well; he was supposed to be resting and wasn't meant to drive. When it was time to leave the restaurant I wanted to call a taxi, but he insisted that he drive me back across town to my hotel. We took a fond farewell of one another.

Eighteen days later, on December 22, 1969, von Sternberg died of heart failure in Los Angeles. He's buried in Westwood Village Memorial Park. Legend pursued him to the end, claiming—erroneously—that his urge to control extended to designing his own tombstone. In fact, Hollywood's master of the visual is memorialized by a simple bronze plaque embedded in a wall among hundreds of others, all identical. It reads simply "Josef von Sternberg 1894–1969." Although Marlene Dietrich, then living in New York, had flown to Paris for the funeral of Coco Chanel, she didn't attend that of the man who had immortalized her and whom she, in turn, had made famous.

In the decades since his death, von Sternberg's fame and influence have increased—not only in cinema but also in the larger arena of visual art. One is likely to see his vision reflected in a Parisian couture gown, a poster for perfume, or a clip by Madonna. Films or musicals set in pre–World War II Germany or Austria frequently strive for the languid sensuality that permeates his films. Generally, they fail. The superficial is easily achieved; the essence eludes them.

In her essay "Notes on 'Camp,'" Susan Sontag was among the first to isolate the cultural importance of his films. "Camp," she writes, "is the outrageous aestheticism of von Sternberg's six American movies with Dietrich, all six, but especially the last, *The Devil Is a Woman*." In a survey that ranges from Antonio Gaudi to Louis Comfort Tiffany, Mae West to Oscar Wilde, Sontag reminds us that "in Camp, there is often something *démesuré* [out of proportion] in the quality of the ambition, not only in the style of the work itself." But although "the hallmark of Camp is the spirit of extravagance," its authenticity relies on sincerity. Von Sternberg's films are never self-knowing or cynical. Like the soft watches of Salvador Dali and the swooning arabesques of Aubrey Beardsley's art, they represent a legitimate vision, intensely felt, that demands, for all its prodigality of resources and its lust for excess, to be taken seriously. The correct response to such immoderation is not amusement but awe at its audacity and applause for the visual and emotional generosity of the artist. Camp is art's red badge of courage— proof that one cares enough to risk absurdity in pursuit of the sublime.

Despite the outrageousness of his ambitions and the scale of his achievement, von Sternberg never ceased to resent his status as a racial and social outcast. It's emblematic of his life that although numerous film personalities are interred at the Westwood Cemetery, only four—Jay C. Flippen, Thomas Gomez, Marc Lawrence, and Miliza Korjus—ever worked with him, and all in minor roles. Even in death, he remains an outsider.

That paradox was encapsulated by an incident during David Stratton's final visit. He fell into conversation with eighteen-year-old Nicholas von Sternberg, already contemplating a career as a cinematographer. *Easy Rider* had just opened, and they discussed the film with enthusiasm as an increasingly irritated von Sternberg watched. After a few moments he asked his son to accompany him into the corridor, and through the closed door, Stratton heard him hiss, "He came to see *me!*"

Acknowledgments

FROM THE MOMENT I met Josef von Sternberg in 1966, I knew I would one day write his biography—no easy task, as it turned out. Not only were scholarly resources severely limited, but in those days of various new waves, von Sternberg himself was regarded by most as hopelessly dated. Fortunately, a chance meeting with Lotte Eisner at the Venice Festival in 1970 resulted in a visit to the Cinematheque Francaise in Paris later that year, and thanks to the generosity of Henri Langlois and Mary Meerson, I was able to view every existing von Sternberg film in pristine 35mm prints. Viennese critic Goswin Dorfler, again with great goodwill, researched von Sternberg's childhood on my behalf, providing me with a copy of his birth certificate and photographs of his birthplace. Armed with this material, I was able to persuade Peter Cowie, then director of Tantivy Press in London, to publish my 1971 monograph *The Cinema of Josef von Sternberg*.

Many of von Sternberg's old friends and adversaries were still alive at that time. In particular, John Kahan, John Grierson, Ivor Montagu, and Marlene Dietrich's daughter Maria Riva shared their memories, and Nagamasa Kawakita and King Vidor responded to inquiries with copious new information. At the British Film Institute, Elaine Burrows untangled the surviving footage from *I, Claudius* for my benefit. The staff of the Information Department and Stills Library provided invaluable assistance, as did the libraries of the Academy of Motion Picture Arts and Sciences, the American Society of Cinematographers, and

270

the Museum of Modern Art in New York. At the Victoria and Albert Museum in London, Brian Reade shared his knowledge of the work of Felicien Rops, and Denise Bethel of Sotheby Parke Bernet was both devoted researcher and friend.

The Cinema of Josef von Sternberg aroused moderate interest, but it was not until Charles Higham and Curtis Harrington introduced me to von Sternberg's son Nicholas in Los Angeles almost ten years later that the ambition to write a full biography germinated. Nicholas's support and generous sharing of information about his father's life have been a source of continuing encouragement. My ambition was paralleled by a widespread increase of interest in von Sternberg's work and an expansion of critical resources. Patrick McGilligan not only recommended the project to the University Press of Kentucky but also alerted me to the many new sources of information available on the Internet. These allowed me to assemble a precise chronology of von Sternberg's peripatetic life and untangle the complications of his genealogy. The Internet also brought me in contact with other von Sternberg scholars, notably, Professor Janet Bergson of UCLA and Drake Stutesman, who widened my understanding and appreciation of von Sternberg's mastery of couture.

I'm also grateful to David Thompson, who provided invaluable assistance in reviewing von Sternberg's films, as well as many significant additions to the text. David Stratton, Kevin Jackson, Kevin Brownlow, Thomas Gladysz, Tony Sloman, and Rory Feldman all added significant new material. Anton Gill, Christopher Jones, and Wolfgang Kuhlmey provided numerous clarifications of Berlin life and language. The American Library in Paris gave me access to books from Marlene Dietrich's library. Joel Finler supplied advice and assistance on stills.

Filmography

Early Work

After working as a film editor, laboratory expert, and assistant to William A. Brady at World Film Corporation in Fort Lee, New Jersey, from 1914 to 1917, von Sternberg served as director and cameraman on training films for the U.S. Signal Corps (1917–1919). He then acted as assistant director on the following films:

The Mystery of the Yellow Room (1919; Émile Chautard)
Twisted Souls (1920; George Kelson)
The Highest Bidder (1921; Wallace Worsley)
The Bohemian Girl (1922; Harley Knoles), *Love and a Whirlwind* (1922; D. Duncan MacRae, Harold Shaw), and other films for Alliance Productions in Britain
By Divine Right (1923; Roy William Neill), *Vanity Fair* (1923; Hugo Ballin), and four unidentified films in Hollywood
Vanity's Price (1924; Roy William Neill)

The Salvation Hunters (1925)

Screenplay: Josef von Sternberg
Photography: Edward Gheller
Assistant director: George Carrol Sims (as "Peter Ruric")
Production/release: Academy Photoplays

Players: George K. Arthur (The Boy), Georgia Hale (The Girl), Bruce Guerin (The Child), Otto Matiesen (The Man), Nellie Bly Baker (The Woman), Olaf Hytten (The Brute), Stuart Holmes (The Gentleman)

The Exquisite Sinner (1925)

Screenplay: Josef von Sternberg, Alice D. G. Miller; based on the novel *The Enchanted Land* (also *Escape*) by Alden Brooks
Photography: Max Fabian
Assistant director: Robert Florey
Production/release: Metro-Goldwyn-Mayer
Players: Conrad Nagel (Dominique Prad), Renée Adorée (Silda), Paulette Duval (Yvonne), Frank Currier (Colonel), George K. Arthur (Colonel's Orderly), Myrna Loy (Living Statue). Most if not all of this film, also known as *Heaven on Earth*, was reshot by Phil Rosen.

The Masked Bride (1925)

Screenplay: Carey Wilson; based on the novel by Leon Abrams
Photography: Oliver Marsh
Assistant director: Robert Florey
Art direction: Ben Carré, Cedric Gibbons
Production/release: Metro-Goldwyn-Mayer
Players: Mae Murray (Gaby), Roy D'Arcy (Prefect of Police), Francis X. Bushman (Grover), Basil Rathbone (Antoine). This film was abandoned by von Sternberg after two weeks of shooting and completed by Christy Cabanne.

A Woman of the Sea (1926)

Screenplay: Josef von Sternberg; from an original idea by Charles Chaplin
Photography: Edward Gheller, Paul Ivano
Assistant directors: George Carrol Sims (as "Peter Ruric"), Charles Hammond, Riza Royce
Art direction: Charles D. Hall

Producer: Charles Chaplin
Players: Edna Purviance (Joan), Eve Southern (Magdalen), Gayne Whitman (The Novelist), Raymond Bloomer (Peter)
This film (aka *The Sea Gull, Sea Gulls,* and *The Woman Who Loved Once*) was withdrawn by Chaplin and never released.

Children of Divorce (1927)

Von Sternberg reshot portions of this film (original director, Frank Lloyd).

Underworld (1927)

Screenplay: Robert N. Lee, Jules Furthman, Charles Furthman; based on the story by Ben Hecht
Photography: Bert Glennon
Art direction: Hans Dreier
Intertitles: George Marion Jr.
Producer: Hector Turnbull
Production/release: Famous Players–Lasky/Paramount
Players: George Bancroft ("Bull" Weed), Evelyn Brent ("Feathers" Mc-Coy), Clive Brook ("Rolls Royce" Wensel), Larry Semon ("Slippy" Lewis), Fred Kohler (Buck Mulligan), Jerry Mandy (Faloma)

The Last Command (1928)

Screenplay: John S. Goodrich, Jules Furthman (uncredited); based on the story by Lajos Biro
Photography: Bert Glennon
Art direction: Hans Dreier
Intertitles: Herman J. Mankiewicz
Production/release: Paramount
Players: Emil Jannings (General Sergius Alexander), Evelyn Brent (Natacha), William Powell (Andreyev), Nicholas Soussanin (The Adjutant), Michael Visaroff (Serge, the valet), Jack Raymond (Assistant Director)

The Drag Net (1928)

Screenplay: Jules Furthman, Charles Furthman; based on the story "Nightstick" by Oliver H. P. Garrett
Photography: Harold Rosson
Art direction: Hans Dreier
Intertitles: Herman J. Mankiewicz
Production/release: Famous Players–Lasky/ Paramount
Players: George Bancroft (Timothy "Two Gun" Nolan), Evelyn Brent ("The Magpie"), William Powell ("Dapper" Frank Trent), Fred Kohler ("Gabby" Steve), Francis Macdonald ("Sniper" Dawson), Leslie Fenton ("Shakespeare" Donovan)

The Docks of New York (1929)

Screenplay: Jules Furthman; based on the story "The Dockwalloper" by John Monk Saunders
Photography: Harold Rosson
Art direction: Hans Dreier
Intertitles: Julian Johnson
Production/release: Famous Players–Lasky/Paramount
Players: George Bancroft (Bill Roberts), Betty Compson (Mae), Olga Baclanova (Lou), Clyde Cook ("Sugar" Steve), Mitchell Lewis (Andy, the Third Engineer), Gustav von Seyffertitz ("Hymn Book" Harry)

The Case of Lena Smith (1929)

Screenplay: Jules Furthman; based on the story by Samuel Ornitz
Photography: Harold Rosson
Art direction: Hans Dreier
Intertitles: Julian Johnson
Production/release: Famous Players–Lasky/Paramount
Esther Ralston (Lena Smith), James Hall (Franz Hofrat), Gustav von Seyffertitz (Herr Hofrat), Fred Kohler (Stefan), Betty Aho (Stefan's Sister), Lawrence Grant (Commissioner)

Thunderbolt (1929)

Screenplay: Charles Furthman; based on a story by Jules Furthman and Charles Furthman
Dialogue: Herman J. Mankiewicz
Photography: Harry Gerrard
Art direction: Hans Dreier
Production/release: Famous Players–Lasky/Paramount
Players: George Bancroft (Jim "Thunderbolt" Lang), Richard Arlen (Bob Moran), Fay Wray ("Ritzy"), Tully Marshall (Warden), Eugenie Besserer (Mrs. Moran), James Spottswood ("Snapper" O'Shea), Fred Kohler ("Bad Al" Frieberg). This film was shot in silent and sound versions, but only the latter had a general release.

The Blue Angel (1930)

Adaptation: Carl Zuckmayer, Karl Vollmoeller, Josef von Sternberg (uncredited); based on the novel *Professor Unrat* by Heinrich Mann
Scenario: Robert Liebmann
Photography: Gunther Rittau, Hans Schneeberger
Art direction: Otto Hunte, Emil Hasler
Costumes: Tihamer Varady, Karl-Ludwig Holub (uncredited)
Songs: Ich bin von Kopf bis Fuss auf Liebe eingestelt ("Falling in Love Again"), *Nimm Dich in Acht vor blonden Frauen* ("Those Charming, Alarming Blonde Women"), *Ich bin die fesche Lola* ("They Call Me Naughty Lola"), *Kinder, Heut'abend such'ich mir was aus* ("A Man, Just a Regular Man") by Friedrich Hollander; German lyrics of all but *Ich bin von Kopf bis Fuss auf Liebe eingestelt* by Robert Liebmann; English lyrics by Sammy Lerner
Producer: Erich Pommer
Production/release: UFA/Paramount
Players: Emil Jannings (Professor Immanuel Rath), Marlene Dietrich (Lola-Lola), Kurt Gerron (Kiepert), Rosa Valetti (Frau Kiepert), Hans Albers (Mazeppa), Eduard von Winterstein (School Principal), Reinhold Bernt (Clown), Rolf Millier (Angst), Roland Varno (Lohman), Karl Balhaus (Ertzum). This film was shot in German (*Der Blaue Engel*) and English versions.

Morocco (1930)

Screenplay: Jules Furthman, Vincent Lawrence (uncredited); based on the novel *Amy Jolly, Die Frau au Marrakesch* by Benno Vigny
Photography: Lee Garmes; additional photography by Lucien Ballard
Art direction: Hans Dreier
Second-unit director: Henry Hathaway
Assistant directors: Bob Lee, Bob Margolis
Unit managers: Dan Keefe, Eleanor McGeary
Editors: Sam Winston, Bob Lee, Dan Keefe
Costumes: Travis Banton
Hats: John Harburger
Producer: Hector Turnbull
Production/release: Paramount
Players: Gary Cooper (Tom Brown), Marlene Dietrich (Amy Jolly), Adolphe Menjou (La Bessière), Ullrich Haupt (Adjutant Caesar), Eve Southern (Madame Caesar), Michael Visaroff (Barratire), Juliette Compton (Anna Dolores), Albert Conti (Colonel Quinnovieres), Francis McDonald (Corporal Tatoche), Paul Porcasi (LoTinto), Émile Chautard (French General)

Dishonored (1931)

Story and direction: Josef von Sternberg
Screenplay: Daniel N. Rubin
Photography: Lee Garmes
Art direction: Hans Dreier
Music: Adapted from Ivanovici (*Donau Wellen*) and Beethoven ("Moonlight Sonata"); additional music by Josef von Sternberg
Production/release: Paramount
Players: Marlene Dietrich (Maria Kolverer, aka X-27), Victor McLaglen (Lt. Kranau, aka H-14), Lew Cody (Colonel Korvin), Gustav von Seyffertitz (Secret Service Chief), Warner Oland (General von Hindau), Barry Norton (Lieutenant of firing squad)

An American Tragedy (1931)

Screenplay: Samuel Hoffenstein; based on the novel by Theodore Dreiser
Photography: Lee Garmes
Art direction: Hans Dreier
Production/release: Paramount
Players: Phillips Holmes (Clyde Griffiths), Sylvia Sidney (Roberta Alden), Frances Dee (Sondra Finchley), Irving Pichel (Orville Mason), Frederick Burton (Samuel Griffiths), Claire McDowell (Mrs. Samuel Griffiths)

Shanghai Express (1932)

Screenplay: Jules Furthman; based on the story by Harry Hervey
Photography: Lee Garmes
Art direction: Hans Dreier
Costumes: Travis Banton
Hats: John Harburger
Design assistants: Peter Ballbusch, Richard Kollorsz
Assistant director: Henry Hathaway
Production/release: Paramount
Players: Marlene Dietrich (Shanghai Lily/Madeleine), Clive Brook (Donald Harvey), Anna May Wong (Hui Fei), Warner Oland (Henry Chang), Eugene Pallette (Sam Salt), Lawrence Grant (Rev. Carmichael), Louise Closser Hale (Mrs. Haggerty), Gustav von Seyffertitz (Baum), Émile Chautard (Major Lenard)

Blonde Venus (1932)

Screenplay: Jules Furthman, S. K. Lauren; based on the story by Josef von Sternberg (and Marlene Dietrich, uncredited)
Photography: Bert Glennon
Art direction: Wiard Ihnen
Songs: "Hot Voodoo," "You Little So and So" by Ralph Rainger, lyrics by Sam Coslow; "I Couldn't Be Annoyed" by Dick Whiting, lyrics by Leo Robin
Production/release: Paramount

Players: Marlene Dietrich (Helen Faraday/Helen Jones), Herbert Marshall (Edward [Ned] Faraday), Cary Grant (Nick Townsend), Dickie Moore (Johnny Faraday), Gene Morgan (Ben Smith), Rita La Roy ("Taxi Belle" Hooper), Robert Emmett O'Connor (Dan O'Connor), Sidney Toler (Detective Wilson), Cecil Cunningham (Night Club Owner)

The Scarlet Empress (1933)

Screenplay: Manuel Komroff, Eleanor McGeary (uncredited); based on the diary of Catherine II of Russia
Photography: Bert Glennon
Art direction: Hans Dreier
Statues: Peter Ballbusch
Icons and paintings: Richard Kollorsz
Costumes: Travis Banton, Ali Hubert
Intertitles and effects: Gordon Jennings
Music: Based on Tchaikovsky, Mendelssohn, Wagner; arranged by John M. Leopold, W. Frank Harling; additional music by Josef von Sternberg
Production/release: Paramount
Players: Marlene Dietrich (Sophia Frederica, later Catherine II), Sam Jaffe (Grand Duke Peter), John Lodge (Count Alexei), Louise Dresser (Empress Elizabeth), Maria [Sieber] (Sophia as a child), C. Aubrey Smith (Prince August), Ruthelma Stevens (Countess Elizabeth), Gavin Gordon (Gregory Orloff), Hans von Twardowski (Ivan Shuvolov), Jane Darwell (Sophia's mother), Davison Clark (Archimandrite Tevedovsky)

The Devil Is a Woman (1935)

Screenplay: Adapted by John Dos Passos from the novel *La Femme et le Pantin* by Pierre Louys
Additional writing: Sam Winston, David Hertz
Photography: Josef von Sternberg, Lucien Ballard
Art direction: Hans Dreier
Costumes: Travis Banton

Music: Rimsky-Korsakov (*Caprice Espagnol*) and Spanish folk songs, arranged by Ralph Rainger, Andrea Setaro; "Three Sweethearts Have I" by Ralph Rainger, lyrics by Leo Robin (another song, "If It Isn't Pain Then It Isn't Love," was deleted before release)
Production/release: Paramount
Players: Marlene Dietrich (Concha Perez), Lionel Atwill (Don Pasquale), Cesar Romero (Antonio Galvan), Edward Everett Horton (Don Paquito), Alison Skipworth (Senora Perez), Don Alvarado (Morenito), Tempe Pigott (Tuerta), Lawrence Grant (Conductor), Charles Sellon (Scribe), Morgan Wallace (Dr. Mendez)

Crime and Punishment (1936)

Screenplay: S. K. Lauren, Joseph Anthony; based on the novel by Fyodor Dostoyevsky
Photography: Lucien Ballard
Set decoration: Stephen Goosson
Music: Louis Silvers
Costumes: Murray Mayer
Producer: B. P. Schulberg
Production/release: Columbia
Players: Peter Lorre (Raskolnikov), Edward Arnold (Inspector Porfiry), Marian Marsh (Sonya), Tala Birell (Antonya), Elizabeth Risdon (Mrs. Raskolnikov), Robert Allen (Dmitri), Douglas Dumbrille (Grilov), Mrs. Patrick Campbell (Pawnbroker)

The King Steps Out (1936)

Screenplay: Sidney Buchman; based on the operetta *Cissy* by Hubert and Ernst Marischka, from the play *Cissy* by Ernst Decsey and Gustav Hohn
Photography: Lucien Ballard
Art direction: Stephen Goosson
Costumes: Ernst Dryden
Ballet: Albertina Rasch
Music: Fritz Kreisler, arranged by Howard Jackson; "Stars in My Eyes,"

"Madly in Love," "Learn How to Lose," and "What Shall Remain?" by Fritz Kreisler, lyrics by Dorothy Fields
Producer: William Perlberg
Production/release: Columbia
Players: Grace Moore (Cissy), Franchot Tone (Franz Josef), Walter Connolly (Maximilian), Raymond Walburn (von Kempen), Victor Jory (Palfi), Elizabeth Risdon (Sofia), Nana Bryant (Louise), Herman Bing (Pretzelberger), Frieda Inescourt (Helena)

I, Claudius (1937)

Screenplay: Lajos Biro, Carl Zuckmayer; additional material by Lester Cohen; based on the novels *I, Claudius* and *Claudius the God* by Robert Graves
Photography: Georges Périnal
Art direction: Vincent Korda
Costumes: John Armstrong
Choreography: Agnes de Mille
Producer: Alexander Korda
Production/release: London Films
Players: Charles Laughton (Tiberius Claudius Drusus), Merle Oberon (Messalina), Emlyn Williams (Caligula), Flora Robson (Dowager Empress Livia), F. Forbes Robertson (Tiberius), Robert Newton (Centurion), John Clements (Valens). This film was discontinued after six weeks' shooting.

The Great Waltz (1939)

Von Sternberg provided addition shooting (original director, Julien Duvivier) for Metro-Goldwyn-Mayer.

New York Cinderella (1939)

Screenplay: James Kevin McGuinness; based on the story by Charles MacArthur Photography: Harold Rosson
Art direction: Cedric Gibbons, Paul Groesse

Music: Bronislau Kaper, Arthur Guttman
Production/release: Metro-Goldwyn-Mayer
Players: Hedy Lamarr (Georgi Gragore), Spencer Tracy (Karl Decker), Verree Teasdale (Madame Marcesca), Kent Taylor (Phil Mayberry), Laraine Day (Linda Rodgers), Mona Barrie (Sandra Mayberry), Jack Carson (Joe), Louis Calhern (Dr. Duveen). Von Sternberg resigned from this film after eight days. It was reshot first by Frank Borzage and then, with an almost completely new cast, by W. S. Van Dyke, It was released under Van Dyke's name in 1940 as *I Take This Woman.*

Sergeant Madden (1939)

Screenplay: Wells Root; based on the story "A Gun in His Hand" by William A. Ullman
Photography: John F. Seitz
Art direction: Cedric Gibbons, Randall Duell
Montage effects: Peter Ballbusch
Music: William Axt
Producer: J. Walter Ruben
Production/release: Metro-Goldwyn-Mayer
Players: Wallace Beery (Shaun Madden), Alan Curtis (Dennis Madden), Tom Brown (Al Boylan Jr.), Laraine Day (Eileen), Fay Holden (Mary Madden), Marc Lawrence ("Piggy" Ceders), David Gorcey ("Punchy")

The Shanghai Gesture (1941)

Screenplay: Josef von Sternberg, Jules Furthman, Geza Herczeg, Karl Volmoeller (uncredited); based on the play by John Colton
Photography: Paul Ivano
Art direction: Boris Leven
Set decoration: Howard Bristol
Murals: Keye Luke
Costumes: Royer (Ona Munson's), Oleg Cassini (Gene Tierney's)
Wigs: Hazel Rogers
Music: Richard Hageman

Producer: Arnold Pressburger
Production/release: United Artists
Players: Gene Tierney (Victoria Charteris/Poppy Smith), Victor Mature (Dr. Omar), Ona Munson (Mother Gin Sling), Walter Huston (Sir Guy Charteris), Phyllis Brooks (Dixie Pomeroy), Albert Basserman (Police Commissioner), Maria Ouspenskaya (Amah), Eric Blore (Caesar Hawkins), Marcel Dalio (Croupier), Mikhail Rasumny (Cashier), Mike Mazurki (Coolie)

The Town (1943)

Screenplay: Joseph Krugold
Photography: Larry Madison
Producer: Philip Dunne. This short film was produced for the U.S. Office of War Information.

Duel in the Sun (1946)

Von Sternberg acted as assistant director for King Vidor on this film by Selznick Productions.

Jet Pilot (1950)

Screenplay: Jules Furthman
Photography (color): Winton C. Hoch
Aerial photography: Philip C. Cochran
Art direction: Albert S. D'Agostino, Field Gray
Set decoration: Darrell Silvera, Harley Miller
Costumes: Michael Woulfe
Editing supervision: James Wilkinson
Editing: Michael R. McAdam, Harry Marker, William M. Moore
Producer: Jules Furthman
Production/release: Howard Hughes Productions/Universal
Players: John Wayne (Colonel Shannon), Janet Leigh (Anna Marladovna), Jay C. Flippen (Major General Black), Paul Fix (Major Rexford), Richard Rober (George Rivers), Roland Winters (Colonel Sokolov), Ivan Triesault (General Langrad), Hans Conreid (Colonel Matoff).

This film was not released until 1957. Portions were reshot by an unknown director.

Macao (1950)

Screenplay: Bernard C. Schoenfeld, Stanley Rubin; also George Bricker, Edward Chodorov, Norman Katkov, Frank L. Moss, Walter Newman (all uncredited); based on the story by Robert Creighton Williams
Photography: Harry J. Wild
Art direction: Albert S. Agostino, Harley Miller
Costumes: Michael Woulfe
Songs: "One for My Baby" by Johnny Mercer, lyrics by Harold Arlen; "Ocean Breeze," "Talk to Me Tomorrow," and "You Kill Me" by Jule Styne, lyrics by Leo Robin
Producer: Sid Rogell, with Samuel Bischoff, Alex Gottlieb, Jerry Wald (all uncredited)
Production/release: RKO Radio Pictures
Players: Robert Mitchum (Nick Cochran), Jane Russell (Julie Benson), William Bendix (Lawrence Trumble), Thomas Gomez (Lieutenant Sebastian), Brad Dexter (Vincent Halloran), Gloria Grahame (Marge), Philip Ahn (Itzumi), Vladimir Sokoloff (Kwan Sum Tang)
Portions were reshot by Robert Stevenson, Mel Ferrer, and Nicholas Ray.

The Saga of Anatahan (1952)

Screenplay: Josef von Sternberg; based on the story by Michiro Maruyama
Narration: Josef von Sternberg
Photography: Josef von Sternberg
Japanese dialogue: Asano
Set decoration: Takashi Kono
Music: Akira Ifukube
Producer: Kazuo Takimura
Executive producers: Nagamasa Kawakita, Yoshio Osawa

Production/release: Daiwa Towa Productions
Players: Akemi Negishi (Keiko), Tadashi Suganuma (Kusakabe, Keiko's "Husband"), Kisaburo Sawamura (Kuroda), Shoji Nakayama (Nishio), Jun Fujikawa (Yoshisato), Hiroshi Kondo (Yanaginuma), Shozo Miyashita (Sennami), Tsuruemon Bando (Doi), Kikuji Onoe (Kaneda), Rokuriro Kineya (Marui), Dajiro Tamura (Kanzaki), Tadashi Kitagawa (self), Takashi Suzuki (Takahashi), Shiro Amikura (Amanuma)
This film is also known as *The Last Woman on Earth.*

Notes

Vienna

1. Von Sternberg, *Fun in a Chinese Laundry*. Unless otherwise indicated, all quotations from von Sternberg are from this work and are used by permission of his estate.
2. Eisenstein, *Immoral Memories*.
3. Bolkosky, *The Distorted Image*.
4. Du Maurier, *Trilby: A Novel*.
5. Ibid.

Love and Other Distractions

1. Zuckmayer, *A Part of Myself*.
2. Interview in *Cahiers du Cinéma* 168 (1963).
3. Riva, *Marlene Dietrich*.
4. Eisenstein, *Immoral Memories*.
5. Maas, *The Shocking Miss Pilgrim*.

An Artist's Life

1. Quoted in Nichols and Bazzoni, *Pirandello and Film*.
2. Lasky, *Whatever Happened to Hollywood?*
3. Letter to the author, 2009.
4. Bruce Bennett, "Capturing Little People with Big Emotions," *New York Sun*, September 8, 2006.
5. Lasky, *Whatever Happened to Hollywood?*

6. Aeneas Mackenzie, "Leonardo of the Lenses," *Life and Letters Today* *14* (1936).

7. Barnet Braver-Mann, "Josef von Sternberg," *Experimental Cinema* 5 (1934).

8. Grierson, *Grierson on Documentary.*

The World, the Flesh, and William A. Brady

1. Kracauer, *From Caligari to Hitler.*

2. Riva, *Marlene Dietrich.*

3. Raymond Durgnat (as O. O. Green), "Six Films of Josef von Sternberg," *Movie* 13 (summer 1965).

4. Henry F. Pringle, "Josef Von Sternberg: All for Art," *New Yorker,* March 28, 1931.

In Uniform

1. Pringle, "Josef Von Sternberg: All for Art."

2. Lasky, *Whatever Happened to Hollywood?*

3. Eisenstein, *Immoral Memories.*

4. Brownlow, *The Parade's Gone By.*

5. Eisenstein, *Immoral Memories.*

6. Grosz, *A Small Yes and a Big No.*

7. Gordon and Gordon, *Star-Dust in Hollywood.*

8. S. J. Perelman, "Vintage Swine," *New Yorker,* September 20, 1952.

9. Grosz, *A Small Yes and a Big No.*

10. Letter to the author.

11. Pringle, "Josef Von Sternberg: All for Art."

Over There

1. Von Sternberg, introduction to *Daughters of Vienna.*

Out There

1. Pringle, "Josef Von Sternberg: All for Art."

2. Riva, *Marlene Dietrich.*

3. Lasky, *Whatever Happened to Hollywood?*

4. Interview in *Cahiers du Cinéma* 168 (1963).

5. Quoted in Beauchamp, *Joseph P. Kennedy's Hollywood Years.*

6. Pringle, "Josef Von Sternberg: All for Art."
7. *New York Times,* October 8, 1924.

Photographing a Thought

1. "Kipps, and the Other Person," *Picturegoer,* June 1922.
2. *Evening News* (London), November 13, 1924.
3. Pringle, "Josef Von Sternberg: All for Art."
4. Ibid.
5. Reeves, *Chaplin Intime.*

A Genuine Genius

1. "Shoestrings and 'Vons,'" *New Yorker,* February 21, 1925.
2. "The Luck of Josef von Sternberg," *Pictures & Picturegoer,* January 1925.
3. Florey, *Hollywood d'hier et d'aujourd'hui.*
4. Ibid.
5. Morris Markey, "The Movies," *New Yorker,* June 10, 1926.

Three Sheets to the Wind

1. Grierson, *Grierson on Documentary.*
2. Ibid.
3. Florey, *Hollywood d'hier et d'aujourd'hui.*
4. Ibid.
5. Robinson, *Chaplin: His Life and Art.*
6. Grierson, *Grierson on Documentary.*
7. Ibid.
8. Eisenstein, *Immoral Memories.*

The Ascent of Paramount

1. Maas, *The Shocking Miss Pilgrim.*
2. Ibid.
3. Ibid.
4. Ibid.
5. Ibid.
6. Gordon and Gordon, *Star-Dust in Hollywood.*
7. *Los Angeles Times,* October 20, 1926.

8. Quoted in Sragow, *Victor Fleming.*
9. Ibid.
10. Ibid.

The City of Dreadful Night

1. Hecht, *A Child of the Century.* Subsequent quotes by Hecht are from this work.
2. Interview in *Cahiers du Cinéma* 168 (1963).
3. Quoted in Brownlow, *The Parade's Gone By.*
4. Quoted in McCarthy, *Howard Hawks.*
5. Capra, *The Name above the Title.*
6. Quoted in McCarthy, *Howard Hawks.*
7. Gordon and Gordon, *Star-Dust in Hollywood.*
8. Braver-Mann, "Josef von Sternberg."

A Great Man

1. *New Yorker,* October 6, 2008.
2. Quoted in Brownlow, *The Parade's Gone By.*
3. *New York Times,* May 28, 1928.
4. Patterson, *Motion Picture Continuities.*
5. Introduction to Josef von Sternberg, *Fun in a Chinese Laundry* (London: Columbus Books, 1987).
6. *Los Angeles Times,* May 23, 1928.

Came the Dawn

1. Quoted in Gordon and Gordon, *Star-Dust in Hollywood.*
2. *New York Times,* June 4, 1928.
3. Brownlow, *The Parade's Gone By.*
4. Card, *Seductive Cinema.*
5. *Los Angeles Times,* December 31, 1928.
6. Quoted in Horwath, *Josef von Sternberg: The Case of Lena Smith.*
7. Ibid.
8. Ibid.
9. Ibid.
10. *New York Times,* January 15, 1929.

The Lady with the Legs

1. John Kahan, conversation with the author.

2. Zuckmayer, *A Part of Myself.*
3. Ibid.
4. Held in Special Collections, American Library in Paris.
5. Dietrich, *Marlene Dietrich: My Life.*
6. Kahan, conversation with author.
7. Ibid.
8. Reinhardt, *The Genius.*
9. Kahan, conversation with author.
10. Lerman, *The Grand Surprise.*
11. Ibid.
12. Riefenstahl, *Leni Riefenstahl: A Memoir.*
13. Kahan, conversation with author.
14. Grosz, *A Small Yes and a Big No.*
15. Ibid.

Falling in Love Again

1. Maas, *The Shocking Miss Pilgrim.*
2. Ibid.
3. Dietrich, *Marlene Dietrich: My Life.*
4. *New York Times,* August 9, 1931.
5. Wedekind, *Lulu.*
6. Durgnat, "Six Films of Josef von Sternberg."
7. Quoted in Higham, *Hollywood Cameramen: Sources of Light.*
8. TV interview with Leni Riefenstahl.
9. Eisenstein, *Immoral Memories.*
10. Bergan, *Eisenstein: A Life in Conflict.*
11. Grosz, *A Small Yes and a Big No.*
12. *New York Times,* April 2, 1930.
13. Special Collections, American Library in Paris.

The Woman All Women Want to See

1. Lerman, *The Grand Surprise.*
2. Ibid.
3. Introduction to von Sternberg, *Fun in a Chinese Laundry.*
4. Ibid.
5. Eisenstein, *Immoral Memories.*
6. Introduction to von Sternberg, *Fun in a Chinese Laundry.*
7. Quoted in Higham, *Marlene.*
8. Ibid.
9. Durgnat, "Six Films of Josef von Sternberg."

10. Quoted in Bogdanovich, *Who the Hell's In It.*
11. Michel Vauclaire, *Le Crapouillot,* October 1931.
12. *Los Angeles Times,* June 5, 1930.
13. Ibid.
14. Lasky, *Whatever Happened to Hollywood?*
15. "Marlene Plus" Web site, http://www.marlenedietrich.org/mdcb.htm.

Spies

1. *Los Angeles Times,* September 15, 1931.
2. Montagu, *With Eisenstein In Hollywood.*
3. Interview with Peter Bogdanovich, *Movie,* December 1962.
4. Peter Bogdanovich, "Encounters with Josef von Sternberg," *Movie* 13 (summer 1965).
5. *Variety,* January 1, 1931.

Talk Like a Train

1. Grierson, *Grierson on Documentary.*
2. Stutesman, *Fashioning Stars.*
3. Ibid.
4. Clive Brook, unpublished interview with Philip Jenkinson, London, 1970.
5. Stutesman, *Fashioning Stars.*
6. Lasky, *I Blow My Own Horn.*

Come Early, Stay Late

1. Quoted in Lea Jacobs, "The Censorship of the *Blonde Venus,*" *Cinema Journal* 27 (spring 1988).
2. Greene, *The Pleasure Dome.*
3. Arthur Millier, "Von Sternberg Dotes on Portraits of Himself," *Los Angeles Times,* June 19, 1932.
4. Eisenstein, *Immoral Memories.*
5. Quoted in Ashton, *A Critical Study of Philip Guston.*
6. Millier, "Von Sternberg Dotes on Portraits of Himself."

Russian Dolls

1. Riefenstahl, *Leni Riefenstahl: A Memoir.*

2. Quoted in Riva, *Marlene Dietrich*.
3. Ibid.
4. Quoted in Thomas S. Hines, "Richard Neutra. Rediscovering the Architect's Vision for Josef Von Sternberg," *Architectural Digest*, January 2007.
5. David Colker, "On the Trail of a Lost Architectural Legacy," *Los Angeles Times*, November 13, 1999.

Moscow Rules

1. Quoted in Geist, *Pictures Will Talk*.
2. Quoted in Riva, *Marlene Dietrich*.
3. *Cinema Quarterly* (summer 1934).

The End of the Affair

1. Quoted in Eyman, *Ernst Lubitsch*.
2. Interview with Jeanne Stein, *Focus on Film* 1 (1970).
3. This report by columnist Robbin Coons was widely syndicated and is quoted here from the *Salamanca (NY) Republican Press*, November 12, 1934.
4. Quoted in Scherba, *Kurt Weill*.
5. *New York Times*, March 3, 1935.
6. *New York Times*, March 4, 1935.
7. *New York Times*, October 23, 1935.
8. *New York Times*, October 24, 1935.
9. *Sunday Times* (London), November 22, 1964.

Cardboard Continental

1. *Los Angeles Times*, June 23, 1935.
2. Arnold, *Lorenzo Goes to Hollywood*.
3. Greene, *The Pleasure Dome*.
4. Moore, *You're Only Human Once*.
5. Ibid.
6. Greene, *The Pleasure Dome*.
7. Capra, *The Name above the Title*.

Far Cathay

1. Maas, *The Shocking Miss Pilgrim*.

The Claudius Trap

1. Lanchester, *Elsa Lanchester Herself.*
2. *Kine Weekly* (London), February 4, 1937.
3. Interview in *Cahiers du Cinéma* 168 (1963).
4. Dietrich FBI file, report to J. Edgar Hoover dated July 12, 1942.
5. Ibid.
6. Tabori, *Alexander Korda.*
7. John Kahan, conversation with the author.
8. Quoted by Kevin Brownlow, conversation with the author.
9. Kahan, conversation with author.
10. Quoted in Eyman, *Ernst Lubitsch.*
11. Riefenstahl, *Leni Riefenstahl: A Memoir.*
12. Tynan, *Diaries of Kenneth Tynan.*

Family Ties

1. Sragow, *Victor Fleming.*
2. Barton, *Hedy Lamarr.*

The War at Home

1. Dietrich FBI file.
2. Nichols and Bazzoni, *Pirandello and Film.*
3. Lejeune, *Chestnuts in Her Lap.*
4. This report by columnist Sigrid Arne was widely syndicated and is quoted here from the *Danville Bee,* November 24, 1941.
5. *New York Times,* December 26, 1941.

Americana

1. Quoted in Colker, "On the Trail of a Lost Architectural Legacy."
2. King Vidor, letter to the author.
3. Ibid.
4. Ibid.

The Seven Bad Years

1. Quoted in Bennett, "Capturing Little People with Big Emotions."
2. Goodman, *The Fifty Year Decline and Fall of Hollywood.*

---

3. This report by columnist Erskine Johnson was widely syndicated and is quoted here from the *Burlington (NC) Daily Times-News,* January 4, 1950.

4. Janet Leigh interview with Rui Noguiera, "Psycho, Rosie and a Touch of Orson," *Sight and Sound* (spring 1970).

5. Server, *Robert Mitchum.*

6. Ibid.

7. Ibid.

8. Eisenschitz, *Nicholas Ray.*

9. Quoted in Bennett, "Capturing Little People with Big Emotions."

10. Lerman, *The Grand Surprise.*

11. Quoted in Eisenschitz, *Nicholas Ray.*

12. Brownlow, *The Parade's Gone By.*

Because I Am a Poet

1. Nagamasa Kawakita, letter to the author.

2. *Los Angeles Times,* June 16, 1951, July 8, 1951, and November 21, 1952.

3. Kawakita, letter to the author.

4. BBC-TV interview with Alexander Walker, 1966.

The Lion Is Loose

1. *Cahiers du Cinéma,* August 1958.

2. *Los Angeles Times,* March 5, 1959.

3. Lerman, *The Grand Surprise.*

4. Manzarek, *Light My Fire.*

5. Bast, *Surviving James Dean.*

"Why Have I Not Been Given a Woman?"

1. Andrew Sarris, *Film Culture* 28 (1963).

2. Higham, *Marlene.*

Bibliography

Arnold, Edward. *Lorenzo Goes to Hollywood*. New York: Liveright, 1940.
Ashton, Dore. *A Critical Study of Philip Guston*. Los Angeles: University of California Press, 1990.
Bach, Steven. *Leni: The Life and Work of Leni Riefenstahl*. New York: Vintage, 2007.
———. *Marlene Dietrich: Life and Legend*. New York: Da Capo, 1992.
Ballard, J. G. *Miracles of Life: Shanghai to Shepperton. An Autobiography*. London: Fourth Estate, 2008.
Barsacq, Leon. *Caligari's Cabinet and Other Grand Illusions: A History of Film Design*. Boston: New York Graphic Society, 1976.
Barton, Ruth. *Hedy Lamarr: The Most Beautiful Woman in Film*. Lexington: University Press of Kentucky, 2010.
Bast, William. *Surviving James Dean*. Fort Lee, NJ: Barricade Books, 2006.
Baxter, John. *The Cinema of Josef von Sternberg*. London: Zwemmer/A. S. Barnes, 1971.
———. *The Hollywood Exiles*. New York: Taplinger, 1976.
Baxter, Peter, ed. *Just Watch! Sternberg, Paramount and America*. London: British Film Institute, 1993.
———. *Sternberg*. London: British Film Institute, 1980.
Beauchamp, Carl. *Joseph P. Kennedy's Hollywood Years*. London: Faber, 2009.
Bergan, Ronald. *Eisenstein: A Life in Conflict*. New York: Little Brown, 1997.
Bernstein, Matthew. *Walter Wanger: Hollywood Independent*. Berkeley: University of California Press, 1994.
Bogdanovich, Peter. *Who the Hell's In It: Portraits and Conversations*. New York: Knopf, 2004.
Bolkosky, Sidney M. *The Distorted Image*. New York: Elsevier, 1975.
Brownlow, Kevin. *The Parade's Gone By*. London: Secker and Warburg, 1968.

Capra, Frank. *The Name above the Title: An Autobiography.* London: W. H. Allen, 1972.

Card, James. *Seductive Cinema.* New York: Knopf, 1994.

Dietrich, Marlene. *Marlene Dietrich: My Life.* London: Weidenfeld and Nicolson, 1987.

Du Maurier, George. *Trilby: A Novel.* New York: Harper, 1889.

Eisenschitz, Bernard. *Nicholas Ray: An American Journey.* Trans. Tom Milne. London: Faber and Faber, 1993.

Eisenstein, Sergei. *Immoral Memories: An Autobiography.* Trans. Herbert Marshall. New York: Houghton Mifflin, 1983.

Eyman, Scott. *Ernst Lubitsch: Laughter in Paradise.* New York: Simon and Schuster, 1990.

Finler, Joel W. *Hollywood Movie Stills: The Golden Age.* London: Batsford, 1995.

———. *Stroheim.* London: Studio Vista, 1967.

Florey, Robert. *Hollywood d'hier et d'aujourd'hui.* Paris: Prisma, 1948.

Geist, Kenneth L. *Pictures Will Talk: The Life and Films of Joseph L. Mankiewicz.* New York: Scribners, 1978.

Gill, Anton. *A Dance between the Flames: Berlin between the Wars.* London: John Murray, 1993.

Goodman, Ezra. *The Fifty Year Decline and Fall of Hollywood.* New York: Simon and Schuster, 1961.

Gordon, Jan, and Cora Gordon. *Star-Dust in Hollywood.* London: George G. Harrap, 1930.

Greene, Graham. *The Pleasure Dome: The Collected Film Criticism 1935–1940.* London: Oxford University Press, 1980.

Grierson, John. *Grierson on Documentary.* Ed. Forsyth Hardy. London: Collins, 1946.

Grosz, George. *A Small Yes and a Big No.* Trans. Arnold J. Pomerans. London: Allison and Busby, 1982.

Hale, Georgia. *Charlie Chaplin: Intimate Close-Ups.* Ed. Heather Kiernan. Lanham, MD, and London: Scarecrow Press, 1999.

Harrington, Curtis. *An Index to the Films of Josef von Sternberg.* London: British Film Institute, 1949 (published as a supplement to *Sight and Sound*).

Hecht, Ben. *A Child of the Century.* New York: Simon and Schuster, 1954.

Higham, Charles. *Hollywood Cameramen: Sources of Light.* London: Thames and Hudson, 1970.

———. *In and Out of Hollywood.* Madison: Terrace Books/University of Wisconsin Press, 2009.

———. *Marlene: The Life of Marlene Dietrich.* New York: Norton, 1977.

Higham, Charles, and Roy Moseley. *Merle: A Biography of Merle Oberon.* New York: New English Library, 1983.

Horwath, Alexander. *Josef Von Sternberg: The Case of Lena Smith*. New York: Wallflower Press, 2008.

Korda, Michael. *Charmed Lives: A Family Romance*. New York: Random House, 1979.

Kracauer, Siegfried. *From Caligari to Hitler: A Psychological History of the German Film*. London: Dennis Dobson, 1947.

Lanchester, Elsa. *Elsa Lanchester Herself*. New York: St. Martin's, 1983.

Lasky, Jesse, with Don Weldon. *I Blow My Own Horn*. London: Gollancz, 1957.

Lasky, Jesse, Jr. *Whatever Happened to Hollywood?* New York: Funk and Wagnalls, 1973.

Lejeune, C. A. *Chestnuts in Her Lap, 1936–1946*. London: Phoenix House, 1947.

Lerman, Leo. *The Grand Surprise: The Journals of Leo Lerman*. Ed. Steven Pascal. New York: Knopf, 2007.

Maas, Frederica Sagor. *The Shocking Miss Pilgrim: A Writer in Early Hollywood*. Louisville: University of Kentucky Press, 1999.

Manzarek, Ray. *Light My Fire: My Life with the Doors*. New York: Putnam, 1998.

McCarthy, Todd. *Howard Hawks: The Grey Fox of Hollywood*. New York: Grove, 2000.

Menjou, Adolphe. *It Took Nine Tailors*. London: Sampson Low Marston, 1950.

Montagu, Ivor. *With Eisenstein in Hollywood: A Chapter of Autobiography, Including the Scenarios of* Sutter's Gold *and* An American Tragedy. London: International Publishers, 1967.

Moore, Grace. *You're Only Human Once*. New York: Garden City Publishing Co., 1944.

Muller, Jorn. *Cabaret Berlin: Revue, Kabarett and Film Music between the Wars*. Hamburg: Edel, 2005.

Nichols, Nina Davinci, and Jana O'Keefe Bazzoni. *Pirandello and Film*. Lincoln: University of Nebraska Press, 1995.

Patterson, Frances Taylor, ed. *Motion Picture Continuities*. New York: Columbia University Press, 1929 (contains Goodrich-Biro script of *The Last Command*).

Reeves, May. *Chaplin Intime*. Paris: Gallimard, 1935.

Reinhardt, Gottfried. *The Genius: A Memoir of Max Reinhardt*. New York: Knopf, 1979.

Riefenstahl, Leni. *Leni Riefenstahl: A Memoir*. New York: Picador, 1995.

Riva, Maria. *Marlene Dietrich*. New York: Knopf, 1993.

Robinson, David. *Chaplin: His Life and Art*. New York: McGraw-Hill, 1985.

Sarris, Andrew. *The Films of Josef von Sternberg*. New York: Museum of Modern Art/Doubleday, 1966.

Bibliography

———. Introduction to Morocco *and* Shanghai Express: *Two Films by Josef von Sternberg*. London: Lorrimer, 1973.

Scherba, Jurgen. *Kurt Weill: An Illustrated Life*. London: Yale University Press, 1995.

Server, Lee. *Robert Mitchum: "Baby, I Don't Care."* New York: St. Martin's, 2001.

Sontag, Susan. "Notes on 'Camp.'" In *Against Interpretation*. New York: Farrar, Straus and Giroux, 1966.

Sragow, Michael. *Victor Fleming: An American Movie Master*. New York: Pantheon, 2008.

Stutesman, Drake. *Fashioning Stars: Dress, Culture, Identity*. London: British Film Institute, 2005.

Tabori, Paul. *Alexander Korda*. London: Oldbourne, 1959.

Tynan, Kenneth. *The Diaries of Kenneth Tynan*. Ed. John Lahr. London: Bloomsbury, 2001.

Von Sternberg, Josef. *Fun in a Chinese Laundry*. New York: Macmillan, 1965.

———. *Macao*. New York: Frederick Ungar, 1980.

———, trans. *Daughters of Vienna*. London, New York, Vienna: International Editor, 1922 (translation of Karl Adolph's *Tochter* [1914]).

Wada, Linda. *The Sea Gull/A Woman of the Sea*. Portland, OR: Leading Ladies, 2008.

Wedekind, Frank. *Lulu*. Trans. Peter Barnes. London: Methuen, 1989.

Zuckmayer, Carl. *A Part of Myself: Portrait of an Epoch*. New York: Harcourt Brace Jovanovich, 1966.

Index

Index

Index

Index